T0354969

GLOBAL GOALS

THE INTERNATIONAL HOCKEY LIFE OF U.S. DEFENSEMAN ERIC WEINRICH

ANDY DEROCHE

iUniverse®

GLOBAL GOALS
THE INTERNATIONAL HOCKEY LIFE OF U.S. DEFENSEMAN ERIC WEINRICH

iUniverse books may be ordered through booksellers or by contacting:

iUniverse
1663 Liberty Drive
Bloomington, IN 47403
www.iuniverse.com
844-349-9409

ISBN: 978-1-6632-6895-2 (sc)
ISBN: 978-1-6632-6894-5 (e)

Library of Congress Control Number: 2024924681

Print information available on the last page.

iUniverse rev. date: 11/15/2024

CONTENTS

INTRODUCTION AND ACKNOWLEDGEMENTS

Eric Weinrich and Andy DeRoche
Early 2000s when Eric played for Philadelphia

For the most part, this book is a scholarly biography of Eric Weinrich, who enjoyed a long career as a defenseman in professional hockey and skated for Team USA in more international tournaments than any other player. In addition to detailing his accomplishments and challenges on the ice, as well as some of the key events in his life off the ice, I attempted to place his story into the broad context of US history during the end of the Cold War and beyond. I have written biographies of other historical figures, and so on one level my work here is nothing new for me and not unique in the fields of biography or sports history.

What makes this a somewhat extraordinary book, however, is the extent to which Eric himself participated. He and his family supported my research efforts from the start, but after I had been doing my usual "historian thing" for a couple of years, Eric told me that he wanted to contribute more of his own recollections. We devised a plan whereby he would read each of the chapters that I had drafted and would add additional memories and insights within the chapter or at the end of the chapter. As a player, his nickname was "Weino," so we decided to call his autobiographical additions "Weino's Wisdom." Fortunately, Eric is much better at writing than I am at skating, so I am quite sure that readers will find his contributions interesting and insightful.

In addition to drafting the "Weino's Wisdom" segments, Eric assisted this project in many other ways. He gave me full access to his personal collection of documents, answered countless questions, and met with my students at the University of Colorado via ZOOM. His wonderful wife Tracy also provided lots of useful information, as did Eric's brothers Al and Jason. The best interview was the day my family and I talked at length with Eric's parents, Sandra and Jack. What a special conversation!

My research and writing would be impossible without the gracious support of my wife Heather. Our children, Ellen and Zeke, add crucial creativity and energy to the DeRoche household in Colorado. My parents, Mary and Wayne, host us when we are in Maine. Having a home base in Bethel has been crucial to the completion of this book. Overall, it is much better because of my family's help. Eric and I first met on a baseball field in Maine in the summer of 1975. This book is dedicated to our Rumford Point little league coaches and teammates.

CHAPTER 1

"From Pond Hockey to World Juniors, 1966-1984"

From the late 1960s to the early 1980s, interest in ice hockey increased dramatically in the United States, as the National Hockey League expanded from the "Original Six" teams to twelve in 1967, then to eighteen teams in 1974, and then to 21 teams in 1979. Most of the new teams were in cities across the USA. More importantly, perhaps, the U.S. men's squad achieved athletic immortality when they upset the mighty team from the USSR at the 1980 winter Olympics and went on to win the gold medal. Countless young boys from Minnesota, Michigan, and Massachusetts (and many other states) learned to skate, handle a stick, and shoot pucks in hopes of one day replicating the 1980 "Miracle on Ice" and facing off against the Soviets.

Eric learning to skate on a lake in Poland, Maine around 1970

One of the boys who would eventually achieve such global goals grew up in Maine, and his name was Eric Weinrich. Eric starred in youth leagues and high school hockey, and attracted national attention when Buffalo attempted to draft him in June 1984. (The pick was nullified because Eric was just seventeen.) Six months later, while still in high school, Eric skated for Team USA at the World Junior Championships in Finland. He played well and demonstrated his diplomatic ability as an unofficial cultural ambassador for the United States. By the end of 1984, Eric Weinrich established himself as a talented U.S. defenseman on the international stage, pursuing his global goals with gusto.

Early Days

In Roanoke, Virginia on 19 December 1966, Eric Weinrich was born. His parents, Sandra and John "Jack" Weinrich, lived nearby in Salem while Jack studied architecture at Virginia Tech University. Jack had grown up in New Jersey where he played football, basketball, and baseball (as well as throwing the javelin) in school. Tragically his dad died when he was eleven and he moved in with his older brother who was busy with work and raising his own kids. No family members ever attended any of Jack's athletic events, and this lack of family support later fed his determination to do things very differently when he had his own children.

After high school Jack joined the military and served four years, then he attended the University of Rhode Island where he played football for a couple of seasons and majored in Chemistry. More importantly during the summer after his sophomore year he met Sandra, a student at Salve Regina College in Newport. Sandra had grown up near Providence, enjoyed dancing and art as a girl, and attended Catholic high school; therefore, Salve Regina (still a girls-only school then) was a natural choice. Soon after Jack and Sandra received their bachelor's degrees in the spring of 1964, they got married.[1] Jack was weighing his options to attend either medical school or

2

architecture school, and the architecture program at Virginia Tech ended up being his choice. The newlyweds moved to the Roanoke, Virginia area. While her husband pursued his next degree, Sandra helped pay the bills by teaching at the Academy Street School. They would not end up staying in the Roanoke area long, but their time in Virginia made a big impact on their lives in part because Jack attended the games of a new East Coast League hockey team in Salem and became a fan of the sport.[2]

After Jack completed his architecture studies in 1968, the family moved to Poland, Maine. Jack's initial interviews after finishing at Virginia Tech had been in Boston on a miserably humid day (made more uncomfortable by young Eric's illness); however, the sessions had not turned out as planned. The interviewers in Boston were impressed by Jack's ability but could tell he did not like the atmosphere of the city. One of them said he had a friend practicing in Maine and asked Jack if he was interested. Jack asked Sandra, and she said "sure!" After a restful night at her parents' house in Providence (where they left young Eric for a day), the couple travelled up to Auburn, Maine. After his first interview Jack got a job offer, but then on a whim stopped at the offices of the Woodward Company and took a position there instead. The Weinrich family moved to Maine and found a friendly place to live not far from Auburn, in Poland.[3]

Poland is a small town in western Maine, on Route 26 between Gray and the Oxford Hills Region. The best opportunities for excitement in Poland, as in most of Maine, are in the outdoors. The Weinrich family lived near Tripp Lake, and during the cold "black ice" winter of 1970, Eric started skating.[4] His parents had purchased skates for the young lad's birthday, and he took to the ice with a determination that would become his trademark. "The little critter wouldn't come off the ice until he could master it," recalled his dad. "By the end of the first day he could skate."[5]

During his early childhood, Eric's hero was the legendary Boston Bruins defenseman Bobby Orr, who could skate and score as well as any defenseman in the history of hockey.[6] Orr was incredibly popular in the early

3

1970s, and a lot of children wanted to play the game like he did. "I learned how to skate when I was four, partly because of him, but also because of my parents. We were living in Poland then, and the whole family went skating on this lake. We stayed there until we knew how to skate," recalled Eric.[7] In addition to learning to skate on the lake in Poland, Eric believed that "it's also where I learned about the basic skills of the game and when I started to love it, playing in pickup games on the frozen lakes and ponds."[8] The biggest challenge in those early days was usually the frigid cold, but hockey captured his imagination and the poster of Orr on his wall motivated him to keep playing, regardless of wintry weather.[9]

In the summer of 1975, the Weinrich family moved from Poland a bit further north into Oxford County, to a small western Maine community called North Rumford that was between Rumford Center and Andover along the Ellis River. Jack and a friend at work named Stephen Moore decided to open their own architecture firm, and since Moore lived in the Rumford Point area, that was where the partners set up shop. Eric quickly caught the attention of local children (including this author) at the Rumford Point baseball field, where summer training was taking place. Coaches Junior Barker and Pete McCluskey quickly realized they had something special on their hands with 8-year-old Eric, who hit, threw, and caught like a teenager already.

First Hockey Teams

Before Eric would get a chance to star on the Rumford Point Little League team in 1976, however, he played on his first organized hockey team in the Squirts division (for players aged 8-10), in downtown Rumford on the outdoor skating rink. He obviously played very well, because at the end of the season banquet which featured as keynote speaker the hockey coach from Bowdoin College, Eric was named the team's most valuable player. It was an auspicious beginning to his career in organized hockey.[10] During

4

the summer of 1976, Eric played his rookie season of Little League baseball for Rumford Point, even though he was only nine and the league allowed players as old as tweleve.[11] While his long-term athletic success would be on the ice, in the mid-1970s many observers believed his future glory might be on the baseball diamond.

Rumford Point little league baseball players, summer 1977
front row: David, Jamie, Andy, and Pete
back row: Russ, Eric, Scott, and Elmer

In the fall of 1976, Eric entered 4th grade at the Rumford Center School, and once again laced up his skates for the Rumford Squirts. In a November 1976 game, the Squirts battled the team from Greene, Maine to a 6-6 tie. Eric starred for his squad with two goals and an assist.[12] This game occurred very close to the 1976 election, which was an event of great excitement in the 4th grade at Rumford Center School. Eric and his classmates held a mock election, and partly due to the influence of their energetic teacher, Carol Starr, voted overwhelmingly for Democratic candidate Jimmy Carter.[13]

In January 1977, Eric clearly demonstrated the spectacular ability that would one day see him in the National Hockey League. In a back-and-forth battle between the Rumford and Gardiner Squirts, Rumford prevailed with only fourteen seconds on the clock by a score of 5-4. Eric rattled home all five goals for the Rumford skaters, including a short-handed goal and the game-winner in the final seconds. His younger brother Alex also played a key role as goalie.[14] During this time, the tandem of Eric and Alex got even more regional notoriety when they competed on television in Boston Garden as part of the Boston Bruins Mini One-on-One competition.[15] Eric soon moved up to the next level, however, competing in the Pee-Wee division for Rumford. He did not miss a beat playing against older kids and contributed one of the goals in another defeat of Gardiner.[16] As Eric rapidly climbed the youth hockey ladder, he established a remarkably consistent and persistent approach to improving his game. For whatever team he skated, he was "always playing the point and thinking the game through."[17]

While it was becoming clear that Eric's best prospects would probably be on the ice, he continued to play many other sports very well. During 5th grade kickball games at Rumford Center School, for example, his ability to blast the ball prodigious distances was amazing. During a 2019 conversation, younger brother Al reminded me just how competitive Eric was at an early age. Having competed in some of their basement tennis ball hockey battles, my recollections support Al's point.[18] He was a very good basketball player, a super tackle football player (which was allowed during recess), and a force in "king of the hill" on high winter snowbanks. In terms of official participation, however, his last great accomplishment while living in the Rumford area would be on the baseball diamond. During the spring and summer of 1978, Eric catapulted the Rumford Point little league nine to a second consecutive championship. He excelled behind the plate as a catcher, pitched several overwhelming complete games including a no-hitter, and hit many long home runs.[19]

Alex, mom Sandra, Eric
late 1970s

During the three years when the Weinrich family lived in North Rumford, it became clear that Eric needed to face better competition on the ice if his hockey game was going to improve sufficiently. The first decision, encouraged by the Rumford coaches who thought Eric was too good to be playing only in their youth league, was whether the Weinrich family would make the commitment to transport Eric approximately sixty miles each way to Augusta three times per week so he could compete in the more competitive league at the Kennebec Valley Ice Arena. "We had a long talk about it," recalled his father, Jack. "We decided to do it."[20]

Playing in the more competitive league in Augusta was very time consuming for the entire Weinrich household, but they were all on board. "My mom and dad drove to a lot of games," remembered Eric.[21] In the summer of 1978, Jack and Sandra decided to move closer to the Kennebec Valley Ice Arena. They bought a home in Gardiner and bid farewell to the Rumford area.[22] Eric's ongoing success in the more competitive league in Augusta had suggested to his parents that the endless driving would not come to an end any time soon, and the likely prospect that their 2nd son

7

Alex (and possibly someday their 3rd son Jason) would also be needing frequent transportation to Augusta convinced Sandra and Jack to relocate to Gardiner.

Weino's Wisdom

It was during this time that my brother Alex and I attended an hour clinic at Kennebec Ice Arena in Augusta which featured Maine's first true hockey star, Waterville's own Danny Bolduc. Bolduc had left his hometown to attend Phillips Exeter Academy in New Hampshire and then went on to be a star at Harvard University. After three seasons at Harvard, Bolduc was selected to play for the USA Olympic Hockey Team and participate in the !976 Olympic Games in Innsbruck, Austria. Though the team didn't medal, Bolduc impressed professional teams and as an undrafted player, he signed a contract with the New England Whalers after the Games were completed. He also played two games in the highly regarded Canada Cup tournament which featured teams from around the world, including a team of NHL players from Canada and the team from the USSR. When Bolduc stepped onto the ice, dressed in his Team USA track suit, the diminutive figure sped around the ice in a fun game of keep away with the 50 or so young players. It was an impressive sight to see how he moved with such speed and power generated from a barely 5'9" frame at nearly 200 pounds!

We chased Bolduc around for a good amount of time until he finally tired out and the clinic resumed. This generous offer of time by Bolduc was the type of moment that leaves a lasting impression on young athletes. It certainly did for me. I wondered what I could do to earn one of those tracksuits and represent my country against the best in the world. Bolduc instantly became an inspiration for me, though in an era long before games and social media were widely televised and available to the public, following Bolduc's stellar but often overlooked ten-year career was not easy. But that moment at the Kennebec Ice Arena in Augusta played a huge role in my ambition to play international hockey and one day face the Big Red Machine of the USSR.

North Yarmouth Academy

The Weinrich boys would all thrive in their athletic pursuits after the move to central Maine, and not only on the ice. Eric continued to excel at baseball during the summer of 1979, his last year of little league. While his former teammates back in Rumford Point were falling short of a 3rd consecutive championship, Eric was a star for his new team in Gardiner, the Elks, winning every game he pitched and even hurling a perfect game with 17 strikeouts. In that same game, he also spearheaded the Elks at the plate with two hits.[23] During the summer of 1979, furthermore, the Weinrich family decided to enroll Eric at North Yarmouth Academy (NYA), in Yarmouth, Maine, about forty miles from their house. The strong academic reputation of NYA impressed Jack and Sandra, and was a key factor in the family decision.[24] As mom Sandra (a teacher herself) later explained, "The family came first, and their education was very important, and sports came after that."[25] Eric certainly did embrace his parents' love of learning; but, at the same time, Eric wanted to play in the top high school hockey league in the state (which NYA was in, but Gardiner was not). He was also excited to skate every day on the school's own rink. "Sure, it was a motivating factor," Eric admitted.[26]

For a variety of reasons, Eric started 7th grade at NYA in the fall of 1979. A few months later, in February 1980, the US Men's Olympic Hockey team shocked the world by upsetting the Soviet team in the first game of the medal round at the Winter Games in Lake Placid, New York, in a match that became universally known as the "Miracle on Ice." The US team, made up entirely of young amateurs, had scraped into the medal round with gutsy play, most notably in a 2-2 draw with Sweden. The Soviet team, on the other hand, was made up mostly of very experienced veterans. They were not technically professionals but played year-round together for state-sponsored teams. They had won gold at the Olympics in 1964, 1968, 1972 and 1976, and were expected by all to do so again in 1980. They won three of their opening round games by a total score of 41-5. After upsetting the Soviets, Team USA would go on to win the Gold Medal.

The Soviets settled for a silver medal at Lake Placid in 1980, but for them it was like coming in last place. Not one of the team's players submitted their silver medal for engraving, and several players threw their silver medals away. After the Soviet team left the Lake Placid Olympic Village, clean-up workers found 121 empty vodka bottles in their rooms. They clearly had taken the loss hard and decided to work for retribution. USSR hockey would come back with a vengeance and not lose any games for five years or any international game for eleven years.[27] Two outstanding young Soviet defensemen, Alexei Kasatonov and Viacheslav Fetisov, played great hockey throughout the games, returned to win Olympic gold in 1984 and 1988, and enjoyed successful NHL careers as the Cold War came to an end and Russian players could move to the western world.[28] Fetisov and Kasatonov would both eventually be teammates of Eric Weinrich on the New Jersey Devils. In February 1980, of course, Eric had no idea that he had seen two future teammates on TV, but he was impressed by the Soviet style of hockey and inspired by Team USA's great upset victory.

Eric, Coach Good, Alex
early 1980s

"We were playing a game the day of the Miracle and the replay was on that night. Some of the families had met on the way home from the game at the ice arena in Augusta and heard the unbelievable news about the game. It was excruciating waiting for the replay that evening even knowing the score. Though the excitement of watching the USA players overwhelmed the evening, it was hard not to notice the technical skills the Russian players possessed and how they dominated the game," Eric remembered.[29] Like almost every young player growing up in the United States, that moment in the winter of 1980 will remain the greatest upset in sports history and the inspiration for the Weinrich boys and a nation of hockey players to dream of one day playing in the Olympic Games and winning a Gold medal.

From the earliest days living in their Gardiner home on Kingsbury Street, all three boys played a lot of hockey at the Kennebec Valley Ice Arena in nearby Augusta. Highlights for the younger brothers included Jason at age 10 representing Maine in the Yankee Conference all-star tournament in Providence, Rhode Island, and Alex at age 13 anchoring the defense for the Kennebec Pee-Wee travel team that won the Division One national title in Buffalo in 1981. A major influence on the development of all three brothers as they spent endless hours at the arena in Augusta was Allan Globensky, a former member of the Quebec Nordiques who ran the rink in Augusta and refereed a lot of the games. He offered advice to Eric and his brothers frequently and assisted their coaches as they strove to help the boys get better.[30] Globensky would sometimes "look the other way" and allow the Weinrich boys and their buddies to use the ice, and overall "his experience as a former pro hockey player was very useful" to Eric.[31]

No one did nearly as much to support the Weinrich boys' dreams of playing high-level hockey as their parents, though. In 2003, while skating for the Philadelphia Flyers, Eric recollected: "It was quite a distance for my parents to drive me to practice and games, but they were committed to giving me every opportunity to improve and enjoy the game."[32] Hockey became a year-round pursuit for the three boys, with winter leagues and summer programs taking them the length and breadth of the northeast and beyond. "When other people were going to the beach," observed Sandra, "we were traveling to ice arenas." She could not count the number of rinks they visited in New England and Canada as her three sons became more and more involved in the game, but she had no regrets. "It was fun," she concluded, "and we traveled together as a family and that was really important to us."[33]

While his family members were unquestionably his biggest supporters and the top influence in his development in all respects, his coaches contributed greatly as well. At North Yarmouth Academy, the hockey coach was Ed Good, a former All-American player who had considerable experience coaching in Massachusetts and in Lake Placid, New York, where he helped prepare future NHL players Chris Nilan and Tom Songin.[34] "Coach Good really started me on the way to becoming a better defenseman," Eric later remembered. "He taught me alignment in the zone, positional play, and a lot of discipline. He taught me a lot of things that will help me down the road, and a lot that have nothing to do with hockey."[35]

The hard work and strong coaching paid off during 1981-82, Eric's first season on the NYA varsity team and ninth-grade year in school. Already standing over six feet tall and weighing 185 pounds, Eric helped NYA reach the state finals against perennial hockey power Lewiston. His great season earned him a place on the All-State hockey team, an incredibly rare accomplishment in any sport for a freshman. "Eric is about as coachable and astute a young man as I've ever coached," commented his high school coach. "His game sense and puck savvy for a 15-year-old kid is incredible. He doesn't cough up the puck much, he's a very astute puck-handler and passer and he has a real hard accurate shot. He's an offensive threat every time he touches the puck," concluded Good.[36]

National Attention

His efforts at NYA and around the northeast paid off in the summer after his freshman year of high school with some national exposure. In August of 1982, the Amateur Hockey Association of the United States invited Eric to a Midget Camp in Colorado Springs, Colorado. Eric played for a week in front of the coaches and staff of the U.S. Olympic Committee, a group that would select the squad for the 1984 Olympics and the teams for the World Championships.[37] For a 15-year-old, the Midget Camp was an incredible experience on many levels. "That's when I first became aware of scouts, of college coaches," he later recalled.[38]

In September 1982, a group of boosters including Jack Weinrich facilitated tryout sessions at NYA for a traveling team of 15-year-old and 16-year-old players, which would be known as the Ice World Midgets of Maine. Some forty players from across the state tried out, and Eric was one of the defensemen chosen. Jack played a key role in helping with the fundraising for the squad, which played twelve games in the fall before high school hockey started, winning nine of them.[39] In April 1983 the Ice World Midgets would get their biggest test and compete in a regional tournament featuring most of the best junior players in New England, where college coaches such as Jack Semler of the University of Maine would be watching closely.[40]

In schoolboy hockey, sophomore Eric and his NYA teammates reached the Maine state championship for a second straight season, but again lost the final to Lewiston. The NYA lads, however, had gotten an excellent bit of experience in a February 1983 exhibition against Mount St. Charles prep from Rhode Island. Considered one of the best high school teams in the USA, Mount St. Charles was led by talented forward Brian Lawton, who had scored forty goals during the regular season and would soon be selected first overall in the 1983 NHL draft by the Minnesota North Stars. Eric's job was to shadow the great Lawton, and he did a very good job. "Several NHL scouts there to take notes on Lawton," observed coach and journalist Joe

13

Clark, "later began asking questions about Weinrich."[41] Lawton himself, who had been steamrolled twice by Eric's hip-checks, recommended Weinrich to scouts back in southern New England who asked if he had encountered any opponents with potential up north.[42]

Completing a great winter season playing both for his NYA school squad and the Ice World Midgets, Eric hoped to get another opportunity during the summer of 1983 to showcase his talents on the national stage. The chance came when the U.S. Olympic Committee called him back to Colorado Springs for a more prestigious National Elite Midget Camp, which took place for ten days beginning on 17 July. Eric's encouraging invitation letter was signed by Lou Vairo, coach of the 1984 U.S. Olympic hockey team. Vairo was with former NHL tough guy and the "Father of Minnesota Hockey," John Mariucci, when first observing Eric in action. Both Vairo and Mariucci were very impressed by the youngster from Maine and believed that his skills and size made him a potential future pro.[43]

Lou Vairo was an excellent judge of talent who had been an advance scout for Herb Brook's Team USA at the 1980 Olympics, and in the case of Eric his prediction was on the money. Beyond his work as a scout and coach, moreover, Vairo had made an incredible (and virtually unknown) contribution to the globalization of hockey and the eventual thawing of USA/USSR relations while coaching a high school team in New York state in the early 1970s.[44] Greatly impressed by a television broadcast of the swirling Soviets and their emphasis on skating and passing, he wrote the USSR coach, Anatoly Tarasov, and asked how he could learn some of the Russian style. Months later Vairo received a reply from Tarasov inviting him to Moscow.[45]

Vairo took out a $3500 personal loan, got a visa from the Soviet consulate in New York City, and flew to Moscow. "Next thing you know," recalled Vairo, "I'm sitting with him in Moscow in his colonel's uniform!"[46] He stayed with the Tarasov family and learned a lot about training and strategy from the Soviet mastermind. Vairo's extraordinary adventure in the early 1970s (as Richard Nixon's policy of détente was just beginning) built some of the very first USA/USSR cultural bonds that would allow hockey to eventually help end the Cold War peacefully. His friendship with Tarasov and contributions to USA hockey before the 1980 Olympics demonstrated that the real history of international hockey was more complicated than the oversimplified "Miracle" of the "good USA" versus the "Evil USSR" at Lake Placid, too.

Employing methods learned in Moscow, Vairo won a high school championship in New York and then a national junior title with a team in Minnesota. His successful and innovative methods attracted the attention of Herb Brooks and a decades-long relationship between Vairo and USA Hockey began. His dedication to the game earned him induction into the USA Hockey Hall of Fame in 2014, and videos of his induction speech and honoring his career on YouTube are fascinating and entertaining. Vairo's enthusiastic attitude and positive influence would be felt by generations of players such as Eric Weinrich, starting with their first encounter in Colorado Springs.[47]

Weino's Wisdom

Lou Vairo was an intriguing character and the biggest thing I remember about the first practice he ran was the somersaults he added to the drills! Of course, no one had ever seen this done in practice, but it was a technique Lou had borrowed from the great Russian coach, Tarasov. He made his players perform these types of moves within the drills to disrupt them and then recover to their feet and keep moving within the drill. Lou had a presence about him and captured your attention. I have never forgotten many of the tips Lou preached during that practice. It was years before we crossed paths again and when we did, the moments we shared are some of my best memories of the game.

Eric played well at the camp; furthermore, doing so against such a high level of competition boosted his confidence. "You look at kids that have made it to the pros, kids that you've played against," he observed, "and you realize you can play with them."[48] More college coaches and pro scouts attended the July 1983 puck rendezvous in the shadow of Pike's Peak, also. Eric described the experience enthusiastically: "Cards were passed around. I remember getting the card of a scout for the Hartford Whalers. That was exciting."[49] Much more attention from NHL teams and USA hockey was soon to come Eric's way, but first he would be focusing on his junior year of high school.

After reaching the state finals two years in a row, going into the 1983-84 season the NYA squad faced the major challenge of replacing several graduates, especially on the offensive end. Coach Good decided to make stingy defense the team's strongpoint. With Eric leading the way and manning the point, NYA sailed through the regular season with a stellar record of sixteen wins, one draw, and one loss. The focus on defense paid off, as they only allowed 29 goals in the 18-game slate. In addition to anchoring the strong defense, Eric spearheaded the offense with 23 goals and 33 assists. "Eric is, without a doubt, the dominant player in the state today," raved Good. "He is unequaled as an offensive threat from the point position, and he has a terrific sense of how the game is played."[50] The spectacular season ended disappointingly for NYA, however, with a third straight loss to Lewiston in the finals and runner-up finish. Eric and his teammates would still have something to shoot for during his senior year.

1984 NHL Draft

While NYA battled their way through the state playoffs in February 1984, the men's US hockey team competed in the Winter Olympics in Sarajevo, Yugoslavia. Pat LaFontaine, who was born in St. Louis in 1965 but grew up in Michigan near Detroit, was the best offensive player for Team USA scoring five goals.[51] LaFontaine had been drafted in the first round by the Islanders in 1983 and would go on to enjoy an incredible NHL career, but his skill was not enough to boost Team USA above a somewhat disappointing 7th-place finish. Another star on the squad, future Hall of Famer Chris Chelios, believed that the public expectations for the team to win another gold were simply unrealistic.

Chelios noted that Coach Lou Vairo was only 38 at the time, and quite different than other coaches the players had encountered. "He owned a memorable Brooklyn accent and a penchant for butchering the English language now and then," added Chelios. Vairo emphasized speed and quickness in hopes of building a squad that would play more like the Europeans and Soviets, and Chelios praised him for treating the players well.[52] Although they had a talented team and an innovative coach, they were no match for the Soviets this time. Nevertheless, the effort of the USA reinforced Eric's dream to play in the Olympics himself. At this point in his career, it was starting to seem more plausible.

In addition to cheering on Team USA and pondering his own possible future participation, Eric noted the dominant play of the Soviet Union, who revenged their 1980 Lake Placid loss by rampaging to the gold. They won all five games in the group stage, outscoring their opponents 42 to five. The USSR juggernaut then shut out Canada and Czechoslovakia in the medal round to take gold. The talent-laden Soviet squad was anchored on defense by two of Eric's future teammates, Alexei Kasatonov and Viacheslav Fetisov.[53] Also packing an offensive punch, Kasatonov scored three goals, and Fetisov's total of eleven points made him the 6th highest scorer in the tournament. The Soviet defensemen in 1984 certainly set the bar high for Eric and other young blueliners.

Eric had little time to be impressed by the Soviet's dominance or feel frustration over another loss in the state hockey finals, though. He had a busy spring maintaining solid grades, playing catcher for the NYA baseball team (his diamond exploits attracted some attention from pro scouts), and preparing for another hectic summer on the ice. Surprising news reverberated through the Weinrich home on 9 June 1984. The new

University of Maine hockey coach, Sean Walsh, called and asked Eric if he had heard about the NHL draft, taking place in Montreal. "Yeah, I guess a couple of New England kids went high," responded Eric. "You got drafted!" exclaimed Walsh.[54] Indeed, the Buffalo Sabres (whose coach and general manager was the legendary hockey figure Scotty Bowman) had chosen Eric in the 9th round with the 186th pick. The problem with Buffalo's selection was that Eric would not turn eighteen until December and was thus two months too young to be eligible. The pick was nullified, but Eric's reputation as a legitimate pro player got another boost.

Being part of the 1984 draft, even as a footnote resulting from Buffalo's gaffe, put Eric in some good company. Future superstars abounded in this draft, such as Mario Lemieux, Brett Hull, Patrick Roy, and Gary Suter. Montreal picked Czechoslovakian youth Petr Svoboda, who had recently defected while playing at the World Junior Championship in West Germany.[55] The Cold War context, which would be a big part of Eric's own experience very soon, was a key aspect of the globalization of hockey in the mid-1980s. Also noteworthy in the 1984 NHL draft was that Los Angeles opted for Tom Glavine in the 4th round, but Glavine decided to pursue baseball instead. Although Glavine would become a superstar pitcher for the Atlanta Braves, he never forgot his high school hockey days.[56]

During the first half of the summer of 1984, Eric competed in the Europa Cup in Wellesley, Massachusetts against other top New England high school skaters. In August, he took part in the Hockey Night in Boston tournament, a high-profile event attended by many college coaches and pro scouts.[57] His hockey stock continued to rise, but with the advent of his senior year at NYA in September, Eric returned to the soccer pitch to compete again in a sport he had embraced late and quickly enjoyed success. The previous year, he had made the all-Maine team as a striker and contributed considerably to NYA's championship.[58] Eric's senior soccer season started strong and NYA won their first eight games, with he and younger brother Alex both playing well. For example, on 24 September they led NYA to a 4-0 win over rival

St. Doms. Eric provided three assists, including one header to Alex who promptly propelled the ball into the net.[59] The two oldest Weinrich boys and their teammates claimed another state title later in the fall of 1984, and Eric was once again recognized with all-league honors.

His brief soccer career had been a very good one, by any standard, but all the while Eric was gearing up for his last rink campaign at NYA. The speed of the top-notch players he had faced in national competitions in Colorado and Massachusetts convinced him that he had to improve his quickness and his lateral movement, and that he should focus on being more defensive-minded. "I think in years to come I'll probably be more of a defensive style player," he commented prophetically as he approached his last year skating for NYA.[60]

World Junior Championships in Finland

In late November, news reached the homestead in Gardiner that Eric would be missing a few NYA games in December, but for a very exciting reason. Word came that Eric had been chosen for the 20-man roster which would travel to Finland for the World Junior Championships. The invitation brought a sigh of relief for the Weinrich family, who had been waiting for three months for the final word. Eric had been one of forty players at a tryout camp in Colorado Springs in July and survived the first cut to 25. He then participated in the second camp during August in Lake Placid and waited. Hints had trickled in, such as an early November call from the team's general manager Keith Blasé, who told Eric that he should get a passport.[61]

When interviewed by journalists in the days following the announcement, Eric was understandably excited. "This meant a great deal to me," he commented. "Some of the best players in the world at my age will be there, so it's the best preparation for college hockey that I can get. It should really help me for next year."[62] About half of his teammates-to-be were already playing Division I college hockey, so his analysis was certainly accurate. In another conversation, he elaborated on the opportunity, with characteristic modesty: "I think it's the greatest thing that could have happened to me. These kids are just outstanding players. Most of them are quite a bit better than me, but it's just so fun to play with kids that are so skilled."[63]

The US squad rendezvoused in New York in mid-December 1984 for two days of practice, then departed for the long flight to Finland. Arriving safely, the team quickly settled into their dorm and a rigorous routine of daily 4-hour practices on the much bigger European-size rink. Eric detailed his experiences thoroughly on a postcard to his family back in Maine. He described the flight over with Team Canada, the dorm rooms and local village, the currency and exchange rate, and of course the food. "A lot of veggies, no salad, sandwiches, stews, porridge, milk, water, goat's milk, a wine-beer mixture (brutal-tasting!), yogurt, and fruit. It's not that bad," he concluded regarding food. Overall, Eric truly enjoyed his first international hockey experience. "Some kids don't like it here, but I love it," he exclaimed.[64]

It would be hard to imagine a better cultural ambassador for the USA than the young NYA defenseman. His younger brother Alex later offered some insights into why Eric shined in this role. He recalled that their family had hosted an exchange student from Finland, and that in general they all "had a soft spot" for engaging with other cultures.[65] Eric took in everything and had only good things to say, even about the Finnish climate. "It's been snowing and cold since we've been here, but it's not a biting cold," he explained. "Everyone skis," he added. His interactions with local Fins were all positive, including when three young children came into the rink for autographs. Eric learned their names and took their pictures. "The people are nice if you get the courage to talk to them," he concluded insightfully.[66]

After about a week of practicing and acclimatizing, games began on 23 December. By then, Eric's dad Jack had arrived, to cheer on Team USA. According to Eric's mom Sandra, "It was a very exciting trip for both of them."[67] Part of the excitement came from being in a tournament against players from the USSR. Eric, who had never seen a Russian in person before, jokingly recalled that "They were like aliens."[68] The Soviet players were guarded closely, but one player managed to show his room number to Jack. Father and son Weinrich decided to sneak up and visit the young Russian.

For his part, Eric was quite nervous going up to the room, worried about the KGB. They made it safely and found two Soviet players in the room, Alexander Semak and Valeri Kamensky, who would both later excel in the NHL. Semak and Kamensky asked Eric for Levi jeans, which he did not have, but he offered them a Levi tracksuit. In exchange, they gave him a set of pins representing teams in the USSR hockey league and a set of photos (resembling hockey cards in the USA) depicting Soviet players.[69] The brief visit showed the potential for unofficial ambassadors, in this case hockey players, to break down Cold War barriers and improve relations between the United States and the Soviet Union.

On the ice, things were not as successful for Team USA, who lost badly to Czechoslovakia, and then played better but still lost to Finland, the USSR, and Canada. Wins over West Germany and Poland boosted the US squad to a 6th place finish, but that was hardly what they and their fans had been hoping for. The Soviets played well in the tournament, as always, but it was Canada who won gold in Finland in January 1985, led by goalie Craig Billington (a future teammate of Eric on the New Jersey Devils). Eric, meanwhile, played in all seven games for Team USA in Finland and acquitted himself well, netting one goal and assisting on another.

Weino's Wisdom

The atmosphere and competition in Finland were beyond anything I ever imagined. When we arrived at the training facility where we would first stay in Finland, the dorm-like setting was dark and desolate in the woods of the countryside. There was a poster in a hallway advertising a Scandinavian stick company featuring the famous "Russian Five" (Krutov, Larionov, Makarov,

Fetisov and Kasatonov) from the Red Army team. I will never forget how impressive the Finnish team looked in practice and how big the European ice surface appeared! I also remember when we stepped onto the ice against the Russian team, the sight of the red CCCP uniforms intimidated us to a point. It is safe to say, the game was virtually over before it started.

For the other teams we played, we believed we could win. The game against Canada, our biggest rival, was 2-2 late in the 2nd period and the puck squirted out to me at the point. I stepped into the shot and scored a goal to put us in the lead going into the 3rd period. But Canada went on to score 5 goals in the 3rd period, led by Wendall Clark, and our hopes of defeating the powerful Canadian team fizzled away. They went on to win the tournament, which was some consolation. The whole experience surrounding international play and the foreign players with skills we had never seen left a lasting impression on my fascination with the training techniques that allowed these foreign players to execute the way they could on the ice. The other takeaway for me was how sullen and stern the Russian players all appeared and that they would hardly ever make eye contact. It was mysterious and a stark contrast to how the other countries' players carried themselves, usually smiling and joking with each other from time to time. The Russian players always seemed to be focused on one thing: preparing for the games and winning. It would be years before I learned about the pressure and expectations that were put on them.

Although Eric and his teammates fell short of replicating the "Miracle on Ice" in Finland, he had made a name for himself in USA hockey circles and opened the door for more opportunities in the future. Eric had come an incredibly long way since learning to skate on a pond in Poland and first competing on a hockey team in Rumford. The hard work at the Kennebec Valley Ice Arena, the endless driving to midget tournaments, the move to Gardiner, and the decision to enroll at NYA, all contributed to Eric's success. Competing at the World Junior Championships in Finland made Eric a truly international hockey player, and it was the first big step towards his global goal of competing with the best.

CHAPTER 2

"Becoming a Black Bear and Competing in Calgary, 1985-1988."

Eric Weinrich, who as a high school underclassman had attracted some national attention at USA hockey camps in Colorado and taken initial strides on the international stage at the World Juniors in Finland, would make a quantum leap towards attaining higher-level global goals starting in the winter of 1985. After picking what college to attend (University of Maine in Orono), he led his high school team to the state championship, and then was drafted by the New Jersey Devils. Although he scored no goals during his first campaign as a Maine Black Bear, he did return to the World Juniors and helped Team USA medal in Ontario. His second season at Orono was much more productive offensively, earning him recognition as an All-American. More importantly, Maine qualified for the NCAA Tournament for the first time.

In August 1987, Eric began battling for a spot with Team USA for the 1988 Calgary Olympics. He earned a place and played three games at Calgary, thus accomplishing one of the global goals he had envisioned since childhood. As soon as Team USA completed its Olympic competition, Eric rejoined his Black Bear teammates for the end of the collegiate season. He made an immediate impact and helped Maine advance as far as the Frozen Four, the semifinals of the NCAA tournament.[70] Between 1985 and 1988, Eric Weinrich enjoyed considerable success such as becoming a Black Bear and competing at Calgary, accomplishing several of his most significant global goals.

College Choice

Upon returning from the World Junior Championship tournament in Finland, Eric faced the daunting challenge of choosing a university while being recruited very aggressively. Hockey powers in the far away west, such as Wisconsin and Minnesota, offered him scholarships; however, he decided to focus only on schools in Hockey East. Eric opted for visits to New Hampshire, Boston University, Boston College, Providence, and Maine. During the process Eric had second thoughts and asked about possibly visiting Minnesota, but his dad reminded him that he had already committed to the maximum five schools for official junkets.

Eric and his dad Jack at 1985 NHL draft

Although some people had advised Eric against attending his own state's university, his trip to Orono sealed the deal quickly. Professors and students made Eric feel at home, and the fans supporting the hockey team were extremely enthusiastic. "I've never seen such a wild crew," Eric exclaimed.[71] The unity of the Black Bears team impressed Eric, as did their young coach, Shawn Walsh, and his assistants. Coach Walsh had high hopes for the Maine hockey program, and Eric decided he wanted to be part of it. He announced his decision to attend the University of Maine in early January 1985. Eric made it clear in several interviews that he was excited about his decision and was proud to play for his state university. The feeling was mutual, as Coach Shawn Walsh explained to the press. "Without reservation, I would call Eric one of the three most highly recruited high school seniors in the country," commented Walsh.[72] The coach contended that signing Eric meant that Maine had landed arguably the top recruiting class in the country. "He will bring size, strength, and smarts to Maine," stated the coach. "He has a tremendous awareness and sense with the puck. There is no question that he will step in and help us out immediately," added Walsh.[73]

Coach Walsh further commented that he was as impressed with Eric's maturity and character off the ice as he was by his ability on it. Walsh also explained that with Eric becoming a Black Bear, the Maine program would benefit greatly from the support of the entire Weinrich family. For their part, Eric's parents were quite excited about his committing to Orono. Eric's father, Jack, described the entire recruiting experience as "interesting and fascinating," and he added that he and his wife had left the final decision in Eric's hands. Mom Sandra was "thrilled about receiving the opportunity to see her son play just an hour and a half from their home in Gardiner."[74] During a lengthy interview shortly after announcing his college choice, Eric assessed his future role playing in Orono realistically. "I don't see myself as being as big of an offensive threat up there as I have been in high school. My main goal is to play solidly. I don't care if I win any awards. I just want to play and do the best that I can. If I'm contributing to the team, I'm going to be satisfied," he stated. His interviewer ended the discussion by asking Eric if he had any advice for aspiring young athletes. Eric explained that his formula for success had been simple. "If you work hard enough," he concluded, "and set your goals high enough, in the end it will be worth all the effort that you've put into it."[75]

State Championship

The most important short-term goal for Eric in early 1985 was to lead the North Yarmouth Academy hockey team to the Maine state class A championship. After missing five games while at the World Junior games in Finland, Eric stepped right back into his role as the anchor of NYA's defense and the catalyst of their offense, getting plentiful ice time including power plays and penalty killing shifts. NYA finished the regular season with thirteen wins and six losses, and they ranked 2nd going into the 4-team state tournament. NYA would be severely tested by St. Dominic (St. Dom's) Academy, a perennial hockey power. On Thursday 28 February 1985, the teams tangled at the Cumberland County Civil Center in Portland. Deadlocked at two apiece after regulation, the boys battled through a couple of intense overtime sessions. The goalie for St. Dom's made several excellent saves on close range blasts by Eric, and the game ended in a tie. Instead of a shootout, Maine state hockey rules required the teams to play another full game, which took place on Tuesday 5 March, once again in Portland. Approximately 1,500 fans witnessed the replay to see who would advance to the state finals against Lewiston, and this time it was no contest. NYA hammered St. Dom's by a score of 5 to 0, and Eric assisted on three of the goals.[76]

Four days later, on Saturday 9 March, Eric and his NYA team defeated top-ranked Lewiston in a hard-fought two to one battle. The victory gave NYA its first ever state hockey crown, and their triumph made them the first school other than Lewiston, St. Dom's, or Waterville to win a Maine title in over 25 years. In the aftermath, Eric was named to the all-state squad, and won the league MVP award. None of that mattered nearly as much to him as his team finally winning the championship. Over thirty years later he still remembered the hectic last week of the 1985 season and recalled that in the excitement on the morning of the final he had forgotten his jersey at home when he drove down to Portland.[77]

Drafted by the Devils

Wearing a new jersey had not affected his play in the state championship and served as something of an omen for Eric as he would soon be trying on a new, New Jersey, jersey. In June, when most high school seniors donned their graduation robes, found summer jobs, and had some final fun with old friends before heading off to college, Eric attended the 1985 NHL draft in Toronto. Early in the 2nd round, the NJ Devils selected Eric with the 32nd pick.[78]

Future famous players selected earlier in the draft included Wendell Clark, who would be a tough opponent playing for Toronto, and Joe Nieuwendyk, who would score nearly 600 NHL goals and win three Stanley Cups. Other notables chosen ahead of Eric included two top-notch goalies, Sean Burke and Mike Richter, whom Eric would get to know well in the years to come. Much later in the proceedings, the Vancouver Canucks drafted Igor "The Professor" Larionov from the Soviet Union.[79] Like his two teammates, Slava Fetisov and Alexei Kasatonov, who had been selected in 1983 by the Devils, Larionov would not be able to move to North America and begin his NHL career until the political situation in the USSR evolved quite a bit further. Eventually, though, these three famous Red Army line-mates would all be star actors in an unfolding end-of-Cold-War drama, and Eric would play a supporting role.[80]

Being a high-ranking pick in the 1985 draft clearly put Eric in very good company, but before turning professional he planned to improve his game at the University of Maine, and hopefully with Team USA. The Devils organization expressed their excitement about signing Eric, but also pledged to support his educational plans. "New Jersey Devils' Draft choices who plan to go to University or College will never be influenced, by any of our people, to leave school in order to get started on a pro career," explained the New Jersey management.[81]

The Black Bears' head coach, Shawn Walsh, was similarly understanding about the strong chance that Eric would not remain in Orono for four years but would instead leave early to play professionally. "I'm happier that we're starting to bring that type of player to Maine than if we didn't have him at all," commented Walsh shortly after the draft. "Sure, it's going to bother you the day that you lose him," he added, "but sometimes it's in a player's best interest to leave."[82] Such decisions seemed a long way's off for Eric going into the summer of 1985, however. In the short term he planned to focus on off-ice training (running, biking, and lifting weights), skate regularly, work at two hockey camps, and then compete at the National Sports Festival in Baton Rouge, Louisiana in late July. A solid performance in Baton Rouge, he hoped, would earn him a second stint with the U.S. Junior National Team for the World Junior Championships in Canada at the end of the year.

Becoming a Black Bear

With the start of the fall semester in September, Eric joined his Black Bears teammates in Orono for preseason training. Games began in late October, and Maine faced tough competition right from the start, playing both Boston College and Boston University in early season matches. The Black Bears were a very young team, and the 1985-86 campaign would be a learning experience, especially for Eric and the other freshmen. Outplayed by their Hockey East rivals, Maine only won two of their first sixteen contests. On the bright side, the Black Bears lost eight of the first sixteen games by only one goal, and nearly upset the number-one-ranked University of Denver Pioneers in a mid-December clash, falling 4-3.

On 20 December 1985, the Maine Black Bears faced off in an exhibition against a tough team from the Soviet Union's top-level Elite Division, Sokol-Kiev. The evening featured considerable pageantry, with national anthems of both the US and the USSR being played, and then the team captains exchanging commemorative pendants.[83] The game itself was not as dramatic, however. Eric and his teammates were no match for the pros from the USSR, and they lost by a lopsided 11-1 margin. This was another good lesson for Eric about the speed and skill of players from the Eastern Bloc. It was also a wonderful opportunity for Eric's dad Jack Weinrich, who joined the Soviet delegation for dinner.[84]

Weino's Wisdom

My father was one of those invited to the meeting of the Maine hockey faithful and the Russian delegation. What a unique experience for the people of the area and in the hockey community to socialize with the delegation of our political and hockey rivals! There was always something mysterious about these kinds of interactions but with the help of some interpreters and Russian vodka, my father had a fun night and enjoyed his experience. I was anxious to play another game against the Russians and the anticipation to compete against players that we knew nothing about.

Our belief that we could skate with our Russian counterparts was quickly put to rest after the puck drop as we witnessed a masterclass of skating and technical play that found us completely over-matched from the get-go. The team from Kiev, comprised of a group of basically professionals, were so well coached and trained, and the technical skills and their attack was incredible to watch. On this night, we were spectators. As frustrating as the game was, where we barely had control of the puck, watching these players was inspiring and fascinating. I found myself absorbed in focusing on how they came up the ice, the way the defensemen used their exceptional skating ability and mobility to defend and breakout and the pace of their play and how fast the puck moved.

That season at Maine, we did not have a lot of success and our skill level wasn't even close to theirs. Furthermore, this team was not the Red Army from Moscow! For our team, the game could not end quickly enough. But even after the game, as an opposing player it was hard not to look back on the game and take away some good lessons in how the game was played. For me, it only increased my desire to compete on the world stage of the Olympic Games and get my chance to compete against the feared USSR.

World Juniors in Ontario

Eric had little time to feel disappointed with the Black Bears' being thrashed by the Soviets, though, as he was soon travelling to Hamilton, Ontario to join Team USA for the World Junior Championships. Eric had played well enough at the summer trials in Baton Rouge to earn an encore with the Under-20 U.S. squad, and he hoped to make more of an impact this time. He did not disappoint, playing in all seven games, chipping in one goal, and helping Team USA win an unprecedented bronze medal. After a tough 7-3 opening loss to the USSR, Eric and his teammates rebounded to defeat Czechoslovakia 5-2, beat West Germany and Switzerland, then earned the bronze by thumping Sweden, 5-1. The bronze represented an important step forward for USA hockey, as no previous squad had ever finished higher than fifth, since the junior tournament began in 1977.[85]

The Junior Worlds in Canada were also something of a personal turning point for Eric, as he approached the second half of the season at Maine with much more confidence. He played more like he had played in high school, remained relaxed rather than uptight, and established himself as the best plus/minus player on the Black Bears. According to Devils' official Max McNab, who was keeping close tabs on their draft pick, "The coach of the junior team said Weinrich was the soundest defenseman in the tournament."[86] Coach Walsh noticed a huge difference in Eric's play after the bronze-medal-winning effort, too. "The biggest thing about Eric is that he was a completely different player before and after the World Junior tournament," observed Walsh. "In the first half of the season, he was a typically inconsistent freshman. Mistakes were getting him down. When he came back, he was able to shrug them off." This drastic improvement occurred even with a serious injury to his back and left shoulder, incurred during the final game against Sweden. The injury convinced Coach Walsh to quietly move Eric from the left side of the Maine defense to the right side for the second half of the college season, and the move worked well for Eric and for the team.[87]

Weino's Wisdom

Our bronze medal achievement at the1985-86 World Junior tournament was a huge step in USA Hockey's development as a program. This group of players was the basis that would make up the next Olympic Team and I started to believe I belonged in this group. We had beaten some opponents that typically we had struggled against. Although we lost the first game to the Russians and then against our northern rivals Canada, finishing 3rd was a major accomplishment in international hockey. The Russian team featured a few of the players from the previous year's team, including Alex Kamensky and Alex Semak, and a player I could not stop watching throughout the tournament, Mikhail Tatarinov. He played defense like me, and I was so impressed by his power and shot and his fearless play even against the Canadian team, who tried to intimidate every team they played. But nothing fazed him, and he led them to the gold medal and earned a place on the all-tournament team. Tatarinov skated for a few years in the NHL. Though we never were friends per se, we recognized each other from that tournament and would always say 'hello' to each other in passing.

The Black Bears played better hockey after the holidays, winning nine out of 22 games. They battled Providence College competitively in the opening game of the Hockey East tournament, falling in a close 5-4 contest. They ran out of steam in game two, losing 5-2, and their season was over. But, as the nation's youngest hockey team, who had lost fourteen games by one goal, they eagerly looked forward to the 1986-87 season. Eric himself had learned a lot about what Division One hockey required. He had logged a lot of ice time, skating during power plays and killing penalties. His plus/minus rating was highest on the team, and he finished fifth with fifteen assists. One possible disappointment for Eric was that he did not score a single goal for Maine during his initial season. "Everybody wants to score his freshman year, but I don't think it bothered him," commented his defensive partner, Jack Capuano, the team captain. "He's a team player, and just having him out there helps because you know he's back there and you've got confidence in him."[88]

After completing his freshman season at Orono on a somewhat positive note, Eric decided to take his summer training to a higher level and work on a part of his game that he thought needed improvement if he was to raise his game another notch. Eric hired a private tutor, Julie Tortorella, a figure-skating instructor whose husband coached the Brunswick high school hockey team. Tortorella tutored the defenseman twice a week for an hour at a time, working on balance, edge work, and a smoother stride. Part of his motivation came from watching Fetisov and Kasatonov of the Red Army. "When I see the Russian players I think, 'Why can't I skate like them?' It's frustrating." His newest global goal, to skate more like the Soviet players, kept him focused. The hard work paid off, too. Unlike other players, observed Maine assistant coach Jay Leach, Eric stuck to his training regimen religiously. "Eric Weinrich goes at it hard. His improvement from the end of March until fall was unparalleled. His skating improved. It was like night and day," raved Leach.[89]

Sophomore Sensation

Maine's new season began on Friday night, 24 October 1986, with a disappointing 8-4 loss in Orono to Boston College. However, Eric's summer training program seemed to give him a boost as he scored his first collegiate goal and added an assist. He was probably happier the next night, though, as the Black Bears rebounded and beat BC. The following Friday in Boston, Maine sent a message to the Hockey East by upsetting Boston University, 3-2. Eric recorded two assists in the big win, and he and the rest of the Black Bears' defense did very well to hold BU to just two goals. The 1986-87 season was off to a flying start![90] On 15 November 1986, the Black Bears took on the University of New Hampshire Wildcats at their arena in Durham, NH. The tight contest stood 2-2 with about a minute remaining and looked like it might go to overtime. Eric controlled a loose puck at the blue line and fired a slap shot past UNH goalie Rich Burchill to give Maine the hard-fought road win. The spectacular play improved Maine's record to six wins and two losses on the season. Eric described the goal as "the biggest of my career." New Hampshire coach Bob Kullen called Eric's game-winner a "pro shot." Maine coach Shawn Walsh exclaimed, "That wasn't a lucky goal; that was a talent goal." During his post-game remarks, Walsh praised Eric as "the best player in the Hockey East."[91]

The Black Bears continued to play good hockey throughout the second half of the regular season, and finished with a record of 22 wins, thirteen losses, and two ties. They ranked third in the Hockey East, which meant they would host Providence College at the Alfond Arena in Orono on 11 March 1987. Eric scored a goal and had two assists, as Maine beat Providence 5-2 for its first ever Division One hockey playoff game victory.[92] In the semi-final game at Boston Garden, Maine beat Lowell 5-4 to advance to the finals. They took an early lead against top-ranked Boston College but ended up falling short by a 4-2 score. Eric was one of six players named to the All-Tournament team, as was fellow Black Bear and long-time friend Mike McHugh. Brian Leetch, star defenseman for BC and future NHL all-star, was named the tourney's MVP.

Based on their very good regular season and their strong showing in the Hockey East tournament, Maine was invited to compete in the NCAA tournament as an at-large bid. The Black Bears travelled to Detroit to play Michigan State in a 2-game series, with the team scoring the most goals in two games advancing to the Frozen Four. Maine gave it the old college try, but only managed five goals in two games versus the eleven scored by Michigan State. A wonderful season for the Black Bears ended, but it represented the breakthrough campaign for a hockey program that would be a national contender for more than a decade to come. Eric, who ended the season with twelve goals and 32 assists in 41 games, was selected by the American Hockey Coaches Association as a 2nd Team All-American. His fellow honorees included future NHL greats such as Brian Leetch, Joe Nieuwendyk, and Eddie Belfour.

Eric was not entirely sure what had made the biggest difference between his freshman and sophomore seasons for Maine, but in any case, he knew that he had "felt relaxed and confident" throughout 1986-87. Regarding the quantum leap in goal production, he attributed it to a couple of things. He believed that being placed low in the slot on power plays had given him more opportunities. He also had shortened up the backswing on his slapshot and just tried to hit the net rather than aim for a precise spot.[93] Whatever the main reasons, his game had reached a very high level, and had attracted considerable positive attention from the NHL. David McNab, a scout for the Hartford Whalers, contended in early 1987 that Eric was the "best defenseman in college hockey."[94]

Not surprisingly, the NHL team watching most carefully was New Jersey, who had drafted Eric in 1985 and held the rights to his potential pro career until at least 1990. David Conte, assistant director of player personnel for the Devils, congratulated Shawn Walsh on the Black Bears' outstanding season. Specifically, Conte informed Walsh that the Devils were "extremely pleased with the progress of Eric Weinrich." Conte acknowledged Eric's "considerable talent" and "exceptional character," but also noted that the good work by Walsh and his staff in Orono had done a lot to accelerate the pace of Eric's development.[95]

Weino's Wisdom

1987 Pravda Cup in the USSR
Eric in center of each photo

A lot had occurred over the season and although a nice mental and physical pause would have been welcome, I received news from Coach Walsh and USA hockey that I had been selected to join a group of college and professional players from the United States to fly to Russia and play in the Pravda Cup against some other international teams and the host team, the Russian National B team. This meant I would have to receive permission from my professors to postpone studies until we returned from the trip. This was an exciting opportunity to further the season and play some meaningful international games before a short break and then summer training. I could not believe I was going to Russia!

We flew to Helsinki and then boarded a small plane with all our equipment and supplies we needed for the tournament. This included lots of water, and the reason for this was we were informed that the water in Leningrad/St. Petersburg had some bacteria that may cause some intestinal sickness. We were given some preventative medication prior to our arrival in St. Petersburg. Our team doctor informed us we should not shower with our mouths open if possible! As we approached the runway, looking out the window of the aircraft provided a glimpse of what we had all envisioned we would see but never really imagined. We landed on a runway not close to the terminals and as we left the plane, we could see the security detail with machine guns. They ushered us into a small building for immigration and they opened every bag and case we had brought with us, confiscating many items including all our VHS movies. None of us had ever been through something like this and it was eye opening and a little unnerving. I did what I was told and said nothing.

The biggest thing I remember about the whole trip was how gray everything seemed. We, of course, were always dressed in our Team USA gear with the bright red, white and blue colors. In that setting where we were staying, it stood out like a sore thumb. I think I was one of the only players who stepped out of the hotel during our stay other than leaving for the games. We always were searching for hidden cameras and recording devices in our rooms, but none were ever found. Still, it was in the back of your mind, all the time. The food wasn't what we were used to, especially their attempt at "pancakes" which were more like a greasy crepe. I wasn't fussy and managed fine. There were always pitchers of water on the tables, and we all were dying of thirst but as we were told before we got there, no water. The only thing we could drink was warm Pepsi and we saved our water for the games and practice.

The games went well, and our team won the tournament, even defeating the host team from Russia. This was my first ever victory against a Russian team. Though it was not the Olympic Games, winning a game against a Russian team in their country was a big moment for us. As the games progressed, I started to feel more confident among my peers and some of the older, more experienced pro players. At the conclusion of the games in Russia, the group went on to Switzerland to play some exhibition games prior to the upcoming World Championships which were to be held in Austria. We flew into Zurich that night and took a bus to the mountain village in Davos. After a long day of travel, climbing into a bed with a down comforter in the cozy inn felt like we had arrived in heaven after the sparse accommodations in Russia. Waking up that next morning to a beautiful sunrise over the alps, it was confirmed, yes, this was heaven!

Olympic Opportunity

In early July 1987, the Amateur Hockey Association of the United States (AHAUS) officially invited Eric to participate in the U.S. Olympic Festival in Greensboro, NC. The AHAUS executive director, Bob Johnson, congratulated Eric on being selected and underscored the fact that the invitation signified that Eric was among the best "amateur ice hockey players in the United States."[96] Eric played well in Greensboro, earning one of the 29 spots at the Olympic Trials in Lake Placid, NY that started on 7 August. The group would be reduced to 25 in September for a rigorous slate of exhibition games, and then finally to 22 for the Olympic games in February 1988. "It's hard to comprehend," commented his father Jack, about the possibility of Eric playing in the Olympics. "It seems so far out."[97]

Eric survived the first cut during the Lake Placid trials and solidified his place among the 25 skaters who would represent the USA during the exhibition campaign. Once again, the New Jersey Devils were watching closely and expressed their approval regarding Eric's progress in a letter to the Olympic hopeful's dad. "The thrill of playing for the United States Olympic Team will be an unforgettable experience – the challenges he will face will mature him immeasurably. We will join you in watching his development with keen and near paternal interest," wrote Max McNab, Devils VP of Hockey Operations.[98]

In late August, Team USA began a ten-day tour of northern Europe, and played several exhibitions in Finland and Sweden. They then returned to Lake Placid and began preparing to play nine games against NHL teams. During a scrimmage against a team of rookie Montreal Canadiens, they lost 3-2 and seemed fatigued from their international travel. One bright spot was that observers described their play as "more like a European team," and that they were "better skaters and moved the puck around more like the Europeans do." They had been practicing that style, which their coach Dave Peterson hoped would make them more competitive in the actual Olympic Games, so it was a positive sign that they were starting to play in live games the same way they were practicing.[99]

On 19 September 1987, Eric and his teammates took on the New York Rangers in Lake Placid, and the Rangers won by a 6-5 score. The next night Team USA faced the Flyers in Philadelphia in front of an enthusiastic crowd of over 12,000. The rowdy atmosphere motivated the Olympic hopefuls and they played the powerful Flyers even throughout, only to lose 3-2 in the final minutes. Eric sustained a 3-inch gash on his cheek. When towering Kjell Samuelsson was upended and fell to the ice his skate sliced Eric's face below his face shield, which luckily protected his eye. Eric skated to the bench and was unaware of the severity of the wound until it was examined by the athletic trainer. The gash took over sixty stitches to close. Although the injury looked nasty, it was not something that would keep Eric from participating in practice and upcoming games, and he remained upbeat. "We moved the puck well," commented Eric after the battle in Philly.

Coach Peterson thought it was their best game yet.[100] Part of the reason for scheduling so many games against NHL clubs in a short period of time was to see if Team USA could stand up to the grind of a professional-type routine, and so they were back on the ice against the Buffalo Sabres in Rochester two nights later. They lost another close battle, 4-3.[101] There was no rest for the weary, though, and next it was off to Washington, D.C., to play the Capitals.

White House Visit

First, however, they went to the White House to meet President Ronald Reagan. A little ice "rink" was set up, and President Reagan shot a few pucks on net. Eric described the experience as follows: "It was neat to see the president. Not everyone gets to meet him face-to-face. I'm not a big Reagan fan, but it was pretty neat to see him. He's a pretty funny guy, he made a couple of jokes." After the short ceremony, Team USA got a special look inside the White House. "I think it was a little different tour than most people get. We got to see where they eat and some of the other rooms. That was really interesting," observed Eric.[102]

Visiting President Reagan in Sept 1987 with Team USA
Eric in red tie 3 to left of Reagan

The day after touring the White House, the US squad played an exhibition against the Washington Capitals, and then within a week squared off against NHL teams from Detroit, Minnesota, and St. Louis. On 2 October in Salt Lake, their opponent was the Calgary Flames. The Flames led 4-2 in the third, and then the Olympians battled back to tie the game and send it to overtime, where Calgary eventually won, 5-4. Eric considered it one of Team USA's most exciting games yet. The next day the US skaters tackled the LA Kings in San Diego, and although they led 4-2, they surrendered four goals in the third period and lost. Eric believed they had simply run out of steam, at the end of a rigorous string of games. He himself chipped in one assist against the Kings, which was only his second point with Team USA. "So, I'm not really tearing up the league in scoring," he observed.[103]

After the Saturday night game against the Kings in San Diego, the team got to remain in the beautiful southern California city for four more days. They practiced each morning, but then had the rest of the day off. It was 95 degrees and sunny each day, so most of the players went to the beach regularly. Eric understood that the team needed some time off, but he believed they stayed too long in San Diego and "forgot about what we were doing out there." He contended that is was good for the team to get back to Lake Placid (just in time for a snowstorm). "We have to get back to being serious," he added. He did find humor in the fact that the players were photographed for TV publicity upon returning to NY from California, and that therefore they would look like the tannest team in the USA, besides the LA Kings.[104]

Return to Orono

After two games in the Lake Placid area, Team USA trekked up to Orono, Maine for a 16 October contest against Eric's former team. Coach Shawn Walsh spoke with Eric during the days leading up to the game and told him how excited he and the Black Bears were about the opportunity. Eric himself was fired up to be back in Orono, but of course also felt a little strange battling his old buddies such as Mike McHugh. He was admittedly homesick but enthusiastic. "This will probably be the highlight of my year until we get to Calgary," he wrote.[105]

Getting back to his old stomping grounds would certainly be enjoyable overall, and he was particularly interested in seeing the new locker rooms at the Alfond Arena because his architect father Jack Weinrich had been hired by the university to design them. The Team USA versus Maine game was also both challenging and exciting for Eric's parents, who continued to support the program by buying season tickets after their oldest son's departure. Jack and his wife Sandra remained close to many of the Maine players. "I know the game is going to be a great thing for Eric and it's also going to be a great thing for them," commented Jack. Mom Sandra described going to the Black Bears' season-opening Blue/White scrimmage in Augusta the previous week, and not seeing Eric, as giving her a funny feeling. "It was kind of sad in a way," she observed.[106]

Before the USA versus Maine game began, the capacity crowd gave Eric a standing ovation. "It sent chills down my spine," he said. The Olympians defeated the Black Bears, 4-1, but it was a better game than the score suggested. In his analysis of the showdown, Eric emphasized that it had been the first game of the season for Maine. He thought they played well and that it would have been much closer if they had had a little more experience before-hand.[107] Eric's play in the encounter impressed his former coach Walsh, who thought it was positive that Eric was being somewhat conservative with Team USA and staying within his capabilities. "He's not trying to be too cute with the puck. He's getting it and moving it quickly to the open man," commented Walsh. Eric was learning to be cautious, and tighter in his coverage, against European players. "You give them too much room, that's just what they want, room to wheel," he concluded.[108]

From Orono, Team USA journeyed to Boston and lambasted Northeastern University the next night by a score of 12-2. The game was a violent affair, especially in the first period. According to Eric, "There were all sorts of penalties and sticks were up." At least six Olympians got cut, and Coach Peterson was furious with the way that Northeastern played in the early going. "It looked like they were just trying to hurt us and I don't know why," added Eric.[109] After the first period Coach Peterson talked with the referee, and the game went more smoothly from then on. Team USA learned a lesson from the game, which was that for the rest of their exhibition schedule they would need to be prepared for this sort of violence, and that they would need to be ready to defend themselves.

Fighting in Hockey

Following the rough clash in Boston, Eric philosophized a bit about fighting in hockey. "If I make it to the pros and have to fight once in every 20 games, I don't think it'll be that bad," he speculated. "I'm not a big fan of fighting, but I guess I'll just have to learn how to defend myself," he added. "I don't think it's anything I'm going to look forward to. It's just something you have to do to make the jump to the pro ranks. It's the thing you must do to be accepted. Once you've done it, people aren't going to test you anymore," he contended. "I've never taken boxing lessons, but I've been told it might not be a bad idea," concluded Eric.[110] Overall, his fall 1987 predictions about the relatively little fighting he expected to do in pro hockey proved to be accurate during his almost twenty-year professional career; however, as fate would have it, a brutal fight tragically ended his playing days in February 2008.

On 24 November, Team USA encountered the Canadian Olympic team at the Saddledome in Calgary, Alberta, Canada. During the previous day, Eric and his teammates toured the Olympic Village, and then watched an NHL game between the Calgary Flames and the New Jersey Devils. NJ President Lou Lamoriello had met with Eric a week earlier and told him the Devils were playing well, so he was hoping to see a good performance; however, the Flames smoked them, 9-1. Eric was happy to see them play but wished they had done better. "The Devils drafted me in 1985," he reminded his readers, "but I'm not sure what will happen after the Olympics."[111]

The USA/Canada game was a hard-fought battle, with Canada winning 5-4. A goal by the USA was disallowed, and the turn of events convinced Eric that they would just need to win games by two goals or more to avoid such disappointments. (Good plan, but it was easier said than done.) From Calgary the squad flew to Los Angeles to prepare for a rematch against Canada a few days later. They practiced in the LA Kings arena in downtown Los Angeles, which Eric described as a tough place to concentrate with so many distractions. The team planned to go to the beach a lot and visit Beverly Hills. Distractions indeed! One highlight of the LA junket was having Thanksgiving in El Toro at the home of goalie John Blue, where the players enjoyed the pool and hot tub. [112]

Battling Illness

After the fun and game in Los Angeles, Team USA took to the ice in Tacoma for a final match-up with Team Canada. From there they went to Kalamazoo to play Western Michigan University, and then to Madison to battle the Badgers. Eric, who had worked hard since October to recover from a shoulder injury, felt good about how he played in late November and believed he was securing himself a spot on the final Olympic roster. However, entering early December, he felt exhausted every day and struggled in practice. His parents called to boost his sagging spirits and told him to "take it as it comes."[113]

In Cleveland, as Team USA prepared to begin an 8-game series against a select team of Soviets, doctors notified Eric that he had tested positive for mononucleosis. They advised him to return home to Maine for a few weeks, and predicted that because they had caught it early, he would recover quickly and probably be able to rejoin his teammates and resume playing at the end of December. Shortly after arriving home on 11 December 1987 Eric remarked, "I'm disappointed I'm not with the team." He could take heart in the fact that he had played well in 28 games for Team USA, notching two goals and seven assists; however, now above all he needed rest.[114]

Home at his family house in Gardiner, Eric did get plenty of rest, sleeping nine or ten hours per night. In addition to the mononucleosis for which he was taking penicillin, he also had contracted strep throat, so he got another medication. More importantly, he enjoyed his mother Sandra's home cooking. "My mom went out and did a lot of shopping and bought a lot of healthy food for me," explained Eric. "She bought a lot of foods the doctor recommended – plenty of fruits, vegetables and carbohydrates." he added. To pass the time during the days at home the Team USA defenseman watched music videos on MTV and hockey matches from the Canada Cup competition, which his parents had recorded for him. As he felt stronger, he went with his youngest brother Jason to the gym to lift weights. Letters and calls from family, friends, and fans cheered him up during his recuperation. "If everyone else is pulling for me, there's no reason for me to feel bad," concluded Eric.[115]

During his second week at home, Eric's health improved rapidly. After getting approval from the Team USA doctors, he started skating again and that lifted his spirits considerably. Correspondence also boosted his morale, including a card from his teammates with funny notes from each player. Danny Bolduc, who grew up in Waterville and played hockey in the 1976 Olympics, called and told Eric how he broke his hand two weeks before the games but still managed to play. Bolduc advised Eric to keep his head up and be thankful the illness had not struck him closer to the Calgary games.[116]

Another local former Olympian, distance runner Joan Benoit, autographed her book *Running Tide* as a birthday present for Eric, who turned 21 on the 19th of December. Benoit wished him a speedy recovery and congratulated him on the Olympic opportunity, emphasizing that it would be a once-in-a-lifetime experience that he would never forget. All of this added to the momentum of his recuperation, as he planned to rendezvous with Team USA on 29 December. He appreciated that he would be fresh and well-rested going into the last six weeks of training before the 1988 Games. He knew these would be the most important games of the entire exhibition schedule, so he intended to "go all out." After a successful recovery period at home, understandably Eric was "looking forward to getting back with the team."[117]

Weino's Wisdom

Little gestures like the one from Danny Bolduc meant the world to me, especially since he was a person I looked up to as a youngster and hoped to follow in his footsteps. Joan was a hero of mine and I always remember sitting on the edge of my chair as I watched her incredible Olympic performance in the first ever women's marathon. Joan had recovered from an injury only months before and soloed to a spectacular victory in Los Angeles. I was proud to be a fellow Mainer and it was a special moment for the state of Maine and for Joan representing the people of the state.

Rejoining Team USA

Team USA's first game after the holiday break was against the University of Minnesota in Minneapolis on 31 December 1987, and Eric was back in uniform. Over the next five weeks, he played in ten exhibition games. He scored a goal and added two assists, bringing his Team USA pre-Olympic totals to 38 games, three goals, and nine assists. The numbers were a far cry from his productivity during the previous season in Orono; nonetheless, his solid defensive play earned him a spot on the roster for the Olympics. After the final exhibition against Sweden in Denver on 8 February 1988, Team USA flew up to Calgary for their opening game on 13 February against Austria.

As the USA skaters defeated the Austrians, 10 to 6, Eric watched from the stands as a healthy scratch. He maintained a positive attitude about

44

being in Calgary and felt prepared for his chance, but of course was not content to sit out the Olympics. "Yes, it's great to be here," he commented to reporters the next day. "But, I want to play, too. It would be one thing if I didn't play at all and came here. But to come this far and not play would be tough." Regarding the fans' expectations for the US squad, he believed they were not too high. "People probably don't expect us to win a gold medal," he observed.[118] With Team USA facing competition including the very best players from the USSR and Czechoslovakia, it was a good thing the fans kept their hopes in check.

Competing in Calgary

Jason, Jack, Eric, Sandra, and Al
Feb 1988 at Olympics in Calgary

Eric first Olympic appearance occurred in the team's 2nd game on 15 February, when they confronted Czechoslovakia. The USA burst out to a 4-1 lead, but then the puck careened off Eric's skate into the net and gave the Czechoslovaks hope. With the US crew holding a 5-4 lead, another lucky Czech goal bounced in off the goalie's pad and then stick. After

Czechoslovakia notched a hard-fought 7-5 comeback victory, some observers (especially USA fans) complained about bad calls by the referee. Eric did not believe that was the issue. "We just didn't hold the lead," he explained.[119] Of course, there was also criticism of Eric because of the goal that deflected off his skate. "You can't think about one goal like that. I haven't thought about it," he contended.[120]

There really was no time to think about it since Team USA needed to get ready to play the Soviets just two days later. In his published diary entry on 17 February Eric pronounced, "We play the Soviets tonight and I know they're the best team I'll ever play against, maybe even if I make it in the NHL." He had first battled two of their star forwards, Alexander Semak and Valeri Kamensky, back at the junior World Championships in 1985, and he conceded that "They're strong players." Overall, according to Eric the USSR would present a formidable opposition: "What makes them so tough is that they regroup on offense and force your defensemen to take them, which is tough on the bigger ice surface."[121]

Although he really relished a rematch with the Soviets, against whom he had played a second time during the 1987 Pravda Cup with a United States select team, Eric was not in the lineup on 17 February when Team USA took on Team USSR.[122] Defensemen Slava Fetisov and Alexei Kasatonov spearheaded the Soviet attack, each scoring two goals, with Fetisov adding three assists for a stellar five-point night. The USSR blitzed the USA for a 6-2 lead, then held off the US comeback to notch a 7-5 victory.[123] A Soviet win should have surprised no one, really. With Fetisov and Kasatonov manning the defense, the Soviets captured six World Championships and two Olympic golds in the 1980s, playing what one historian described as a "flawless, balletic game."[124] For Eric, the silver lining in the disappointing evening (although he probably did not think about it at the time), was that he had gotten a close look at the tremendous talent of two of his future fellow Devils defensemen.

Although Eric spent more time in the stands watching than he would have preferred during the first week of the Olympics, he managed to appreciate the overall experience. "We live in a beautiful place," he wrote. "People who have been to the Olympics before say this Olympic Village it the best they've seen."[125] He and five other players shared a large and comfortable apartment. They were able to watch a lot of different sports on the TV in their living room, including the downhill skiing. Eric planned to visit with his parents, who were staying in town with an Adopt-A-Family, again during the second week. He and his roommates also hoped to run into the glamorous East German figure skater Katarina Witt, but to no avail. They had better luck befriending US speed skater Bonnie Blair, who lived on their floor and won a gold medal in the 500-meter race.[126]

On Sunday 21 February when the USA confronted West Germany, Eric returned to the ice. He and his fellow blueliners played reasonably well, but the forwards fell flat and only scored once in a very disappointing 4-1 loss which eliminated the USA from medal contention. "I really don't know what happened to us against West Germany," admitted Eric.[127] Sportswriters argued that Team USA had not played tough enough competition during their exhibition schedule and applauded the Soviets as the cream of the crop at Calgary.[128] During the few days following the Germany game, Eric spent some time with his family and attended the bobsled competition and ski jumping. At these venues, they got to watch the infamous Eddie "the Eagle" Edwards, the English ski jumper, and the Jamaican bobsled team in action.

On 25 February, Team USA took on Switzerland in a game for 7th place. Although it was a consolation game, according to Eric and his teammates, "it meant something to us." Before the encounter they discussed the fact that it would be their last time playing together and promised to give it their best shot. They played well and won handily by a score of 8-4 to finish in 7th place, equaling their predecessors' result in 1984. The morning after the final game, as he flew to Bangor and prepared to rejoin his old friends at the University of Maine for the remainder of the NCAA season, he was tired. "People had the idea that it was a vacation up here," he explained about the Olympic experience, "But it was work."[129] It had not been easy, but Eric had accomplished one of his most cherished global goals of playing hockey for the United States in the Olympic Games.

Weino's Wisdom

The game against the Soviets was a hard game to watch. As a teammate, I hoped they would play well and pull off a massive upset. On the other hand, it was amazing to see the talent and skill the Russian team possessed. Even in defeat, our scoring five goals proved our team also had some special players. The final Olympic game was a bittersweet moment. When I look back on the actual Olympic experience, I have some regrets, the biggest was not winning a medal. But, in the heat of competition, you lose sight of the fact that there are hundreds of other special athletes who have trained their whole life to reach this moment as I and my teammates had, and for many of them this was the pinnacle of their careers. My dream had been to win a gold medal like the team in 1980. When that did not happen, mentally I just wanted to leave the experience behind. We had an opportunity to stay until the closing ceremonies and watch other events and then celebrate the games with the rest of the athletes. I made the choice to return to University of Maine and join my teammates there for the remainder of the season. In hindsight, I often wish I stayed until the closing ceremonies and took in the full Olympic experience.

Rejoining the Black Bears

The plan to get some rest quickly took a back seat upon returning to Orono, and Eric rode the bus with his fellow Black Bears down to Rhode Island to play against Providence on Sunday 28 February. During only his second shift back in college hockey, Eric blasted a slap shot from the left circle into the net. On the same spectacular shift, he assisted on a second Black Bears' tally. Later in the first period he added another goal. "I didn't have a very good year offensively with Team USA," Weinrich said. "This will really help my confidence."[130] It was not only a boost for him, but also for his team as they trounced Providence 10-2 and earned a bye in the first round of the Hockey East tournament with an incredible regular season record of 29 wins, six losses, and two ties.

The Black Bears' regular season success garnered them a home ice advantage in the 2nd round of the Hockey East tournament. They played Providence in a two-game, total goals series. Maine won the first game on March 8th, 6-5. They hammered the Friars in the second game the next night, 11-2, and Eric registered one goal and two assists, putting the Black Bears into the Hockey East final on 14 March at the Boston Garden. Northeastern University outplayed Maine in the finals, winning 4-3, but the Black Bears nevertheless received an invitation to the NCAA Tournament, and a first-round bye.

On 25 March, Maine defeated Bowling Green 5-1. The next evening, they beat Bowling Green again, 4-3. These wins earned them a trip to the Frozen Four, a first for the Orono program. Eric's return to the collegiate ranks had helped his team accomplish another global goal, qualifying for the final four at the NCAA tournament and getting one step closer to a championship (Eric's youngest brother Jason would be a dependable defenseman for the first Maine team to win an NCAA championship in 1993). Eric contributed an assist in the semifinal match against Lake Superior State; however, it was not enough, and the Black Bears fell 6-3. Maine's wonderful 1987-88 season came to an end, as did the amateur career of Eric Weinrich.

The exciting period from January 1985 to April 1988 provided Eric with innumerable opportunities to skate at the highest levels of amateur hockey, both on the global stage and stateside. He had helped his teams win a state championship, a World Juniors medal, and reach the Frozen Four. As a member of Team USA, he had battled against some of the best players in the world. At the end of what he described as the 1985-88 "glory days," Eric was ready to tackle his next global goal: becoming a professional hockey player.[131] No one knew how successful he would be in the New Jersey Devils organization, nor did they realize how much globalization would impact his early pro career.

CHAPTER 3

"Going Pro as Hockey Globalizes, 1988-1990"

From summer 1988 until summer 1990, Eric Weinrich accomplished several notable milestones and attained several more of his global goals. He decided to forego his final year of eligibility of college hockey and sign a contract with the New Jersey Devils organization. He hoped to make the NHL club, but instead was assigned to the Utica Devils in the American Hockey League (AHL). He played very well for Utica in 1988-89, and even got called up to the NHL for 2 games late in the season. Another positive development during the first year in Utica, more important in the long run than anything on the ice, was that Eric met Tracy Martin and the couple began dating.

During the Devils' September 1989 training camp Eric nearly made the parent club, but was the last player cut and sent back to Utica. He played extremely well during the first few months of his second year in the AHL and was promoted to New Jersey in February 1990. "Weino" was a key part of the NJ squad as they battled their way into the post-season, and he chipped in a key goal in their second playoff game against Washington. Eric headed into the summer of 1990 confident that he would be a respected NHL player for the foreseeable future.

In addition to the significance of these two seasons for Weino's career advancement, the years 1988-90 were also crucial in terms of the relationship between NHL hockey, globalization, and the end of the classic Cold War. As Eric was earning his way from Utica to New Jersey, stars of the Soviet Red Army team such as Viacheslav Fetisov and Alexei Kasatonov were fighting for their freedom and a chance to play in the NHL. By the time Weino got the call to NJ in February 1990, both Fetisov and Kasatonov were already there. For a young player like Eric to make it into the NHL with any club would be exciting, but the chance to play with an international, globalized, diverse squad such as the Devils was that much more incredible.

Going Pro

After the 1988 NCAA tournament, Eric Weinrich decided to leave the University of Maine and its hockey program which he had done so much to boost. In mid-July, Eric signed a multi-year contract with the New Jersey Devils organization, which had drafted him in the 2nd round in 1985. He hoped to jump from college directly to the NHL; however, in late September the parent club released Eric and assigned him to the Utica Devils of the American Hockey League, one notch below the NHL. The AHL Devils had only been in Utica one year, and they were coached by Tom McVie, a legendary hockey figure.

McVie, described in a preview of the 1988-89 AHL season as "one of the craziest men in professional hockey," was a grizzled former minor league player.[132] He had coached the Washington Capitals, Winnipeg Jets, and New Jersey Devils in the late 1970s and early 1980s before taking the helm in Utica. Eric perhaps would have preferred playing for New Jersey in the fall of 1988; but, if he was going to have to earn his shot in the NHL by first skating in the AHL trenches, he was lucky to have a coach such as McVie.

Fetisov

As the end of the 1980s approached, big changes occurred around the globe which eventually reverberated in the rinks of the USA and Canada. With Mikhail Gorbachev initiating reforms in the Soviet Union, star players on the great Red Army team looked to the West with high hopes, and hockey officials in the West were looking back at them. Among the Soviet players, Viacheslav Fetisov attracted the most attention, particularly from the team which had drafted him in 1983, New Jersey. While Eric would face obstacles in his path before suiting up for the senior Devils, his journey was not as complicated as that undertaken by his future teammate Fetisov.

Going into the 1988 Calgary Olympics, Fetisov believed that if he played well and helped win another gold medal for the USSR, that he would be allowed to move to North America and compete in the NHL. He did indeed lead the Red Army to gold in Calgary, but soon afterwards was informed by Coach Viktor Tikhonov that USSR hockey needed him for another year and so he could not make the move. The Soviet government honored him with the prestigious Lenin Medal in spring 1988; however, it would not allow him to ply his trade in the NHL and instead would keep him on as the Red Army captain – or so they thought.

The plot thickened soon after the Lenin Medal ceremony, when New Jersey general manager Lou Lamoriello arrived in Moscow to meet with Fetisov and Soviet officials to discuss the player's future. Lamoriello, after a successful career as athletic director at Providence College, had been hired in 1987 by NJ owner John McMullen to get the Devils on the winning track (in their five seasons since moving from Colorado the team had not made the playoffs). Lamoriello decided quickly that one way to strengthen the team would be to get some of their draft picks from the USSR over to the USA and onto the ice. He started working on this project by first talking with Soviet officials at the Calgary Olympics, then meeting with the Soviet ambassador in Washington, Anatoly Dobrynin, and finally deciding to go to the USSR.[133]

Landing in Moscow in June 1988 with great expectations and a contract for Fetisov in hand, Lamoriello got help arranging the rendezvous from international chess champion Gary Kasparov. Upon arriving at the meeting place alone, Lamoriello walked up four flights of stairs and met his female interpreter. The two entered a smoky room and found Soviet generals in uniform seated at a table. Fetisov entered and shortly thereafter one of the generals announced that the Red Army captain would not be allowed to leave the Soviet Union. Fetisov and Lamoriello walked down the stairs together, making eye contact at the bottom. Later that night Fetisov snuck into Lamoriello's hotel with another interpreter, and the two men agreed to continue pursuing a deal.[134] About a month later Lamoriello released some details about his Moscow mission, optimistically opining that Fetisov would be skating with the Devils during the upcoming NHL season.[135] Although the general manager was correct about the defenseman joining NJ, it would take a year longer than he predicted.

Debate over Soviet Players in NHL

Not everyone associated with the NHL anticipated the arrival of Soviet players with the enthusiasm of Lou Lamoriello, of course. The debate had heated up around the time of the Calgary Olympics, as rumors flew about the USSR allowing players to leave. Larry Robinson, then a standout defenseman for the Canadiens who would eventually be inducted into the Hockey Hall of Fame, spoke out strongly against a Soviet influx. One of Robinson's concerns was the expectation that the players who came from the USSR would be required to return a substantial amount of their money to the government at home to fund developmental hockey. "Why should we be helping them get better at hockey?"[136] he wondered. Robinson's argument was based on bitter experience, as he had battled the Soviets for Team Canada in several international competitions with limited success, and he knew as well as anyone the effectiveness of their program.[137]

A strong counterpoint was presented at the time of the Calgary Games by hockey fan and journalist Nate Dow, who believed that allowing the Soviets to play in the NHL would make it a truly international sport. He contended that relatively few players would leave the USSR, so they would not take large numbers of jobs and Robinson's concern about subsidizing the Soviet program would not be a major issue. According to Dow and like-minded supporters of the efforts of Lamoriello, there would never be an influx. "But there are a precious few," observed Dow, "and if they can come to the 'Promised Land' and play hockey as they've been taught to play, provide us with a few passing thrills and human insights, and make our children want to emulate and even surpass their skills, we will have found the greatest tool for international diplomacy ever conceived." Dow was quite insightful on this point about cultural diplomacy, but he concluded on a level that the average fan might better appreciate: "And, gee, the hockey would be pretty damn good, too."[138]

Weino's Wisdom
(Comments from Eric "Weino" Weinrich himself)

I have the greatest respect for Larry Robinson as a person and a player. I would have to respectfully disagree with his initial objection to Russian players coming to play in North America and I would guess in time Robinson changed his opinion. Robinson was one of the fortunate players in the world of hockey to have competed against the best Russian players in the Canada Cup and other international games. And I imagine he appreciated the grace and skill of his Russian counterparts and enjoyed his moments working alongside them as a coach. In the era of great NHL defensemen, we all can look back toward the end of Robinson's career and the number of tremendous defensemen which included the likes of Fetisov and his counterpart, Alexei Kasatonov. The New Jersey Devils organization and the rest of the NHL community would have been robbed of their contribution to our wonderful game.

Glasnost

For players, coaches, and observers in North America the debate over whether the Iron Curtain should come down was about competition for jobs and playing time, money for development in the USSR, improving a struggling team like the NJ Devils, or making the NHL truly international and facilitating a bit of cultural diplomacy. For players on the Soviet Red Army team, however, the debate was about human rights. The leader of the USSR, Mikhail Gorbachev, had proclaimed a new age of Glasnost, meaning "openness," implying a step towards free speech and freedom of the press which the Soviet Union had never allowed. While these freedoms had been extended to many aspects of life in the USSR, there had been no such progressive reform in the hockey program. In October 1988, star Red Army forward Igor Larionov decided to call for similar changes in hockey.

Larionov penned a long letter to Red Army coach Viktor Tikhonov, and the incendiary document was published in a mass-circulation magazine named *Ogonyok*, meaning small fire. His statement, which blasted the archaic methods of Coach Tikhonov, stoked an inferno. Larionov wanted the world to know that while Glasnost was bringing change and opportunity to many Soviets, it was not being offered to the national heroes of hockey. He revealed Tikhonov's tight control over their eating, sleeping, and training. He decried the fact that Red Army players spent about 11 months each year in camp without friends or family. He underscored the endless time away from spouses, and poignantly pointed out that "It's a wonder our wives manage to give birth."[139]

The October 1988 letter from Igor Larionov infuriated Coach Tikhonov, and he responded by cutting Larionov from the Soviet team. Slava Fetisov supported Larionov's stance and announced that he would not suit up for Tikhonov's Red Army squad while the situation remained the same.[140] Both Fetisov and Larionov were around 30 years old, and they hoped to move to the NHL before Father Time dimmed their skills too much. For Larionov, moreover, it was clearly a fight for human rights in the context of the reforms in the USSR initiated by Gorbachev. This epic showdown between Soviet players and Tikhonov intensified in fall 1988, but it would not be resolved until the following year.

Weino's Wisdom ────────────────────────────────

Igor Larionov, known as "the Professor", was always such an interesting player to watch and listen to and garnered the upmost respect from his teammates and contemporaries. His style of play was so methodical and was closer to the game of Wayne Gretzky with a blend of technical skill and vision. His small stature for the NHL game at that time was overcome by his intelligence and his years of training in Russia. His account of the experience he had in his time with the Red Army team, CSKA, details a regimented training schedule and lack of access to his family.

It must have been such a joy for him to play the game he loved with the freedom he was afforded in the NHL. It was a pleasure to watch his skill but not as much fun to play against. Interestingly, Igor has recently offered his services to the Russian Federation as a coach and mentor to up-and-coming players in Russia. He was coaching a player from the team I have been working for in a European tournament. After watching the games that weekend, I wondered how frustrating it must be for a player who prided himself on execution and precision during his time in Russia, and coaching players with far less skill. I admire him for returning to his country to help grow the game back to the level of his era. I also appreciated his allowing us access to his players and his greeting me like we were longtime friends. His bold views that he expressed, before he came to North America, showed great courage.

First months in Utica

The possibility of skating for New Jersey someday with legendary players such as Fetisov, after the political and personality disputes in the USSR were resolved, excited Eric Weinrich greatly, but first he had to earn his way onto the NHL club himself. While Larionov and Fetisov were taking on Tikhonov in October 1988, Eric was playing his initial month of professional hockey for the Utica Devils in the AHL. The young defenseman entered October with a bang in an exhibition against the rival Rochester Americans before 1,500 fans at Ritter Arena on the campus of the Rochester Institute of Technology, as he scored a goal in Utica's 4-2 loss.[141]

By the time regular season games kicked off later in October, Eric had cemented a place in the starting line-up for Utica and set about establishing himself as a steady presence on the blueline. In early November, he started chipping in a bit more on the offensive end, assisting on goals in two straight games.[142] December saw Eric really come into his own and make major contributions such as when he scored the winning goal for Utica in a 6-4 victory over the Adirondack Red Wings. Opponent Murray Eaves, a Red Wings forward, took the blame for the winning goal and acknowledged that Eric "blew by me."[143] Eric netted a short-handed goal in a 6-1 victory on 18 December, and had a goal and an assist in an 8-2 victory on 24 December. With Eric becoming an AHL star, the Utica Devils went into the 1988 holiday break riding a 7-game unbeaten streak.

Tracy

As noted above, Eric had hoped to play the 1988-89 season with the New Jersey Devils in the NHL and so was not completely thrilled with his assignment to Utica. Nonetheless, he made the most of the opportunity on the ice, improving his game against AHL opposition. More importantly for the long-term course of his life, moreover, Eric made the most of an opportunity outside the rink, by getting to know the General Manager of the Utica office of the Metro Based Cable Advertising company. Her name was Terese Renee Martin, but she prefers to be called Tracy.

A local girl born and raised in upper New York state, Tracy attended school in the village of Poland, which is about fourteen miles from Utica. Tracy had one older sister named Denise. Their dad worked in the packaging business, and his company created the beer ball. Their mom taught reading at Poland Central school, which Tracy attended from kindergarten through grade twelve. In high school, Tracy played soccer and participated in cheerleading. She was an honor student, in the French Club, and on the Student Council. With only about sixty students in her graduating class, she knew everyone. After graduating from Poland Central, Tracy attended Ithaca College.[144]

After earning her bachelor's degree from Ithaca in 1986, Tracy started working for Metro Based Cable Advertising in sales. By 1988 she was overseeing the Utica office, and one of her projects was to create television commercials for the Utica Devils. Among the players, one impressed her immediately – Eric Weinrich. The feeling was mutual, and shortly after Christmas the two went out for drinks. They met again the next day for lunch at a Chinese restaurant, and Tracy (not a big hockey fan, yet) asked if Eric "hoped to play pro" someday. He explained that he did get paid by Utica! Evidently, he was not at all bothered by Tracy's lack of expertise regarding pro hockey and may have been charmed by it instead. The couple started dating regularly.[145]

Weino's Wisdom

It was ironic how things turned out that season, and meeting Tracy was almost by accident. But it all occurred during a time in my career when things started to come together and with the help of Tom McVie, I learned how to be a better pro and my game took off. Until then, I felt mired in mediocrity and never felt quite comfortable on and off the ice. But during the month we first met, I was in a good place mentally and our relationship certainly made my time in Utica much more special.

First NHL Games

Back on the ice in January 1989 after the holidays, Eric played spectacular hockey for Utica. He scored both goals in a 4-2 loss to Rochester on the

13th. Then, he upped the ante with a hat trick in a 7-4 win over the Hershey Bears on the 18th. In the win over Hershey, which snapped a 4-game winless streak for Utica, Eric's teammate Claude Vilgrain, who was born in Haiti, added two goals.[146] (Claude would later play with Eric in New Jersey, adding to the cosmopolitan global diversity of that team.) During Utica's 20 January battle against Rochester, the rookie defender from Maine scored on the power play, giving him a remarkable eight goals in seven games.[147] In 42 games for Utica, Eric had accumulated twelve goals and thirteen assists.

Such a stellar performance, not surprisingly, attracted attention from the parent club, and on 23 January 1989 Eric was recalled to the New Jersey Devils. That evening in the Meadowlands, he played against the Minnesota North Stars in his first NHL game, wearing uniform number 4. One of his biggest global goals since childhood, to play in the NHL, had been accomplished. No one could know at the time that this game marked the beginning of an NHL career for Eric that would span well over 1,000 games and nearly two decades, and it turned out to be an inauspicious debut indeed. Minnesota trounced NJ 7-2, and early in the game Eric slipped and fell in his own zone facilitating a North Star goal.[148] The young defender eventually would get plenty of chances in other NHL games to make up for his stumble, but in the short run it was back to the AHL for him. On 28 January he returned to Utica.

After two more weeks toiling in the minors, Eric was called up for a second time on 10 February and played in his second NHL game. He did not score a point, but on the other hand there is no record of him committing any costly errors. Nevertheless, the Devils soon returned the 22-year-old blueliner to Utica, where he remained for the rest of the season. He was credited with the winning goal when he was the closest attacker to an own-goal in Utica's 3-2 victory over Baltimore on the last night of February, helping his team stay in the hunt for an AHL playoff berth.[149] He scored a couple more times down the stretch, simultaneously playing tough defense.

Weino's Wisdom ————————————————————————

My first NHL game was nerve wracking, and I made it harder on myself with that mistake on the goal against where I stumbled over my own feet and while trying to recover back to the net ran into my teammate in front of the net and made things worse. But I chalked it up as a learning experience. I ended up hitting the post on a shot from the blue line and in the second half of the game felt a little more comfortable. My partner on defense that night, Ken Daneyko, did his best to help me stay calm even after my blunder. While I was starting to play well at the AHL level, I still had a way to go before I was ready to play full time at the NHL pace. Still, it was the thrill of a lifetime.

AHL Playoffs

Eric and his teammates won the regular season finale in Rochester on 2 April 1989, 6-5, snatching a playoff spot out of thin air.[150] In their first foray into AHL post-season play, however, the Devils were eliminated in the opening round by Hershey. Eric played in all five contests and notched one assist. Utica of course would have preferred going further in the playoffs, but they certainly could look back on a much better season than the senior Devils in New Jersey, who did not come close to the playoffs. Eric had been a very big part of Utica's success, moreover, and he hoped that his strong AHL season would get him a spot on the NJ roster for the 1989-90 NHL season.

Leaving the USSR

Another defenseman who hoped to suit up for the NJ Devils in the fall of 1989, meanwhile, was Slava Fetisov. After his initial meeting with NJ general manager Lamoriello in June 1988, and the explosive letter by Larionov in October, the pressure on Soviet officials to allow at least a few of their best players to enter the NHL increased. Lamoriello continued his cultural diplomacy, meeting again with Fetisov in Germany while the Red Army were there training. At that point, he asked the Soviet superstar to defect, but Fetisov declined. As Lamoriello remembered the conversation Fetisov said: "He couldn't do it. In the position he was in, captain of the Red Army team and someone who was looked upon as he was, it wasn't something he wanted the young Russian players to follow. He wanted to do it the right way."[151]

As his bitter standoff with Coach Tikhonov continued unabated into the spring of 1989, Soviet officials started to panic about the approaching World Championships in Sweden. They promised Fetisov and his four "Green Unit" comrades Alexei Kasatonov, Igor Larionov, Sergei Makarov and Vladimir Krutov, that they could sign with NHL clubs after competing one more time for the USSR in Sweden.[152] They played better than ever, winning ten straight games by a combined score of 47-16 for a gold medal. Fetisov was named the Defenseman of the Tournament. It was a glorious end to his tenure with the USSR national team, and excitement in NJ mounted.

Although he knew his veterans would leave, Tikhonov was pleased with the Soviet's 21st gold medal at a hockey World Championship and believed his talented young players would guarantee another decade of domination. He treated the team to the usual celebration banquet on 1 May 1989, then granted them two "shopping days" in Stockholm. But Tikhonov was soon in for another shock. When the team boarded the bus on 4 May to begin their return to Moscow, one of their most promising young forwards, Alexander Mogilny, was missing. He had jumped the gun and defected to join the Buffalo Sabres. It would be the youngster Mogilny, not Fetisov, who was the first to leave the USSR and sign with an NHL club.[153]

However, when the 1989-1990 season opened, Fetisov would also be competing in the NHL. During the summer of 1989 he worked out the final details and got official permission to leave the USSR. One of the sticking points was the Soviet government's insistence that Fetisov forward most of his salary to them, which he refused to do. Resolving this required a tense meeting with Soviet Minister of Defense Dmitry Yazov, who threatened to send Fetisov to Siberia if he would not accept the Soviet government's requirements.[154] Fetisov did not back down, and shortly after the meeting he received his passport and a work visa and was on his way to the USA. He laced up his skates at the NJ Devils training camp and set about demonstrating that he belonged.[155]

Weino's Wisdom

Alexander Mogilny was the youngest member of the 1988 Russian Olympic Team when I competed in Calgary. Because of his age, he had to wear a full cage on his helmet. He didn't play regular time but was spotted in the games throughout the tournament. A selection on the team assembled for the 1988 team was a tremendous honor for such a young player and a sign he was the future star of Russian hockey. His talent was evident and instantly he made an impact in the NHL with his speed and skill. I remember watching the Russian Olympic team practice one day in Calgary. After the rest of the players left the ice, Mogilny was left with one of the goalies and his task was to beat the goalie with every puck on the ice and he couldn't leave until it was complete. I sat and watched him go through this process to the point of exhaustion. With the introduction of Fetisov to the New Jersey Devils, I was both excited and a bit frustrated. I knew the depth chart on defense suddenly included a player that was going to be on the roster and made my task of earning a spot on the roster that much more difficult. Still, the thought of practicing and possibly playing alongside the great Slava Fetisov was very intriguing. The NHL was about to see one of the greatest hockey players of all time and one that many fans had never seen play.

Last Devil Cut: Back to Utica

Eric Weinrich was also at the NJ training camp, and his next global goal of securing an NHL roster spot as one of the Devils' defensemen was made more difficult by the arrival of Fetisov. As things turned out, Eric was the last player cut from the squad, and on 2 October NJ assigned him to Utica once again. An article previewing the AHL season cleverly commented on Utica: "This team could have a devil of a good time this season. Coach Tom McVie has turned the Devils from a group of rookies to a potential powerhouse in a hurry." The arrival of Fetisov in NJ meant more talent in Utica, noted the preview article, which characterized Eric as "one of the AHL's best defenseman."[156]

Regardless of a talented roster, the Utica squad started the AHL regular season slowly with losses to Rochester and Hershey. Weino recorded assists in both of those games, and then another assist when his slapshot was tipped into the net in the junior Devils' first win, against Baltimore. Eric's best game in October came on the 29th in another win over Baltimore, when he racked up a goal and two assists in the 8-2 triumph.[157] Moving into November 1989, incredible international developments heralded the end of the classic Cold War, and these dramatic changes would have a big impact on the NHL.

Weino's Wisdom

Of course, I was disappointed, but I wasn't stupid. I believe I could have played at the beginning of the season and earned a spot, but I also knew that there were veteran players ahead of me and with the addition of Fetisov, one more to leapfrog. Knowing Tracy would be in Utica along with many of my old teammates, the drive back to Utica after my meeting with Lou Lamoriello had a little less sting. Little did I know that year would bring a few more surprises.

Cold War Context

After Gorbachev visited East Germany, demonstrations forced hardline leader Eric Honeker to resign. On 9 November his replacement allowed East Germans to pass through the gates of the Berlin Wall without visas, and the process that would lead to a reunified Germany had begun.

Nearby in Czechoslovakia, demonstrations and a general strike convinced the communist government to resign. In late December, the parliament elected progressive poet Vaclav Havel as prime minister, and this smooth process in Czechoslovakia became known as the Velvet Revolution.[158] As the Iron Curtain came crashing down, scores of talented Russian and Eastern European hockey players prepared to crash the NHL party.

In Utica, which was not nearly as tumultuous as Berlin or Moscow, Eric had a strong November and was determined to break through the logjam on the NJ roster, sooner rather than later. His performance took a quantum leap in December. In a 3-game stretch he notched six assists and three goals, including a 5-point game (one goal, four assists) in a win over Moncton. The AHL honored him as player of the week, and Coach McVie commented that the defender was "right on the edge" of being promoted to NJ.[159]

Kasatonov

The competition for spots on the blueline with the parent club intensified further in December, however, as the other elite Soviet Red Army defender, Alexei Kasatonov took advantage of Gorbachev's ongoing Glasnost and signed with the Devils. There was no question about Kasatonov's ability to play hockey at the NHL level, but the cultural transition would be a challenge. During a short stint with Utica, during which he and Eric first got to know each other, Kasatonov's inexperience with North American hockey traditions became clear. Eric recalled that when Alexei received the post-game "first star" for playing a great game, he seemed to think he was going to get a prize and skated around the Utica rink waiving.[160] Eric would do as much as anyone to help Alexei adjust to life in the USA and they would develop a solid friendship, but that would not be until after they both earned a roster spot in NJ.

In early January 1990, Kasatonov suited up for NJ, joining his long-time Red Army teammate Fetisov.[161] Journalist Colin Stephenson insightfully analyzed the situation in a 7 January column, noting that the two had not been on speaking terms for a year and that Fetisov was extremely bitter towards Kasatonov because he believed his former friend had betrayed him and sided with the Soviet government against him. Stephenson pointed out, moreover, that the arrival of Kasatonov might motivate Fetisov to play harder so as not to be shown up by his fellow Russian. Stephenson also argued that in addition to these two international superstars, furthermore, NJ would need to figure out how to carve out some ice time at the NHL level for Eric Weinrich. Through 3 January in 36 games with Utica, Eric had amassed 35 points. "Logic says that room has to be made for him in New Jersey sometime soon," concluded Stephenson.[162]

Weino's Wisdom

I first saw Alexei in Calgary during a meal at the athletes' village. He was a mountain of a man and sitting in the same dining hall with him and the other members of the Russian team was intimidating. I had been an admirer of how both he and Fetisov played the game in tandem and became big fans of them during the !987 Canada Cup series. To this day I still feel that was the best hockey ever played. Alex played a different style than Fetisov, and as a more powerful man he was not afraid to throw his body around. But make no mistake, his game was distinctly Russian trained. There is no doubt that Fetisov was the most skilled defenseman in Russia at the time, but I always felt that Alexei respected him and may have played in his shadow his whole career. When he came to North America and was assigned to Utica to get acclimated, we all were in awe of his ability. The first day he came straight from the airport in Newark to Utica. He then proceeded to practice with us, and Tom McVie put him through some extra skating which he handled with ease. But it wasn't only he who arrived that day.

Another veteran of the Red Army team, Sergei Starikov, also signed a contract with New Jersey. Again, we were all aware of the situation. There were always rumors that more were coming, and the appearance of both players was not a shock. After the first game they both played, it was more than evident that Alexei was too good for our league. He dominated play and was named first star. We all got a chuckle as he skated around the ice waving to the crowd after being honored as the first star. Little did we know in Russia that was what players did after the game. But who were we to stop him enjoying the moment?

As I remember, that was New Year's Eve, and the team was set to gather at a local restaurant. The two Russians joined along and enjoyed the festivities that night. Both Alexei and Sergei showed us how to celebrate in style...While neither of them had even the slightest grasp of English, we all found a way to communicate and enjoyed the night together. It has always amazed me how sport brings cultures together. And even though I knew both players were creating a logjam for my promotion to New Jersey, I wanted to befriend both players and learn about them as people and about their hockey. When they both left for New Jersey, it was bittersweet for me. I tried to soak in what they did on the ice and did my best to make them feel comfortable.

Breaking into the NJ Line-up

Lamoriello and the rest of the NJ management clearly agreed. When the Devils played an exhibition against Moscow Dynamo on 7 January, Eric got a chance to play and assisted on the first goal. Kasatonov was also in the Devils lineup, and he registered a goal and an assist in the 7-1 NJ victory. After the exhibition, however, NJ sent Weino back to Utica again. It would be the last time. In a win over Rochester on 12 January his point slapshot was tipped into the net, earning him an assist. On 20 January he helped Utica beat Binghamton, scoring on a 5-foot wrist shot.[163] About three weeks later, on 16 February 1990, Eric was promoted to NJ, and he would remain in the NHL for the next sixteen years.

The Devils, who were in the race for a playoff spot, lost on the 16th to the Rangers, 2-1, with Fetisov scoring the only goal. Perhaps the arrival of Kasatonov had motivated him to play better, after all. The NJ management was not pleased with the performance of some of their other defensemen, however, and after the Rangers game decided to give Weinrich his shot. Sportswriter Alex Yannis of *The New York Times* thoroughly detailed the summons, noting that Lou Lamoriello called Weino at 1:30am Saturday morning to get down to NJ for that night's game.[164] He made it, joined the NJ lineup on 17 February in a 5-4 loss to Toronto, and assisted on a powerplay goal. The *Daily News* commented that Eric and fellow blueliner Bruce Driver both "played exceptional offensive games."[165] NJ coach John Cunniff strongly indicated that Eric was in the NHL to stay and praised his play against Toronto: "He did a good job of moving the puck, and that's one of the things we want to do."[166]

About a week later the Devils battled the New York Islanders to a 3-3 tie, earning an important point in their quest for the playoffs. Weino snapped a "perfect pass" in the neutral zone, hitting John MacLean in stride as he broke free to score a key goal. The second assist on the goal came from Kasatonov, who started the break with a pass to Eric.[167] The fact that one of the Soviet Red Army's most famous players passed to a former USA Olympian to set up a goal spoke volumes about how fast the world was changing in 1990 in terms of the Cold War concluding. Fetisov also chipped in with an assist on another goal during the game, moreover, further underscoring the impact of post-Cold War cultural connections on hockey and vice versa.

Weino's Wisdom

It's hard to explain the excitement of getting the call to the NHL. Tom McVie drove me to the airport in Syracuse, NY during a snowy night. He didn't say much but let me know he didn't think I was coming back. It was fitting that Tommy drove me and all the other players to the airport when they got the call. He was a mentor to all of us and sort of a father figure. I may not have ever gotten this chance without his helping me get my career in order. Those last twenty or so games were a blur but having the chance to play with all the great players we had in the lineup including Fetisov and Kasatonov was the thrill of a lifetime.

I should also mention that Starikov was sent back to Utica to play, and we had many shifts on the ice together while I was still there. In the language of athletes, we found a way to work together on the ice and I learned some subtle techniques by watching him in certain situations of the game, especially on the penalty kill, an area I would never play in New Jersey, but later in my career was one of the staples of my game. Although maybe past his prime physically, you could see the intelligence and skill he once had though his legs couldn't get him where he once could go. It was quite an education playing with Sergei, who had once been a fixture on the great Soviet era teams.

Cultural Ambassadors at the Cold War's End

While some players and other NHL personnel had resisted the arrival of the Russian players, Eric had never expressed any negative opinion on the subject. To the contrary, he was excited about the possibility of playing with Fetisov and Kasatonov and viewed it as an incredible learning opportunity. He enthusiastically recalled that the presence of the Russians only added to his excitement when called up to the Devils in February 1990: "I couldn't believe Kasatonov was there!" While Weino had tremendous respect for Fetisov as a player, he developed more of a personal bond with Kasatonov, whom he described as "very friendly." Alex taught Eric a lot about the game on the ice, and perhaps even more about off-ice training. Kasatonov pushed him constantly to improve, and if the young US player slipped up, the former Soviet superstar would "scold" him.[168]

In Eric's view, the Russians made a positive impact on the Devils' performance. They might not have been able to alter the overall style of play that North Americans had developed over many years, but they did help all the Devils improve their skills. In his 1990 autobiography, Wayne Gretzky made similar observations. "We've learned from the Soviets how to handle the puck, how to be creative on offense," commented Gretzky.[169] Hall of Fame goalie Ken Dryden, in his acclaimed book *The Game*, offered insightful analysis of the impact of Russian players coming to the NHL. Interestingly, he contended that Gretzky played the Soviet passing style, "giving, not receiving." In Dryden's opinion, it was Gretzky who made Soviet-style hockey acceptable in North America. Additionally, the legendary Canadiens netminder argued: "Nobody has been more affected by the Soviet impact than the U.S. player." Learning from the Russians allowed U.S. players to escape from the long shadow of Canada.[170] Dryden's assessment applied very well to Eric's situation in March 1990.

Weino's Wisdom

I had lots of success in my year and half in Utica and started to play a more complete game that second season. But taking the step to the next level meant even more attention to detail and less margin for error. Watching Slava and Alex play the game, they were a defensive pair for the Devils although they never spoke off the ice, the tandem was magical in the way they read off each other. You can't appreciate the skill of professional athletes unless you are around them every day. All their life playing in Russia they had been held to such a high level of perfection and everything they did in practice and in games was very precise.

If I missed a pass or slipped up, they let me know about it. This accountability was something I thought I practiced but they took it to another level. I was starting to understand the type of scrutiny and pressure that these former Russian players had experienced while playing for Tikhonov. I often wondered what Slava and Alex thought about the NHL game? There were many players in our league that could never perform like their teammates and many of the New Jersey players had far less skill than those from the Red Army. For me, I appreciated how they played the game and though I could never adopt most of the techniques they had perfected over the years, I still learned something new every day watching my Russian teammates.

Clinching a Playoff Spot

During the last month of the regular season the battle for playoff spots heated up, and Eric boosted the Devils' cause. On 25 March 1990 he scored his first NHL goal on a power play in the second period.[171] His goal increased the NJ lead over Buffalo to 4-1, and they held on for a 4 3 victory and clinched a place in the postseason, only the second playoff qualification in franchise history. Two days later Eric registered his second NHL goal in a 4-1 win over the Washington Capitals. According to the *Asbury Park Press*, "Working a perfect give-and-go with Brendan Shanahan at the Capitals' blueline, Weinrich drilled a shot from 35 feet that beat Liut between the pads."[172] Outfoxing a top-notch netminder such as Mike Liut, a former all-star and league MVP, signaled that Eric belonged at the highest level of hockey. These first two markers in the NHL, moreover, catapulted the Devils back into the playoffs and represented the accomplishment of another major "global goal" for Eric.

In their last regular season game at home, the Devils squared off against the Detroit Red Wings and hammered the men from the Motor City, 5-1. Kasatanov notched three assists and Fetisov had two, working some of their magic that had made the Soviet Red Army so dominant. Eric also contributed when his powerplay slapshot bounced off the skate of Peter Stastny and into the net, earning Eric an assist.[173]

Stastny and the Diverse Devils

Assisting on a goal by Stastny linked Eric to one of the all-time greats, and to another player who had come out from behind the Iron Curtain. Stastny, whom NJ had acquired in March in a trade with the Quebec Nordiques, had defected from Czechoslovakia with his brother Anton in August 1980 in an extremely dramatic chain of events that sounds like it came from a Cold War spy thriller.[174] After an all-star decade with Quebec, Stastny was still a standout when he joined the Devils. Eric later described Stastny as "a super-talented old-school tough guy."[175]

These were thrilling times for Eric in many ways. Not only was he evidently in the NHL to stay, which would have been exciting under any circumstances, but he was part of a very talented team about to compete in the playoffs. The situation was made more amazing by the presence of Fetisov, Kasatonov, and Stastny, who all were key players in the end-of-the-Cold War drama that was unfolding at the dawn of the 1990s. The Eastern Bloc trio not only reflected the way that the end of the Cold War would impact hockey (and popular culture in general), but also demonstrated how hockey players could be cultural ambassadors and help facilitate the transition to a new post-Cold War reality.

The end of the Cold War was a crucial part of the historical context that shaped Eric's experience with NJ in spring 1990, but there were other forces at play that were reflected in the makeup of the Devils' roster. Globalization and a new wave of immigration combined throughout the 1990s to bring about the "internationalization of the United States."[176] Ethnic and racial diversity increased considerably in the USA during the decade, and these developments already could be seen on the Devils in 1990. Although most of the players were from Canada and the USA, the roster listed three Russians, three Swedes, two Fins, one Czechoslovakian, and one Haitian (Claude Vilgrain, who had scored a key goal late in the season). Eric befriended them all. For the 23-year-old defenseman from Maine, the Devils' globalized roster presented him with unlimited learning opportunities, both on and off the ice.

Weino's Wisdom

As a life-long Boston Bruins fan, I had the pleasure of watching Peter Stastny and his two brothers play for the Quebec Nordiques. A little-known fact about Peter is that he was the second leading scorer in the NHL during the 1980s. Peter was such an interesting person as well as one of the greatest players in history. He spoke many languages and was a wealth of knowledge. Peter was one of the most respected people in our locker room and when he had something to say it was always well thought out and meaningful.

Peter came from another eastern bloc country where practice and perfection were held at a high regard. Peter was one of the first players I saw that took his off-ice and on-ice training very seriously. He recorded every day of practice on and off the ice in a notebook and did some training techniques that were only adopted in North America later in my career. Peter was not only one of the most skilled players in the game but also one of the fiercest competitors. Most of all, he always had time to help a player with a skill or talk him through something that happened in a game.

Peter assisted on my first NHL goal. I never tired of listening and learning from Peter. Post-career he became a politician in his country of Slovakia. You never made the mistake of calling him a Czech. And if you did, he would make sure you never did it a second time. He was and will always be one of the most passionate people I've ever been a teammate of in my career.

Devils v. Capitals

Eric's next educational experience occurred in the intensity of a tough NHL playoff series against the Washington Capitals. On April 5 in Washington, the Caps opened with a grueling 5-4 win in overtime at the Brendan Byrne Arena in the Meadowlands of NJ. Two nights later, the Devils scraped and clawed to a gutsy 6-5 victory. Eric blasted home a goal from the top of the right faceoff circle to give NJ a 5-4 lead as Brendan Shanahan pestered the Caps' goalie Don Beaupre, who complained to no avail that Shanahan had interfered with him. Eric's first career NHL playoff goal was a remarkable one, for sure. Stastny slotted home a wraparound marker a few minutes later that proved to be the winner. Stastny also had an assist, as did Fetisov and Kasatonov.[177] Eric and the globalized Devils had won an NHL playoff game.

Game three took place on 9 April, and NJ took a 2-1 lead in the best-of-seven series with a 2-1 victory. Eric assisted on a powerplay tally by Shanahan in the second period, which proved to be the winning goal. Washington stormed back with three straight triumphs, however, ending the Devils season on 15 April with a 3-2 win. Eric assisted on a goal by Stastny in the third period to get NJ within one, but that would be the Devils final goal of the season. The 1990 NJ/Washington series had been exciting, dramatic, and hard-fought. Eric played well, skating in all six games including on the powerplay. In his initial NHL playoff experience he notched a goal and three assists, as well as showing some grit while racking up seventeen penalty minutes.[178]

Undoubtedly all the Devils were disappointed that the Capitals overcame their 2-1 lead to win the series; but, for Eric there was much for which to be thankful entering the post-season. His former international rival turned NHL comrade, Alex Kasatonov, invited him to a celebratory dinner where the two blueliners enjoyed caviar and gin.[179] They had each come a long way since the start of the season — one from Utica in the AHL and the other from a disintegrating Soviet Union. Both could be proud of what they accomplished, on the ice as players and off the ice as cultural ambassadors at the end of the classic Cold War.

The 1989-90 accomplishments by the young blueliner from Maine did not go unnoticed in the hockey community. In June at the American Hockey League's annual banquet in West Springfield, MA, Eric was awarded the Eddie Shore Trophy as the AHL's top defenseman. Players and media voted, and they selected Eric as the winner by a "wide margin." Weino was also named to the AHL's all-star first team.[180] During his stint with Utica he scored twelve goals and added 48 assists, thus totaling sixty points in only 57 games. After his call-up to NJ, he registered two goals and seven assists in nineteen regular season games and then another goal and three assists in the playoff series against Washington. Weinrich, more importantly, had cemented his place in the talented and diverse NJ lineup and could look ahead to the upcoming NHL season with confidence.

Weino's Wisdom ——————————————————————

My first playoff series was an unbelievable experience, and I had no idea how the intensity picked up compared to the regular season. I had some meaningful moments in the series and after it was over, I was just happy to have been involved. It wasn't until my fifth playoff season that I won a series and started to realize what that feeling was like. After the last game, when we arrived back in New Jersey, Alexei invited me to his home and his wife, Jeanette treated me to a Russian specialty of thick, white bread covered with butter and caviar on top. We washed it down with a glass of gin. Never in a million years would I imagined this moment would have occurred when I was watching the !987 Canada Cup series in Lake Placid, NY that August. That was when I became fascinated by the Russian players and most of all, Slava Fetisov and Alexei Kasatonov. And despite the deep political and cultural divides that had been created years before, athletics once again allowed people from two extremely different cultures and backgrounds to come together as teammates and friends. This is something I have truly missed after my retirement from the game.

Conclusion

The period from summer 1988 to summer 1990 was critical for Weino's career development, as he starred in the AHL, earned a shot in the NHL, and contributed to a playoff run and hard-fought series. These years were also key for his personal life and long-term happiness, as he met his future wife, Tracy Martin. In the broader context of history, moreover, Eric played a part in the drama of players from behind the Iron Curtain moving to the NHL. He befriended former Soviet players, especially Alex Kasatonov, and thus once again acted as a cultural ambassador. Playing with a diverse and globalized Devils team, Eric relished the opportunity to learn both on and off the ice from Kasatonov and others such as Fetisov and Stastny. His friendliness and respect surely also helped them adjust to life in the USA. During his first two years in pro hockey, Eric Weinrich accomplished many more of his global goals as part of a truly diverse organization.

CHAPTER 4

"Competing with the Best as the Cold War Ends, 1990-1991."

After working hard during the summer of 1990, Eric "Weino" Weinrich solidified a spot with the New Jersey Devils in training camp. By mid-season he emerged as one of the most successful rookies in the NHL. Weino remained a key defender for the Devils down the stretch as they qualified for the playoffs and in the dramatic 7-game defeat to Pittsburgh. He then flew to Finland to skate for Team USA in the World Championships. In June he was named to multiple NHL all-rookie teams. In July things got even better when he married Tracy Martin. Returning to the ice in August, Eric earned a place on the US squad competing in the prestigious Canada Cup. Team USA won a silver medal, and Eric played well. Throughout the long season of 1990-91, as the Cold War was ending and the Soviet Union was disintegrating, Eric Weinrich demonstrated repeatedly that he could compete with the very best hockey players in the world.

Summer 1990

After getting a chance to skate with the Devils for the last few months of the 1989-90 regular season and during a playoff series against Washington, Weinrich pushed himself during the summer of 1990 with hopes of cementing a spot in the NHL. He stayed in Orono, Maine and trained with his former college teammate Mike Golden, who was recovering from an injury. "Working out with Mike was great because we pushed each other," commented Weino.[181] In addition to lots of running, lifting weights, and skating, Eric took summer courses at the University of Maine. He had completed about half of his bachelor's degree and intended to keep working on it.

Global Goals for a New Season

As the summer came to an end, Weino's enthusiasm and anticipation regarding the Devils' training camp in New Jersey increased. He decided to show up a few days earlier than the 6 September veterans' deadline in order to skate with new players and rookies. This partly reflected his excitement, but also his desire to show that he was not over-confident. "I don't want to treat it like I've solidified a position," he explained. "I'm going down there with the attitude that I have to earn a spot on the roster even though in the back of my mind I know that I'd have to play myself out of a position."[182]

In addition to solidifying a place with New Jersey, he intended to focus on improving his physical strength through hard work and his mental strength through additional experience at the highest level. Because he was entering the option year of his contract, he hoped to complete negotiations for a new contract before the regular season started. Weino's agent, Bob Goodnough, also represented Brett Hull. Hull had recently inked a multi-million-dollar deal with St. Louis. In response to a question about whether he thought Goodnough could get him a similar deal Eric laughingly replied: "Hull scored more than 50 goals last year, I had three. I've got a way to go."[183]

Scoring goals like Brett Hull, or in a more appropriate comparison for a defenseman, like Bobby Orr, would have required a quantum leap by Weino. His more realistic goal was to work hard and play good hockey and earn a place on the Devils for the opening day of the 1990-91 season. He started strong, notching a goal and assist in New Jersey's second exhibition game against the Islanders on 16 September. The winning goal in the 4-1 victory was the first NHL goal by rookie Zdeno Ciger, who had recently arrived from the Czech Republic. Peter Stastny registered the opening goal of the game and was serving as Ciger's interpreter. If Eric survived the cut and skated with the Devils, he would be part of an even-more-international squad in the globalized NHL.[184]

A Spot with the Devils

When Devils' management trimmed the roster to thirty players on 24 September, they included Eric among the nine defensemen remaining in New Jersey. During a 27 September exhibition win over the rival Rangers, Weino and his friend Alexei Kasatonov joined a 5-man swarm on net that resulted in a goal by John MaClean and an assist for Eric. Observers at that point speculated that Weino would be paired with Bruce Driver, and also predicted that the duo would get some power-play minutes.[185] A season preview on 30 September reiterated the prediction that Weino would partner with Driver, but emphasized that the former Soviet Red Army tandem of Kasatonov and Viacheslav Fetisov most likely would be the cornerstone of the Devils' defense. The sportswriter noted that Fetisov had played solid hockey the year before; however, he praised Kasatonov as NJ's best blue-liner and a potential all-star. The scribe concluded with a key question: "Have the Soviet defensemen adjusted to life in the NHL?"[186]

The same question could also be asked about relatively inexperienced Eric Weinrich, who was still classified as a rookie. Previewing the opening game of the regular season on 4 October, a journalist noted that although Weino had not yet signed a new contract with New Jersey, his potential value to the team in his official rookie season was significant. "The defensive corps is deep, talented, intelligent, and versatile. Driver, Fetisov, Kasatonov, and Weinrich are capable of scoring 50 points apiece this season," concluded the optimistic scribe.[187] The opener against Detroit ended in a 3-3 draw, and Eric did not figure in the scoring. Another rookie, however, did score. One of the Red Wings' goals came from Sergei Fedorov, who had recently defected from the disintegrating Soviet Union while his club CSKA Moscow was playing an exhibition in Oregon. Fedorov turned out to be one of the most talented former Soviets to play in the NHL, racking up 483 regular season goals during his Hall-of-Fame career.[188]

Weino's Wisdom (WW)

Sergei Fedorov was one of the new Russians that we didn't know much about, but soon learned of his talents. For me, I always was fascinated by the unknown players from Europe who were just getting a chance to come to the NHL and play in the best league in the world. I felt fortunate that we had some of the best to ever play such as Fetisov, Stastny, and Kasatonov. What a shame it would have been to hockey fans everywhere if they never were given the chance to play here. Fedorov and Mogilny were the next generation of Russian stars with many more to come.

Rapid Change in the USSR

Entering the 1990-91 season, former Soviet players such as Fedorov, Kasatonov, and Fetisov had extra motivation to succeed in the NHL because it was becoming increasingly clear that the situation in the Soviet Union was changing rapidly. It seemed more and more likely all the time that there would not be a Soviet hockey system to rejoin if playing in the NHL did not work out. Indeed, early in the summer of 1990 the leader of the USSR, Mikhail Gorbachev, had officially expressed his willingness for recently re-unified Germany to join the North Atlantic Treaty Organization (NATO).

During an Oval Office meeting on 31 May 1990, President George H.W. Bush had asked if a re-unified Germany would have the right to choose which alliance to join, and Gorbachev had nodded his head in agreement.[189] It had been a startling turning point in world history, signaling the end of the Cold War. The Gorbachev regime's earlier decision to grant Fetisov a work visa and permission to negotiate his own contract with the Devils had similarly signaled a shift in the circumstances in the USSR, but a re-unified

Germany joining NATO had impact much broader than the fate of a single hockey player. About six weeks later in mid-July, Gorbachev had made it official by issuing a formal statement acknowledging Germany's right to join NATO if it saw fit.[190] According to esteemed scholar Robert McMahon, this decision by Gorbachev regarding Germany's ability to join NATO, more than any other event, meant the end of an era.[191] As the new season dawned, therefore, the former Soviet players possessed extra motivation to prove they belonged in the NHL.

Limited Playing Time

While Weino did not have the same stress as the former Soviets regarding a quickly evolving political landscape at home, he still felt pressure to prove he belonged in the NHL. In any long career, there are bound to be ups and downs, with occasional bumps in the road, and Eric's hockey experience was no different. When the Devils played on 11 October 1990, Coach John Cunniff decided that Eric would be a "healthy scratch" for the second straight game. Being a healthy scratch means a player does not suit up in a uniform and sits in the stands, but not due to injury. Understandably, Weino was "unsettled by the move." Coach Cunniff explained: "We wanted Eric to watch a little." When questioned about the situation Eric commented, "I don't think I was hurting the team."[192]

On Saturday 13 October, the Devils' coach reinstated Weino to the lineup for a game against Calgary, but the rookie was still uncertain about why he had been benched in the first place. Sportswriter John Dellapina examined the situation thoroughly in a piece published the next day. He explained that Eric was relieved to be back on the ice but still "mystified" why had spent two games in the stands. "They just gave me a little time to think, but I don't know about what," stated Weino. He reiterated his earlier comment that he did not feel that he had been hurting the team, but then upon further reflection he added: "Maybe I just wasn't helping enough."

Dellapina concurred with that assessment and contended that Cunniff and the Devils' management expected great things from Eric based on his performance in both Utica and New Jersey the previous season.[193]

Cunniff did not want only "damage control" from Eric; instead, based on his potential as a skater and passer, he wanted much more. This line of reasoning made some sense to Eric, who answered: "Cunnie wants me to control games." Although he hoped to be able to perform at that level, similar to his former Olympic teammate Brian Leetch (who had dominated games for the Rangers from day one), he honestly wasn't sure he was ready to do that yet. He hoped that if given the chance to play regularly for a full NHL regular season that he would get to the point of being comfortable in every situation. "I guess it's probably better that this happened at the beginning of the year than at the end," he reasoned. "I just want to play," he concluded.[194]

WW

It's ironic now that my role with the New Jersey Devils is to help players with their transition to different leagues after the draft and ultimately make it to the NHL. Shame on me for not always looking to push myself but to instead allow myself to get "comfortable" as a player. I only had to look around the room and see some of my heroes in the game and veteran players always doing the extra work on the ice and in the weight room. It seemed like every step in my career I had to take a moment and go through a learning experience to open my eyes again. The more I learned about the training that the European players went through, especially the Red Army players in Russia, I had a long way to go before I could be comfortable as an NHL player. Once I learned that coaches and general managers are always looking for their players to perform at their best consistently, and that "okay" is not good enough, I changed as a player and took a different attitude. I owe much of that to teammates such as Scott Stevens, Bruce Driver, Ken Daneyko, and the Russian and European players who had spent countless hours practicing and honing their skills that we all marveled at when they arrived on the scene.

Back in the Lineup

Coach Cunniff decided that Weino needed a little more time observing before becoming an automatic inclusion in the lineup, and so he scratched Eric on 20 October for the 4th time in the first nine games of the regular season. Back on the ice against the Islanders in the Devils' win on 23 October, Eric chipped in with an assist. Four nights later when New Jersey beat Pittsburgh 7-5, Eric gave the Devils an early lead when he blasted home a 45-foot slap-shot for his first goal of the season. The refs whistled Weino for two penalties in the rough-and-tumble affair. The multi-national Devils demonstrated the benefits of globalization in the NHL, with newly-arrived Czech Zdeno Ciger scoring a goal and with assists in the game coming from Stastny, Fetisov, and Kasatonov. As October wound down, the Devils were riding high at home with an undefeated record in the Brendan Byrne Arena of seven wins and one tie.[195]

Weino's prime-time performance against the Penguins had evidently convinced the Devils' management that he was ready to be a regular, and he contributed to the attack with an assist in a 6-3 loss to the Islanders on 7 November. A week later in a 6-3 win over the legendary Montreal Canadiens, Weino intercepted a pass and hit John MacLean in stride for the Devils' fifth goal with seven minutes remaining. The end of the Cold War again benefitted globalized New Jersey, led by the former Red Army blue-liner Kasatonov, who shined at both ends and scored his third goal of the season. Fellow immigrants from behind-the-iron-curtain, Fetisov and Stastny, recorded assists in the impressive victory.[196]

A few days later when Hartford knocked off New Jersey 4-2, Eric assisted on both goals. One of the goals came from Ciger assisted also by Kasatonov, demonstrating yet again the international makeup of the team. On 17 November 1990, the Devils rebounded and beat the Flyers in a tight 3-2 battle with Weino assisting on the opening marker by Stastny on a power-play.[197] Five nights later the Los Angeles Kings held off the Devils, 5-4. Weino registered an assist, but Wayne Gretzky had 2 assists and a goal. While being outdone by Gretzky, arguably the greatest hockey player of all-time, was nothing to be ashamed of, a tight loss was disappointing regardless. The Devils ended November drawing 5-5 with Philadelphia in a game which they led at one point by three goals. A late penalty by Weino put the Flyers on a power-play and they capitalized on the chance to earn the tie. Expressing his frustration afterwards Eric accurately observed: "We had the lead. We should have been able to hold it."[198]

December Success

Any Devils' disappointment with the way November ended quickly disappeared as New Jersey hammered the St Louis Blues 4-1 on 1 December. One minute into the third period Weino netted his second marker of the season, and then he assisted on MacLean's goal with three minutes left to seal the win. In Winnipeg two nights later, Eric blasted home another goal in a 4-4 draw with the Jets.[199] At that point in the campaign, Weino's plus/minus ranking was an impressive plus-24, meaning he had been on the ice for 24 more even-strength or short-handed goals for New Jersey than even-strength or short-handed goals allowed by New Jersey. He ranked first in plus/minus among NHL rookies, and second overall in the league![200]

When the Devils lost to the Islanders 3-2 on 10 December, Weino assisted on a power-play goal by Claude Lemieux which had tied the score, but to no avail. Ten days later in an overwhelming 4-1 triumph in Quebec, Eric again assisted on a goal by Lemieux. Stastny contributed a goal and assist against his former team who had facilitated his defection from behind the Iron Curtain. The lone Nordiques score came from future Hall-of-Famer Guy Lafleur, who as a long-time star for Montreal had been a hero to Eric as a youngster growing up next door in Maine.[201]

A New Year's Eve showdown with the rival Rangers ended in a dramatic 2-2 draw. Eric assisted brilliantly on the second New Jersey goal, scored by Kirk Muller. A sportswriter described it as a lucky/pretty goal: "The pretty part was the springing pass that Weinrich banked off the left boards to send Muller in on Vanbiesbrouck."[202] This entertaining goal from Muller gave the Devils a two-goal lead, but the Rangers battled back to earn a tie as the dramatic and historic year of 1990 wound down. The classic Cold War had ended, for all intents and purposes, and the Soviet Union itself was teetering on the brink of final collapse. "The year 1990," concluded historian Robert McMahon, "truly marked the end of the Cold War."[203]

Fittingly at such a historic juncture, early in 1991 the Devils hosted the Moscow Dynamo for an exhibition. In the 2-2 draw on 6 January, Weino assisted on the second New Jersey goal which was scored by recent immigrant Ciger. Alexander Semak, whom Eric and his dad had covertly visited in the hotel room during the World Junior Championships in Finland back in 1984, scored one of the Moscow goals. (The Devils had drafted Semak in 1988 and he would join them for the 1991-92 campaign.) A few days later when the regular season resumed, St Louis beat New Jersey 5-3. Eric recorded an assist, but the Devil who really shone with a goal and an assist was Kasatonov, perhaps rejuvenated by the recent exhibition battle against his countrymen.[204]

Plus/Minus Debate and Award Speculation

With the regular season approximately half-completed, journalists began evaluating mid-year statistics and speculating on potential award-winners. In his first forty games of the campaign, Eric had recorded three goals and 21 assists. His plus-minus ranking, moreover, was an incredible plus-23, which ranked forth in the entire NHL. One of the sportswriters who paid close attention was Dave Greely, and he emphasized that the season's success had given Weino the confidence to move out of the Turtlebrook Inn (where new Devils usually stayed) and into a condo. Tracy Martin, whom Eric had met during his stint in Utica, was an ever-more-frequent visitor. The couple felt optimistic about the future in all respects and were planning a July wedding.[205]

Greely's mid-year piece on Weino painted a very positive picture about his progress both off and on the ice. Greely extensively quoted Coach Cunniff, who praised Eric's consistent play, especially for a rookie, and for being very sound on the defensive end of the rink. "His forte is moving the puck out of the defensive zone and up to the forwards," observed Cunniff. "That's one of the reasons he has such a high plus-minus rating." Greely also pointed out that a daily sports publication called *The National* had recently ranked Weino as the top rookie in the Patrick Division for the first half of the season. When asked if he had a chance to win Rookie-of-the-Year for the NHL, Eric said that he would be happy to finish in the top five. "I'd like to be the top rookie defenseman," he concluded, "but I've always put team goals ahead of individual goals."[206]

Greely's article strongly suggested that even if Weino did not place a high priority on individual awards, he still might end up winning some. Not all observers were singing Eric's praises as loudly as Greely, however, and one who penned a more critical assessment of Weino at mid-year was Colin Stephenson, who covered the NHL for the *Asbury Park Press*. Stephenson critiqued the Devils' efforts at drawing attention to Weino's strong first-half performance and their emphasis on his high plus/minus ranking. SportsChannel, which broadcast New Jersey's games, had recently suggested that Eric be considered for the Calder Trophy, given to the NHL's Rookie-of-the-Year. The Devils' radio commentators had raised the possibility that Weino be named to the NHL All-Star team. For Stephenson, arguments for Eric as Rookie-of-the-Year or All-Star were not convincing and he exclaimed: "Let's stop that right now!"[207]

Stephenson questioned the judgement of other observers who were considering Weino for possible awards based on plus/minus. At the outset of his article he quoted Coach Cunniff, who applauded the statistic and pointed out that winning teams always had lots of players with a good plus/minus. Stephenson compared that argument to the classic "chicken or egg" conundrum, and wondered whether "plus" players make good teams, or do good teams make "plus" players? He acknowledged that plus/minus was a useful statistic but should not be over-emphasized and in fact could be deceiving. He contended convincingly that even the weakest players on good teams often ended on the plus side, whereas the very best players on unsuccessful teams often finished on the minus side.[208]

"So Weinrich's plus/minus rating is an interesting stat," continued Stephenson, "but it shouldn't – and won't – determine who makes the All-Star team or wins the Calder." He identified several defensemen including Ray Bourque, Paul Coffey, Brian Leetch, Kevin Hatcher, and Alexei Kasatonov whom he believed should be chosen before Weino for the All-Star game. For top freshman in the running for the Calder Trophy he pointed to Ed Belfour, Sergei Federov, and Rob Blake as top contenders and suggested that Mike Richter and Mike Ricci could be ranked ahead of Eric as the top rookie.[209]

Stephenson concluded his insightful and thought-provoking analysis of the plus/minus statistic on a light-hearted note, revisiting Eric's remarkable rating (plus-26 at the time he wrote the article). Stephenson noted that no one was quite sure how Eric amassed such a high plus figure. Evidently, some of the other Devils jokingly called him "Renaldo," in reference to the former 49ers wide receiver and record-holder in the 100-meter hurdles, Renaldo Nehemiah. According to these Devils' humorous explanation, Weino's hurdling technique launched him off the bench and onto the ice just before a NJ goal, and similarly removed him from the ice and onto the bench just before they surrendered one.[210]

An Exciting Regular Season Resumes

Regardless of all the joking by teammates and critical analysis by the media, Eric Weinrich had certainly enjoyed a very strong first half of his rookie NHL season, and he was excited to get the second half under way. In a tough battle against the Pittsburgh Penguins on 22 January 1991, Weino put NJ on the scoreboard with a power-play goal early in the third period. Pittsburgh's offensive juggernaut (led by Mario Lemieux and Jaromir Jagr) nevertheless prevailed by a 5-3 score.[211]

On 26 January 1991, in a 3-1 loss to the Minnesota North Stars, Weino got the puck from Doug Brown and promptly assisted skillfully on a Devils' goal by Jeff Madill. "Brown passed back to Eric Weinrich at the right point," described a sportswriter, "and his perfect pass to the left post bounced off Madill's stick and in." Two nights later back on the ice for an impressive 6-2 win over the Detroit Red Wings, Eric assisted on NJ's final goal half-way through the third period, a power-play marker by John MacLean (his 31st of the season). The benefits of globalization at the end of the Cold War were once again on full display as the cosmopolitan Devils got their opening goal from Kasatonov and their fourth goal from Stastny, assisted by Fetisov and Kasatonov. Perhaps Detroit learned a lesson that night, because their Stanley Cup winning team several years later would feature an entire 5-man unit of former Soviet players including Fetisov.[212]

As the long NHL season ground on, the Devils hoped for a sweep of back-to-back games against the Nordiques in Quebec and at home against Vancouver during the second weekend of February. They fell 3-1 in Quebec on February 9 but managed to bounce back with a 2-0 win the next night in Brendan Byrne arena against the Canucks. "It is disappointing," commented Eric to the press. "We knew what we had to do this weekend and we didn't do it."[213] About a week later in a 3-3 draw against Winnipeg, one of the Jets goals ricocheted off Weino and into the net. Eric had learned early on that such unlucky bounces were a part of the game and did not let it bother him. In earning the tie, the diverse Devils had again benefitted from the end of the Cold War, with Fetisov and Ciger netting goals.[214]

Two nights later the Devils got back on track with a hard-fought 3-2 win over the Flyers. The winning goal came from the stick of Zdeno Ciger, the recent immigrant from Czechoslovakia, with an assist from Eric. Fortunes took a turn for the worse on 19 February, when the Edmonton Oilers handed NJ a 4-0 drubbing. Eric nearly scored seven minutes into the game, but his shot was stopped by a spectacular save on the part of Edmonton's great goalie, Grant Fuhr. Perhaps pressing to get NJ on the scoreboard, Weino committed a costly mistake a little later in the game. "Defenseman Eric Weinrich made a poorly timed attempt at intercepting an Edmonton pass in the neutral zone," noted a sportswriter, "leading to Joe Murphy's goal, which made it 2-0."[215]

Playoff Battle

Disappointing February efforts such as the Edmonton loss raised questions about NJ's season, and moving into March the Devils found themselves in a tight battle for the final playoff spot in the Wales Conference. On 3 March, their record stood just over .500 at 28 wins, 27 losses, and eleven ties. NJ ownership, not satisfied with the mark and hoping to rejuvenate the team, fired Coach John Cuniff on 5 March 1991 and replaced him with Tom McVie, who had been Eric's coach in Utica the previous season. In addition to being a familiar face for Weino and a few others who had played for him in the minors, McVie brought a wealth of experience in hockey and an irrepressible love for the game. The NJ brass hoped he could guide the Devils into the post-season.

Taking stock after a few games with McVie at the helm, sportswriter John Dellapina found considerable hope among the NJ players. With ten games left and the Devils still clinging to the final playoff spot, the pressure was on. "I think the guys believe now that we're going to make it," defenseman Eric Weinrich said. In his analysis heading into the final ten games of the campaign, Dellapina lauded Weino as "a voice of common sense all season." Eric told the reporter that he had seen an improvement in team chemistry since McVie took over. "A little tension has been lifted," stated Weino. "I think some of the guys feel a little more at ease." In Eric's assessment, the Devils were playing with desperation but not tension. "There's a little more jump. You can see guys picking each other up on the bench and on the ice," concluded Weino. The new coach echoed Eric's optimism. "I see great signs, really good signs," commented McVie. "But we've got to win and win now. We're running out of games. We've got to win." If they didn't earn some key victories down the stretch, as Dellapina underscored at the end of his article, they would get to start summer break early and sleep through the playoffs.[216]

Fortunately for the Devils and their fans, they fought back from an early 2-0 deficit at home against Toronto and gave McVie his first win as coach of NJ. Except for a rocky opening, the Devils played "solid hockey." The victory lifted NJ to sole possession of fourth place in their division and back into a playoff spot. The former Soviet Red Army tandem made the difference in this crucial game, moreover. Fetisov's interception of a clearing attempt led to the tying goal, and then Kasatonov pounced on a loose puck in the slot and fired home the winning wrist-shot. Weino, though not involved in the scoring, played a good defensive game and his picture was featured in the sports pages the next day, dramatically sprawled on the ice. None of the Devils felt any need to apologize for how they beat Toronto, emphasizing only that they got a huge win.[217]

Crucial Points down the Stretch

About ten days later NJ once again rallied from a 2-0 deficit, this time in the fabled Forum in Montreal, and rescued a critical point in the playoff race by tying the Canadiens 3-3. The Devils third goal was scored by the famous Slovak defector Peter Stastny, who tucked home a rebound after a drive by Weino had been deflected by the great goalie Patrick Roy. This crucial contribution represented one of the most important plays of Eric's NHL career up to that juncture.[218] Helping score against Roy in the Forum to improve his team's chances to make the post-season demonstrated Weino's ability to compete with the best hockey players in the world.[219]

The Devils battled for another important point a few days later, on 26 March at Madison Square Garden in New York, drawing 3-3 with the

Rangers. Weino again chipped in with a timely assist, this time on a power-play goal by Claude Lemieux in the first period. Every point was invaluable as NJ fought tooth-and-nail with Philly for the final post-season slot. "Wasn't it great," exclaimed Coach Tom McVie. "That was playoff hockey. It's a point and it was fun to be in."[220] If Eric had been interviewed following that game, then he almost certainly would have agreed with his coach.

On 31 March, the Devils lost their final regular season game to the Islanders, but they had done just enough down the stretch to qualify for the post-season. Their 79 points from a record of 32 wins, fifteen ties, and 33 losses put them in fourth place in their division and pitted them against the Pittsburgh Penguins in the opening round of the playoffs. Overall, they had not lived up to pre-season expectations, finishing with the thirteenth best record out of 21 teams in the NHL; however, their defense had been very good, only allowing the seventh most goals in the league at 264. The Devils' blue-liners could take some pride in that accomplishment. Individually, Eric finished with a plus-10 ranking, four goals, and 34 assists to rank third in scoring by a NJ defender behind Kasatonov and Driver. The Devils had no time to dwell on such statistics, however, as their attention immediately turned to the dangerous Penguins.

Playoffs versus Pittsburgh

The series opened in Pittsburgh on 3 April, and the Devils stunned the Penguins 3-1. Peter Stastny hammered home the winner early in the second period, with an assist by Weino. There was no question that the playoffs had begun, and a lot was on the line, as a whopping 56 minutes of penalties were allotted in the third period alone, including two minutes to Eric for elbowing. The Penguins fought back for a grueling 5-4 game two victory in overtime, when young Jaromir Jagr, recently arrived from Czechoslovakia, scored the winner. It was another intense affair, with 74 minutes of penalties, including two minutes on Weino for roughing at the end of regulation.[221]

Game three of the series, at Brendan Byrne Arena in NJ on 7 April, was an incredibly dramatic heart-breaking 4-3 loss for the Devils, with Weino in the middle of the maelstrom. The Penguins took the initial lead and then NJ tied it up in the first period. The pattern repeated in the second and third periods. With less than two minutes on the game clock, the Devils' Doug Brown thought he had scored the potential winner on a wrap-around move. However, the referee ruled that the puck had not crossed the goal-line and waved off the score. About thirty seconds later, Pittsburgh's Mark Recchi won the game with a fluke goal after Eric tried unsuccessfully to catch a puck descending in the NJ end.[222]

Recchi slotted home the winner after teammate Phil Bourque flipped the puck high in the air out of the Penguins defensive zone in the final minute to run time off the clock. "Weinrich, a most dependable defenseman, skated backward under the falling puck," described a journalist. "About 15 feet from his own goal, he extended his left hand trying to catch it." Eric explained his thinking: "I wanted to catch it and bat it into the corner." Instead, the puck grazed his fingertips and then bounced crazily towards the NJ goal. Recchi swooped in and jabbed it past goalie Chris Terreri into the net. After the game, the Penguins admitted that they had gotten lucky. For his part, when asked what happened, Weino politely responded to the reporters: "You saw it." Fellow defenseman Bruce Driver spoke up on Eric's behalf, saying that it was not a mistake but rather "an unfortunate thing." Weino added: "The guys understood." They had told him "It could have happened to anyone."[223]

Of course, losing game three on a fluky bounce was frustrating nonetheless, but all Weino and his buddies could do was try to put it behind them and prepare for the next game. The Devils did exactly that, pounding the Penguins 4-1 in game four at Brendan Byrne Arena. Their final goal by Claude Lemeiux was on a power-play, and Eric assisted. Two nights later, on 11 April in Pittsburgh, the Devils triumphed again, by a 4-2 margin, for their third win in the series. They only needed one more victory to eliminate the Penguins and advance, but that would prove easier said than done.

Game six shifted back to Brendan Byrne Arena in NJ. After a quick score by John MacLean gave the Devils an early lead, the high-powered Penguins came roaring back with four straight goals including one from Jagr. The Devils did not quit, and Weino pulled them within two goals with a slap-shot blast on a power-play about half-way into the second period. Claude Lemieux cut the Penguins lead to one about a minute later, but that was the end of the scoring and Pittsburgh held onto a 4-3 victory that tied the series at 3 games apiece.[224] The stage was set for a showdown seventh game in Pittsburgh, but it turned out to be anti-climactic with the Penguins skating away from the Devils 4-0 and winning the series. Weino's first full NHL season ended abruptly, but the rookie defender was not nearly finished competing against the best in 1990-91.

WW ──

That series was a big disappointment for me, especially the game I turned over the puck after we had just scored a short-handed goal to get back in the battle. After the season I had where I went through stretches when I felt I was a legitimate NHL player, I made some mistakes and decisions that I wasn't accustomed to making. I just didn't perform up to my ability. But watching the Russian players on our team perform each night was a real learning experience for me. It amazed me how calm and poised they were. It took me back to the day I watched the Russian Olympic Team practice in Calgary. The precision and skill in every drill was exceptional and intimidating. Each day both Alex and Slava would challenge me to get better.

World Championships

The Devils convened one last time for an end-of-season team meeting on 17 April 1991. Their inconsistent regular season and first-round playoff exit made off-season roster changes very likely, but such concerns could wait. Most players were shifting into vacation mode already, but Weino was not among them. In what would become a frequent decision for him, he had accepted the call to national team duty.[225] "Oh, some were busy," observed a reporter. "Sean Burke and Eric Weinrich packed their equipment bags for the trip to the World Championships in Finland, where Burke will tend goal for Team Canada and Weinrich will play defense for Team USA."[226]

The 55th edition of the World Ice Hockey Championships took place in Finland in the cities of Turku, Helsinki, and Tampere, beginning on April 19. Returning to play again in Finland, where he had participated in the World Junior Championships back in 1984-85, was a nice turn of events for Eric. The 1991 senior competition featured eight nations who played each other once in the opening round with the top four advancing to the medal round. Weino and his US teammates split their first six games evenly, with two wins (including an impressive 4-1 victory over Czechoslovakia), two losses, and two draws. In their seventh game they defeated the host nation Finland 2-1, earning a place in the medal round.

The Soviets, playing in the World Championships for the last time as a unified nation, beat the USA in the opening medal-round game on 30 April, 6-4. The USA then lost badly to Sweden 8-4 on 2 May and were defeated even worse by silver-medalists Canada 9-4 on 4 May, finishing in fourth place. Sweden, led by teenager Mats Sundin who scored the most points of any player in the tourney, grabbed the gold. Weino's fellow Devils, Fetisov and Kasatonov, both skated for the bronze-winning Soviets and earned spots on the all-tourney team. Eric did not take home any hardware, but he had held his own against the world's best, playing in all ten games for the USA and chipping in two goals and an assist.[227]

All-Rookie Teams

Returning from Finland, Weino got some rest and had time to re-evaluate his rookie NHL performance. While Eric could be one of his own toughest critics, others saw much to praise in this first full season with NJ. On 21 June 1991, Upper Deck and the NHL honored him in a ceremony at the

Buffalo Convention Center, announcing that Eric was one of six players selected to the NHL All-Rookie team by the Professional Hockey Writers' Association. The other five chosen were Boston's Ken Hodge, LA's Rob Blake, Detroit's Sergei Fedorov, Pittsburgh's Jaromir Jagr, and Chicago's Ed Belfour. The six rookie honorees each received $1,000 to donate to charity, a commemorative jersey, and a specially commissioned crystal keepsake.[228] Weino's winning the same award as Jagr (from Czechoslovakia) and Federov (from the USSR) again demonstrated the changing face of the NHL as the Cold War concluded and globalization accelerated.

The writers of *Hockey Digest* also recognized an NHL all-rookie team in early summer 1991, and Weino again found himself in rare company (and even more international). In addition to Eric this squad included four other repeats from the Upper Deck choices: Blake as the other defenseman, Belfour as net-minder, and Jagr and Fedorov up front. The one new face was Sweden's Mats Sundin (whose spectacular performance at the World Championships had just been witnessed by Eric first-hand) who was chosen as the third forward. Commenting on what explained his successful season, Weino contended that his late-season stint with NJ the previous spring had given him a real boost going into the fall of 1990. "I wasn't confident that I had a spot on the team in training camp," explained Eric, "but I was confident that I could play against people on this level."[229]

Now, after playing a complete regular season, a 7-game series against Pittsburgh, and an intense World Championship tourney, there was no doubt whatsoever that Weino could compete against the very best and was in the NHL to stay. The jury was still out, however, regarding how well several of the former Soviet players could adjust — not so much to NHL play but rather to life in North America. The early summer issue of *Hockey Digest* graded the recent immigrants from the USSR, awarding both Alexander Mogilny and Kasatonov the highest marks at B+, giving the 1990 Rookie-of-the-Year Sergei Makarov a B, and being a bit tougher on Fetisov and Igor Larionov with C marks. Sergei Priakin scored lowest with a D, and a few other players such as Vladimir Krutov had not done enough in the 1990-91 season to even merit a grade.[230]

A Wonderful Weinrich Wedding

Part of the explanation for the relatively smooth transition by Alexei Kasatonov could be found in his good relationship with Devils from North America such as Weino. Eric had been an unofficial Cold War cultural ambassador since the World Junior Championships in 1984-5, when he and his dad visited two Soviet players in their hotel room. Reaching out to Kasatonov five years later with the Devils, therefore, came naturally to Weino. Their friendship, moreover, extended beyond the ice, and so on one level it was not surprising at all that Kasatonov attended Eric and Tracy's mid-summer nuptials.[231] On the other hand, the fact that one of the star players from the 1988 USSR gold medal winners was a guest in 1991 at the wedding of a player from the 1988 Team USA squad elucidated how much the world had changed in three years.

Eric and Tracy's wedding July 1991

The wonderful wedding of Terese Renee Martin and Eric John Weinrich took place on 6 July 1991 at the Hamilton College Chapel in Clinton, NY.[232] The reception was nearby in Utica. The maid of honor was Tracy's sister Denise, and the best men were Eric's brothers Alex and Jason. Alex, drafted in the twelfth round in 1987 by Toronto, had recently completed his freshman season at Merrimack College. After high school he had played in the Central Canada Hockey League, so he entered university the same year as his "little" brother. Jason, the tallest of the three boys at 6'3", had been drafted by the Rangers in the sixth round in 1990 and had just completed his freshman year at the University of Maine. During his toast at the reception, Jason correctly characterized his eldest brother Eric as a "role model."[233]

After the wedding, Eric and Tracy honeymooned in Banff National Park, west of Calgary, Alberta. Tracy enthusiastically stepped into her role as a Devils' wife, participating regularly in community service events. She befriended Alexei Kasatonov's wife, Jeannette, and vividly described taking her to the grocery store for the first time. "She filled the cart with meat," recalled Tracy, "because she never could count on it in the Soviet Union." Communicating with the Russian wives was more difficult than with those from Finland, Sweden or Czechoslovakia, as their English was generally not as strong. Nevertheless, Tracy believed that being in the NHL was a positive experience for former Soviet players because they were able to spend a lot more time with their families than they had in the USSR.[234]

WW ——————————————————————————————

It was special for Tracy and me to have Alex and Jeannette Kasatonov at our wedding. I had only known Alex for about a year and a half and having watched both Slava and him play against the best-ever Canada team in the 1987 Canada Cup and then at the Olympic Games, I had so much admiration for their play. Getting to know the person was fascinating. Even with the language barrier, Slava and Alex found a way to communicate and I learned even more about their culture and what they had been through as players on the Red Army team. Alex and Jeannette were always so kind to Tracy and me and we were thrilled to see them at the wedding. During our reception, we had tables set up with different kinds of food and appetizers. One contained some seafood and caviar. It was not the quality of the caviar I had been served at the Kasatonov house one night, and Jeannette came up to Tracy at the reception and exclaimed that the caviar was "no good." We got a kick out of that! Just a few years before we all considered the Russians as our enemies and new we were friends and teammates.

More Chaos in Moscow

Living in North America and playing in the NHL presented the former Soviet players with a wide array of challenges. While some of them were unable to make the adjustment, a large number would eventually be successful. In late summer 1991, however, their lives grew even more complicated as the political situation at home got more chaotic. When President George H.W. Bush visited Moscow in late July, the tension between Soviet leader Mikhail Gorbachev and the new Russian president, Boris Yeltsin, was palpable. Bush intended to keep working closely with Gorbachev as long as he held power, but it was clear that Yeltsin was on the ascendency. The USSR still technically existed, but a new agreement decentralized much of the power to the governments of the republics. In reaction to this trend, hard-liners and military leaders such as Defense Minister Dmitri Yazov (who had tried to prevent Fetisov from joining the Devils back in 1989) attempted a coup against Gorbachev, hoping to re-instate centralized Soviet rule, on 17 August 1991. The coup fizzled quickly, and Gorbachev temporarily returned to office, but the USSR's days were clearly numbered.[235]

The 1991 Canada Cup

The impending disintegration of the USSR meant that the 1991 Canada Cup would be the last major senior tournament in which a Soviet squad participated.[236] The team would not be full-strength, however, as the political uncertainty in Moscow convinced many top players to opt out. Kasatonov and Federov did play, but other big names such as Mogilny, Fetisov, and Pavel Bure stayed away. Weino, recently returned from his honeymoon in Alberta, traveled to Pittsburgh in mid-August intent on earning a roster spot. He was not guaranteed a place by any means, so "he simply went out and earned one."[237]

Team USA opened the tourney in Pittsburgh on 31 August 1991 against a strong Swedish squad led by Mats Sundin, earning a decisive 6-3 victory. After falling 6-2 to Canada on 2 September, the US crew ran off three straight wins over Czechoslovakia, the USSR, and Finland to qualify for the semi-finals. They again met the super-talented Fins, whose stars included Jari Kurri, Esa Tikkanen, and a teenage Teemu Selanne. On 11 September in Hamilton, Ontario, Team USA finished off the high-flying Fins, 7-3, to reach the finals versus host Canada, who beat Sweden in the other semi-final game. The Soviets, playing with a watered-down roster due to the political chaos in Moscow, uncharacteristically failed to reach the medal round in their final major international tournament. Hockey reflected the momentous changes unfolding in the world.

Canada and the United States squared off on 14 September in Montreal, and although Weino had done well in the first six games, he only played a couple of shifts in this one. The big story, though, involved another US defender, Gary Suter, who checked Wayne Gretzky hard into the boards from behind, knocking him out of the game and the rest of the series. "I don't believe he intended to hurt Gretzky, but he became Public Enemy No. 1 in Canada," recalled Chris Chelios. "He even received death threats. The first person we saw the next day when we walked into the rink was Gretzky, who had his arm in a sling, and Suter walked right up to him and apologized."[238]

The second matchup between the neighboring nations occurred on 16 September in Hamilton, and even without Gretzky the Canadians prevailed 4-2 to win the 5th and final Canada Cup. With Brian Leetch injured, Weino got a lot of ice time and played very well in defeat. According to Team USA assistant coach Jay Leach, Eric "was tremendous in the second game against Canada. He was one of the best three defenseman on the ice."[239] Considering the caliber of players on the US and Canadian squads, that was saying a lot. This tourney in general, and this last game particularly, demonstrated as much as any example from Eric's career that he could compete with the best.

For Team USA overall it had been a great performance and winning a silver medal against such a field was quite an achievement. According to a Team Canada website: "The Americans, accurately dubbed as 'the best U.S. team ever' by general manager Craig Patrick, were inspired by their dying coach Bob Johnson, who fell ill with a brain tumor as the tournament began. They put in a gutsy effort, very deserving of their second-place finish."[240] Forward Jeremy Roenick, who scored a team-leading four goals and was named to the all-tourney team, did not always enjoy his international experiences with USA Hockey; but, he had very fond memories of the 1991 Canada Cup. "That was the tournament," exclaimed Roenick, "where the younger American players began to believe that we were going to eventually be a world... power in hockey!"[241]

In his summation of the USA performance in the Canada Cup, Weino seconded JR: "We gave it our best shot and I think we proved to a lot of people that we're an up-and-coming hockey nation." Although he had a few low points such as being steamrolled by big Eric Lindros on 2 September and not playing much in the first finals matchup against Canada, overall Weino's own experience was very positive. "I thought I had a pretty solid tournament. I didn't do too much offensively. We had enough guys who could do that. My role was to play defense and help kill penalties," he observed.[242]

Eric had watched the 1987 Canada Cup on TV and never seen such a high level of play. He expected fast-paced action in 1991 and was not disappointed. "To play in the tournament was a dream come true," stated Weino. He explained that you really could not predict what would happen on the ice the way you could in regular season NHL games. "These were some of the most creative players ever seen and you knew you were never going to have an easy shift out there. It was every bit as intense as they said it was going to be," he concluded. Maine journalist and hockey enthusiast Larry Mahoney summed up the story nicely: "The Canada Cup was everything hockey was meant to be. And there was Gardiner's Weinrich right in the middle of it."[243]

WW ——————————————————————————————————

Talk about a dream come true! Having witnessed the best tournament ever played in 1987 between Canada and the USSR, putting on the Team USA jersey and playing amidst the world's greatest players for the best hockey-playing countries was a great honor. I hadn't expected to be part of the team but when a couple of US players weren't able to play, it opened a door for me, and I wouldn't have missed the chance. Looking back on the Russian team's roster, a few of the top players decided to sit the tournament out, namely the four players who had left the Red Army team coached by Tikhonov and only Kasatonov played in 1991. As I went through the roster recently, there were many familiar names of younger Russian players who had not made the jump to the NHL yet. But it would not be long before they came over. A few would later become teammates such as Semak, Zhamnov, and Malakhov.

Conclusions

Between September 1990 and September 1991, Eric Weinrich accomplished several major global goals both professionally and personally. He earned a spot at the beginning of the NHL season with the increasingly international New Jersey Devils. By the season's start, the Cold War had ended for all intents and purposes because Soviet leader Mikhail Gorbachev had conceded the right for a unified Germany to join NATO. This development, in conjunction with the looming disintegration of the Soviet Union, meant there would be a bigger wave of players arriving from behind the Iron Curtain with a major motivation to be successful – it seemed very likely that soon there would be no Soviet hockey system to return to if they failed in North America. Weino experienced this firsthand, both with teammates Fetisov and Kasatonov and opponents such as Detroit's Sergei Federov.

Al, Eric, and Jay
early 1990s when Merrimack played Maine

After a slow start which included several frustrating healthy scratches in early October, Weino contributed some key goals and assists in late October and November against the Penguins and Canadiens. Eric scored two more goals in early December and bounced a beautiful pass off the boards for an assist in a 2-2 New Year's Eve tie in Madison Square Garden against the Rangers. Eric fit in well with the globalized Devils who featured many recent arrivals from the USSR and other Soviet-controlled areas, as his emphasis on skating and passing, rather than fighting, matched their style.

Going into the second half of the NHL season and the playoff race, Eric continued to play well. Much of the Devils offense came from immigrants such as Stastny, Ciger, Fetisov, and Kasatonov. Eric collaborated well with these imports, most notably helping earn a crucial tie in Montreal on 23 March 1991 when his blast bounced off legendary Patrick Roy and was tucked home by Stastny. Eric's excellent regular season had demonstrated that he could compete with the world's best, and he helped the Devils qualify for the playoffs. In their intense 7-game series against Pittsburgh, Eric contributed a goal and two assists, but the Penguins prevailed.

Weino's season was far from over, however, and in what would become an admirable habit for him he accepted an invitation from Team USA to compete in the World Championships in Finland. He played all ten games and chipped in two goals and an assist. He helped the US qualify for the medal round but they were defeated by the Soviets, who were led by Fetisov and Kasatonov. Upon returning from Finland, Weino received the honor of being named to two NHL all-rookie teams. Eric's presence in select company with the likes of Jagr, Federov, and Sundin was a great honor, and reflected the rapidly globalizing NHL at the end of the Cold War.

As he had done since high school, Eric continued to serve as an unofficial cultural ambassador, and that would even carry over to his July wedding where Alexei Kasatonov was a guest. Weino and Kasatonov had clicked since Alexei's arrival in the USA and Eric's friendship surely helped Alexei adjust to life in North America, so in some respects it was no surprise to see the Red Army star at the wedding. On the other hand, his attendance clearly demonstrated how much the world had changed since 1988, as would the ensuing friendship between Eric's wife Tracy and Jeannette Kasatonov.

The changes, moreover, were not finished. The Soviet Union teetered on the brink of collapse in August when military hard-liners attempted a coup. The plotters failed in their effort, but the damage was done and the Soviet team competing in the September 1991 Canada Cup would be the last senior hockey team from the USSR to ever play on the world stage. Eric earned a roster spot on a stacked squad that many hockey fans consider the best US team ever. The USA beat powerhouses Sweden and Finland, among others, and earned a silver medal. Eric handled the challenge well, particularly in the final match against Canada. This tourney, and especially the last game, underlined Eric's ability to play at the highest level. Throughout the long season of 1990-91, as the Cold War was ending and the Soviet Union was disintegrating, Eric Weinrich demonstrated repeatedly that he could compete with the very best hockey players in the world.

WW

Having been to the USSR in 1987, watching from afar what happened in Russia was interesting. When we played the games in the Pravda Cup against the USSR and when we were in the hotel in Leningrad, it was hard not to be a little nervous about the situation and where we were. We felt like outsiders and enemies. But when the Russian players began to integrate into the teams in the NHL as teammates, you held no ill-will if they could help the team win. And in the end, they were just people like us who had been through different experiences in life in a different culture. The 1987 Canada Cup was about as thrilling a series as there ever will be. There was no clear winner, even with Canada technically prevailing. The players of that era paved the way for future stars from Russia and not only in hockey; moreover, it opened the door for other athletes to participate in other international sports.

CHAPTER 5

"Embracing 'Home' in Chicago, 1991-1997"

Between 1991 and 1997, Eric "Weino" Weinrich established himself as a dependable NHL defenseman who skated and passed well, was not afraid to play physical hockey, and occasionally displayed an offensive flair. After another year with the cosmopolitan and globalized Devils, he was traded to the Hartford Whalers where he started slowly but displayed his high-level skills nicely during the second half of the campaign. The next season, in the fall of 1993, the Chicago Blackhawks acquired Weino and he immediately felt at home in the Windy City. For five years he played a key role on a strong Blackhawks team that included many "home-grown" players born in the USA. While he occasionally displayed his offensive ability at key times and in playoff games, Eric mostly played a conservative, defensive-minded style of hockey. As a stay-at-home defender, as a homeowner, and more importantly as a husband to Tracy and a father of Ben and Emily, Eric Weinrich increasingly embraced the concept of home during his five years in Chicago.

Final Year as a Devil

After his incredible 1990-91 campaign that culminated in a strong performance at the Canada Cup, Weino confidently laced up his skates for New Jersey in the fall of 1991. The Devils again featured a very globalized roster that played exciting and high-quality hockey. New Jersey was led by forwards Claude Lemeiux (from Canada) and Peter Stastny (from Slovakia), who scored 41 and 24 goals respectively, and defensemen Scott Stevens (from Canada) and Alexei Kasatonov (from Russia). Weino enjoyed a stellar sophomore season, tallying seven goals and 25 assists in 76 games. Other international members of the cosmopolitan Devils included Alexander Semak and Slava Fetisov from Russia, Zdeno Ciger from Slovakia, and 19-goal scorer Claude Vilgrain from Haiti.

During the 1991-92 NHL regular season, New Jersey won 38 games while losing 31 and tying eleven. (Though little noted during the season but of great significance in future years, Martin Brodeur and Scott Niedermayer each made their NHL debuts, appearing in four games for the Devils during the regular season. Niedermayer's potential had a major impact on the trajectory of Weino's career.) New Jersey's 87 points earned them a fourth place finish in their division and a playoff matchup with the division-winning New York Rangers. The Devils and Rangers battled tooth and nail for seven games. After New York won the opener, the Devils fought back and won games two and three. Weino notched assists in both of those wins, including his helper on Vilgrain's insurance goal in a 3-1 victory in game three. After the Rangers triumphed in games four and five, the Devils won game six to force a rubber match which New York won to advance, sending the Devils on vacation earlier than they had hoped. Weino headed for Orono to take a summer class. During his time in Orono he trained with former Black Bear teammates and his brother Jason, who had just finished his sophomore season at the university.

Traded to Hartford

As summer wound down, Eric and Tracy received the news on 28 August 1992 that New Jersey had traded Weino to the Harford Whalers. New Jersey acquired Bobby Holik and a draft pick in exchange for Eric and Sean Burke. The Devils had decided to give the promising youngster Scott Niedermayer a chance to prove himself, so Eric would have seen a significant reduction in playing time. On September 12 he joined the Whalers for training camp in

Burlington, Vermont and spoke to the press. "I was shocked when I heard," Eric stated. "I think every player, even if they are expecting it, is shocked. I wasn't disappointed in the trade. I was disappointed that I won't be around all the good friends I've made with the Devils."[244] Weino was looking on the bright side in that the trade to the Whalers would give him more playing time; however, his biggest concern (which proved prescient) was that the team would lose a lot of games and not draw large crowds.

During the first two months of the season, Hartford did indeed lose a lot of games and attracted "dismal" attendance; however, Weino clocked a lot of ice time and played solid hockey. By mid-December he had accumulated ten assists, and his plus/minus rating was at minus 5, which was not bad considering how poorly Hartford was playing overall. He was still waiting for his first goal as a Whaler. "I feel like I'm playing well, I just can't put the points on the board," he commented. One low point of the season came on 25 November against Montreal when he got up-ended by a Canadiens player and hit his head on the ice, suffering a concussion. As a result, he sat out the next two games, which was the first time he missed any games as a professional due to injury. After recovering and returning to action Eric contributed assists in three straight games and expressed optimism that Hartford could get on a roll and perhaps catch fourth-place Buffalo for the last play-off spot.[245]

His hopes that Hartford might claw back into postseason contention would turn out to be overly optimistic, but there were occasional bright spots such as an impressive win in Montreal on 21 December over Patrick Roy and his Canadiens, who would go on to win the Stanley Cup at the end of the season. The game entered the final period knotted at two apiece, when Weino snatched a pass from Geoff Sanderson on the fly and skated into the slot where his rising shot beat Roy just inside the post. Eric's first goal of the season proved to be the winner as the Whalers ended up on top, 5-2.[246] Scoring the decisive goal against the legendary net-minder Roy on his home ice was an accomplishment to remember, for sure.

At the halfway point of the season, a sportswriter for the *Hartford Courant* provided a lengthy analysis of Eric's offensive performance up to that point. His single goal and twelve assists through forty games were less than the Whalers had hoped for, but to be fair he was not getting much time on the powerplay. He also believed that it reflected the team's overall struggles, which necessitated a focus on defensive play to stay in games. "If things were going well for us," observed Weino, "I think we would be more creative, guys would be a lot more relaxed... Things would be going easier for us, and there may be more opportunities for that." He concluded the interview by looking at the glass as half full, pointing out that he was much more productive with the Whalers playing at even strength than he had been during his seasons with the Devils.[247]

World Championships in Germany

During the second half of the season, the Whalers did not fare much better. They won fifteen games, tied two, and lost 27. Weino improved his offensive production considerably, however, scoring six goals and chipping in with seventeen assists to finish the 1992-93 with 36 points, the second highest total of his entire NHL career. As he would do so many times over the years, instead of packing up his gear and heading for the golf course or the fishing boat when his professional season ended, Eric accepted the call from USA Hockey and laced up his skates for the 57th Men's Ice Hockey World Championships which took place in Germany. Weino appeared in all six games in Germany for Team USA, who performed quite well in the group stages with wins over France and Norway and hard-fought ties with Finland and the Czech Republic. They did lose badly to host Germany, but their record was still good enough to get them into the medal round where they were eliminated by a strong Swedish squad who ultimately finished second to Russia. Eric contributed an important assist in the 1-1 draw with Finland in Dortmund on 20 April, when his blast from the blue line was tipped into the net by Ed Olczyk.[248]

Tracy Weinrich witnessed Eric's solid play for Team USA from the packed stands, as she and three other wives (including the wife of Bob Beers, another former Maine Black Bear) journeyed to Germany for the tournament. Tracy ranked this trip as her favorite of all the World Championships that she attended, and she went to many of them. One highlight that she enthusiastically recalled was a late-night knock on the hotel door by legendary tennis superstar and Connecticut resident Ivan Lendl, who was a minority owner of the Whalers and a big hockey fan. He was delivering tickets for the next game for Tracy and her three fellow travelers. Tracy's strong agreement with Eric's inclination to play for Team USA in such championships was a key reason for his ongoing participation over the years. She considered these tourneys a wonderful opportunity for family travel, and she found the intense level of pride among fans from other nations quite impressive and admirable.[249]

Arguably the rowdiest fan base was in Canada, and they were surely disappointed by their team's 4th-place finish after winning all five games in the group stage. Eric Lindros, a 20-year-old forward who had just completed his rookie season with the Flyers, gave Canadian fans a lot to cheer about by leading all scorers with eleven goals and six assists. Canada also got an exciting boost from flashy 18-year-old Paul Kariya, who was among the scoring leaders with two goals and seven assists. The Weinrich family was not surprised by the high-octane performance from Kariya, whom they knew very well because he had just completed his freshman year at the University of Maine where he was a teammate of the youngest Weinrich brother, Jason.

NCAA Championship for the Maine Black Bears

Jason, a junior Black Bears defenseman, and freshman forward Kariya had enjoyed an incredible season in Orono. Maine blew by their regular season opponents, winning 21 games while only losing one game and tying one game. They beat rivals Boston University to win the Hockey East tournament, and then won Maine's first ice hockey national championship by beating Lake Superior State 5-4 in the finals of the Frozen Four. To beat Lake Superior, the Black Bears needed to come back from a two-goal deficit in the 3rd period. They did so thanks to three straight goals by future NHL player and coach Jim Montgomery, with all three markers being assisted by the mesmerizing Kariya.[250] Big Jason, the tallest Weinrich brother at 6'3", had been a tough and steady defender for the Black Bears all season, playing in 38 games and notching one goal and eight assists.

Jason's steady play meant the Weinrich family had a direct role in Maine's first championship, but undoubtedly the family's long-term indirect contribution to the title went back to Eric's decision to attend his home state university in the spring of 1985. According to Jason, Eric playing in Orono "solidified it as a legitimate destination" for the best players from Maine and across New England.[251] Eric's decision to attend Maine, and then his great play for the Black Bears for two plus seasons, greatly increased the credibility and leverage of Coach Shawn Walsh. There was no question in the minds of young fans in Orono, such as David Benjamin, how important Weino had been for the Black Bears' rise to prominence. Benjamin's encounter with Weino was detailed in the pages of *Yankee* magazine. "I saw Eric Weinrich at the outdoor rink once," said Benjamin, recalling a conversation with the former Black Bear sensation. "He was skating with us, passing us the puck, just like we were equals, you know?" I tried to be all cool about it. I said, 'My name's David Benjamin.' He said, 'I'm Eric Weinrich.' I said, 'I know.' And then I said it: 'I'm a big fan of yours.' He smiled."[252]

Jason characterized Coach Walsh, for whom he toiled for four seasons, as a super innovator who adopted Soviet tactics. Jason further praised his coach as a marketing genius who was able to galvanize everyone to pull together for one purpose, and an exceptional recruiter.

Walsh secured no better recruit than Kariya, who accumulated a mind-boggling 100 points (25 goals and 75 assists) during his first year as a Black Bear, earning him the Hobey Baker Award and leading Maine to its first national title.[253] Jason described Kariya's skill level as out-of-this-world. For example, many great stick handlers can do tricks such as flipping the puck through their legs up into the air and catching it, but in Jason's long career the only person he ever saw do such tricks while skating full speed was Kariya.[254] Not surprisingly after his award-winning season in Orono, the speedy forward starred in multiple Olympics and World Championships for Canada and amassed 989 points in just 989 NHL regular season games, earning induction into the Hockey Hall-of-Fame in 2017.

While the entire extended Weinrich family took pride in Jason and his teammates earning an NCAA title, there was no rest for the weary for Eric and he quickly turned his attention after the World Championships to his off-season training regimen. Lifting weights, skating, and cycling kept him busy for another summer as he prepared to start his second season as a Hartford Whaler. At summer's end he joined the other Whalers for training camp in Vermont and experienced a slight setback when he sprained his ankle on the last day. Then a few weeks later he hit another bump in the road when he strained a medial collateral ligament in his knee. Approximately one month into the season, Hartford was struggling with just three wins, nine losses, and one tie. Due to injury Weino had missed five of the games. In the eight he played, he had one goal and one assist. On the personal side, Tracy was working hard on a master's degree in business and the couple was starting to think seriously about having children. Eric pondered his future after hockey, hoping Tracy would let him stay home as a "Mr. Mom." He also explained that his appreciation of a "robust Stout" had convinced him to consider starting a brew pub when he retired.[255]

Sweet Home Chicago!

Ben, Eric, Tracy, Emily in Chicago mid-1990s

Just after returning to action from the disabled list, Weino scored his first goal of the season in a 4-2 loss to St. Louis. The following day, on 2 November 1993, the Whalers traded Eric to the Chicago Blackhawks as part of a major multi-player deal that featured all-star winger Steve Larmer. While being swapped a second time in a little over a year may have been discouraging for some, for Weino there was no doubt that going to the Windy City was a great opportunity. "I found out about the trade at practice," said Weinrich from his home in Connecticut. "I'm really excited about it. I think along with Boston, that Chicago's one of the greatest sports cities in the world."[256] For the next five years, Weino would call Chicago home and skate with a very talented bunch of Black Hawks, most notably Chris Chelios and Jeremy Roenick.

The Blackhawks drew heavily on USA Hockey to produce a "homegrown" roster that was popular with their midwestern fans: Chelios, Roenick, Weino, tough defender Gary Suter, speedy forward Tony Amonte, and Keith Carney (another defenseman from the University of Maine). The

Blackhawks played very sound hockey, starting with a talented goalie in Ed Belfour who was supported by a strong cast of blueliners. Eric fit in well and got a lot of ice time in his first few months, but sadly a puck struck him in the face on 24 February 1994 and he was sidelined with a broken jaw. Up until then he had been partnering with Chelios and playing "his best hockey," notching two goals and 24 assists while averaging thirty minutes on the ice per game. At the time of his injury he thought he only needed stitches, and he returned to the fray to contribute his third assist in a 6-3 win over Winnipeg. After the game, the extent of his injury became evident, and he would not return to action for about six weeks.[257]

On 3 April in his first game back, Weino helped Chicago grind out a hard-fought 2-1 victory over Calgary and snap a 6-game winless streak. Darryl Sutter, the Blackhawks coach, hoped that "Eric Weinrich could help stabilize a defense riddled by injury and inconsistency."[258] Eric did just that, hitting his stride immediately after the lengthy lay-off. On 12 April in Toronto, he contributed to the Hawks' impressive 4-3 victory by notching the winning goal on a third period powerplay, assisted by fellow Maine alum Keith Carney. Toronto beat them in the regular season finale in the Windy City, 6-4, on 14 April. At season's end, Chicago finished with a solid record of 39 wins, 36 losses, and nine ties. They finished in sixth place in the Western Conference and would face the very same Maple Leafs in a best-of-seven playoff series. On 15 April, the Blackhawks enjoyed a day off by attending a baseball game at Wrigley Field, witnessing a 19-5 shellacking of Chicago by the Atlanta Braves and their star pitcher Tom Glavine. Eric got to talk with Glavine after the game, and they reminisced about their days as high school hockey players in New England.[259]

The playoffs began on 18 April in Toronto in a very disappointing fashion for Chicago, as they were thrashed 5-1. Game two on 20 April was a much tighter affair, with the Maple Leafs prevailing in overtime 1-0. In the third game, at home in the Windy City, the Blackhawks earned a hard-fought 5-4 win, and Weino assisted on two of Chicago's goals. In game four, Chicago won again by a score of 4-3 in overtime to even up the series. The Blackhawks defense played very tough in the final two games, but the offense sputtered, and Toronto won both contests by 1-0 scores to advance to the next round and end the Blackhawks' season earlier than they would have wished. Game six on 28 April 1994 was the last game ever in historic Chicago Stadium, as the Blackhawks would be moving into the brand-new United Center in the fall.

Baby Ben and a Lockout

Eric and Tracy spent much of the summer on the coast of Maine, close to Eric's parents and a short drive away from Tracy's parents in New York. Family bonding time and support were more important than ever, as Tracy was pregnant and expecting their first child. Eric as usual stayed in top physical condition, and early in the summer he had a fun opportunity to watch the best soccer players on the planet when he attended a World Cup match. As August passed, the time to return to Illinois for another season fast approached. On 24 August 1994, Tracy flew to Chicago by herself. The plan was for Eric to drive out in their SUV loaded with belongings. She recalled the dramatic turn of events: "The day I flew into Chicago for the season, my water broke six weeks early for Ben. I went by ambulance to have our premie!" Instead of driving out, Eric changed plans and flew out with Tracy's mom. To this day he does not remember how the SUV got to Illinois.[260] Welcome to the chaotic life of first-time parents with a newborn!

After the arrival of the newest Weinrich, Eric started his first training camp with the Blackhawks. Unfortunately, as camp went by, it became clear that a major labor dispute threatened the season. Indeed, on 1 October 1994 the owners announced a "lockout" which would postpone the start of regular season games. Some of the key issues included the owners' desire to impose a luxury tax on higher salaries, their hope to impose a salary cap, and goal of asserting more control over free agency. As months passed, some of the bigger market team owners decided they were losing more by not having games than they stood to gain from any potential new agreement with the players' organization, and they took the lead in ending the lockout on 11 January 1995. Plans were quickly hammered out for a shortened regular season (48 games) and a later start for the play-offs.

The first puck of the season dropped on 20 January 1995, with Weino in the line-up that night and every subsequent game until the end of a long playoff run. Although Eric only scored three goals in the 48-game regular season, they were all important starting with a power-play marker in a 4-3 overtime win at Calgary. On 26 February in Dallas, Weino assisted on Chicago's first goal and then scored the winning goal in a 2-1 victory over the Stars. The winner was an unassisted even-strength goal in the first period. He tickled the twine a third time in the regular season finale at home against the Los Angeles Kings, notching the game-winner in a 5-1 triumph. The Blackhawks had won their last five games to finish with a record of 24 wins, 19 losses, and five ties, which was good enough for fourth place in the Western Conference. During their first regular season in the new United Center, they drew an average of over 20,000 fans per contest. The excitement for Weino and his teammates, however, was just beginning.

Long Play-off Run

In the opening round of the 1995 playoffs, Chicago faced off once again with Toronto, who had finished fifth in the conference. Weino assisted on the first goal of the series in the opening game in the United Center, but Chicago ended up losing. The Blackhawks also lost game two at home before winning the next two in Toronto. The series unsurprisingly went to seven games, when Chicago triumphed by a score of 5-2 to advance. In the seventh game, Eric scored the third goal of the game to give the Blackhawks a 2-1 lead, and then assisted on the fourth Chicago goal to give then a 4-1 lead as they cruised to a 5-2 win. As in the regular season, his 1995 playoff goals/ assists were not very numerous but were very important.

In round two, the Western Conference semi-finals, Chicago faced Vancouver who had upset St Louis. As the higher-ranked squad the Blackhawks got home ice advantage and proceeded to win the first two games in the United Center. Weino and his teammates then finished off Vancouver in their arena by winning two straight overtime battles. Chris Chelios scored both overtime winners and reminisced in his autobiography that the Blackhawks "swept the Vancouver Canucks in the second round, and I had two overtime game-winners in that series. Those may have been my two most important goals as a Hawk. They came in Games 3 and 4 in a series that was actually much tighter than a sweep would indicate." Chelios convincingly contended, however, that at least as important as his two OT goals was his role in defusing the explosive Vancouver winger Pavel Bure, holding him to just one assist in the series after he had roasted St. Louis with seven goals in the opening round.[261]

After vanquishing Vancouver, the Blackhawks faced the Red Wings in the Conference finals. This was the fourteenth time that Chicago and Detroit butted heads in a playoff series. In game one at the Joe Louis Arena in Detroit, Weino assisted on the opening goal on a first period powerplay. Unfortunately, the Red Wings battled back and won in overtime. They also triumphed in game two by a 3-2 score, their only win in regulation. Game three in Chicago saw the Red Wings win in double overtime. The Blackhawks thrashed Detroit, 5-2, in game four; however, the teams returned to the Motor City for game five and the Red Wings again came out on top in double overtime to advance to the Stanley Cup finals. In the words of Chelios, "It was our misfortune to be in the same conference as Detroit, because we were playing well before facing the Red Wings in the conference final."[262]

Scotty Bowman's Detroit squad relied heavily on imports from the former Soviet Union. Slava Kozlov scored the winner in game 5, while

Vladimir Konstantinov had done likewise in game 3. Sergei Federov chipped in with 3 assists, and Eric's former New Jersey teammate Slava Fetisov added 2 assists. The following season they would acquire Igor Larionov and be able to skate a full Russian Five line as they won the 1996 Stanley Cup, demonstrating more than anything else the effects of globalization and the end of the Cold War on NHL hockey. The Blackhawks, for their part, showed the incredible upswing in talent produced at home, with six of their important players during the lengthy 1995 playoff run being from the United States. The two top stars, Chelios and Jeremy Roenick, were from the USA. In the words of Roenick, "The Blackhawks were an Original Six team led by two American stars. Who would have thought that possible even 15 years before?"[263] Other major USA-born contributors included Weino, Gary Suter, Tony Amonte, and Keith Carney.

1995-96 Season

The same heavily homegrown cast of characters returned for another campaign in fall 1995 for a new coach named Craig Hartsburg, and Weino arrived for camp in top condition and feeling confident. "I felt great," he recalled. "I was ready for anything. I was in as good shape as I've ever been in and felt good on the ice." Observers believed that in the first month of the season, Eric was the Blackhawks' most solid all-around defender after Chelios. That was saying a lot on a blueline corps that also included Gary Suter, Steve Smith, and Keith Carney; however, things changed in a split second on 1 November at Dallas when a stick blade caught Eric on the right eye lid. He only missed three games, but the two-week layoff hurt his conditioning. When he returned to action, he was wearing a face shield (in fact he decided after nearly losing an eye to wear a shield for the remainder of his career). His play seemed tentative, and if he made a mistake then on the next shift, he was pressing to make up for it. Coach Hartsburg explained that "Weino's strength is that he's a strong guy who can finish checks and hit in our end and he's a good skater and can move the puck." The team missed his steady play while he struggled to get back in the groove through the holiday season, but fortunately by the end of January 1996 when Chicago prepared for the last big road-trip of the regular season Hartsburg could definitively state about Eric, "He's back!"[264]

The road trip went very well for the Blackhawks, and then at home on 18 February they defeated Edmonton by a 4-1 score to improve to 32 wins and sixteen losses, their best winning percentage of the year. Weino scored the first Chicago goal against the Oilers to knot the score at 1-1 on an unassisted marker in the first period. It was his fifth and final goal of the regular season. Captain Chris Chelios scored the third and fourth goals for the Blackhawks. At season's end, "Cheli" led the Blackhawks with 72 points and won another Norris Trophy as best NHL defenseman. Chicago ended with a strong record of 40 wins, 28 losses, and fourteen ties. They finished third in the Western Conference behind Detroit and the new Colorado Avalanche, who were in their first season in Denver after moving from Quebec. Eric had played in 77 games and accumulated ten assists to go with his five goals.

4-point Playoff Game and a Showdown with Colorado

In the first round of the playoffs, Chicago squared off with the Calgary Flames, and the Blackhawks triumphed in the first two games at home by wide margins, 4-1 and 3-0. When the series shifted to Calgary for game three on April 21, a lively 7-5 goal festival resulted. Weino played one of the best games of his entire career, assisting on Chicago's first two goals and again on their fifth goal. Furthermore, he scored the Blackhawks' fourth goal about two minutes into the second period on a powerplay. Racking up a goal and three assists in an NHL playoff game was a night to remember for Weino, no doubt. Fittingly it happened in the Saddle Dome in Calgary where he had skated for Team USA in the 1988 Olympics, and close to Banff national park, where he and Tracy had gone for their honeymoon. Chicago then won game four in overtime to advance to the second round against the high-scoring Colorado Avalanche.

The series opened on 2 May 1996 in Denver, and the Blackhawks won a very tough 3-2 battle in overtime when Jeremy Roenick beat the great Avalanche goalie Patrick Roy, with assists by Chris Chelios and Tony Amonte. Three of Chicago's stars, all born in the USA, had shined brightly and given the Blackhawks a super start. Colorado bounced back and trounced Chicago 5-1 in game two, but when the series moved to the Windy City the Blackhawks rebounded with a 4-3 overtime win and a lead in the series. Unfortunately for Weino and his teammates, however, the Avalanche got a winning goal from Joe Sakic in triple overtime of game four. Emerging victoriously from that epic battle gave Colorado a momentum boost and they won the next game in Denver handily, 4-1. Eric assisted on the Blackhawks' only goal, which Roenick scored. Weino logged tons of ice time throughout the brutally intense series, including a lot of minutes on 13 May in Chicago in game six, which the Avalanche captured by a 4-3 score in double overtime to advance to the conference finals.

According to Chris Chelios, being eliminated by Colorado was one of the more disappointing experiences in his career. In his view, because the Avalanche went on to win the Stanley Cup, if Chicago had defeated Colorado, they may well have won the championship. While it is impossible to prove of course, it is a reasonable point worth considering. What made it so frustrating for Chelios, moreover, was that he missed the crucial fourth game due to a doctor's error. "The loss to the Avalanche was particularly hard to take," wrote Chelios, "because I had missed a game after our team doctor, the late Dr. Louis Kolb, stuck a needle in the wrong place when he was attempting to freeze my groin before the game."[265]

Chelios had a sports hernia and believed he could play at full strength if that area of his body were numbed. It went badly wrong. "I could walk fine," he explained, "but as soon as I got on the ice and pushed my leg to the side I fell down. I thought I had just hit a rut. But when I got up and tried again, back down I went. I realized quickly that I had no feeling in my leg when I tried to skate." He was unable to play at all that night and instead was forced to watch the triple overtime game from the locker-room. As the Blackhawks best defender and leading scorer, Chelios may well have been able to lead them to victory and a nearly insurmountable 3-1 lead in the series if he had played. He believes he would have done it, and that the Blackhawks could have gone on to win the Stanley Cup. "That needle being pushed in the wrong place on my leg may have cost us the Stanley Cup," he surmised.[266] As things turned out, Chelios would win two titles with Detroit; however, Weino would never reach the finals to get a chance at the cup. A sad twist of fate indeed!

There was a bit of humor in the showdown with Colorado, and it also centered on the epic fourth game that Chelios missed. During the first overtime period, Roenick (who had beaten Roy on a breakaway in game three) got behind the Avalanche defense and broke in alone on the all-star netminder. Before he could fire a shot, however, he was taken down from behind by defenseman Sandis Osolinsh. No penalty was called, regardless of boisterous protestations by the Blackhawks. Roy commented afterwards that Roenick got caught from behind because he was uncertain of his next move and added that he did not think the Chicago forward would have scored anyway. Roenick quickly quipped, "I wonder where he was in game three? Probably getting his 'jock' out of the United Center rafters." Roy then finished the exchange with one of sports all-time great rejoinders: "I didn't really hear what Jeremy said because I had my two Stanley Cup rings plugged in my ears."[267] Roenick described the incident thoroughly in his autobiography and explained how there were no hard feelings between the two: "As we got to know each other through the years, I told Roy that was the funniest line I had heard in my career."[268]

Hockey Royalty

A verbal showdown with the NHL's greatest goalie was classic Jeremy "JR" Roenick, who played as hard as anyone on the ice and partied as enthusiastically as anyone off the ice. "Chelios and I were treated like royalty everywhere we went, he explained. "As a general rule the Blackhawks always had a good time away from the rink. Chelios and I had a better time than most." JR enjoyed encounters with celebrities such as the Canadian comedy actor John Candy, who invited JR and his wife to visit him in his trailer on the set of a movie that was being filmed in Chicago. They sat down and "helped him drink the tub of beer he had on ice." JR spent a lot of time with Michael Jordan and Dennis Rodman, but his most notable experience with an NBA star was his relationship with Charles Barkley. The great Sir Charles came to a Blackhawks game and afterwards burst into the locker room and exclaimed: "I want to meet that Roenick kid!" It turned out that Barkley thought JR played hockey with the same high-energy enthusiasm with which he had played basketball. During a trip to the 1996 Olympics in Atlanta with his wife, JR was surprised to be picked up from behind and whipped around by a big man who turned out to be Barkley. One of his favorite outings occurred in Toronto at comedian Dan Aykroyd's local bar, where the Saturday Night Live legend and the Blackhawks jammed on stage late into the evening.[269]

Chris Chelios elaborated on the exciting encounters enjoyed by many Chicago players, especially he and JR. "Life in the Blackhawks dressing room was never dull. At one point, the late comedian Chris Farley got interested in the team and started coming to our games. Once, he came into our dressing room, climbed on a stationary bike, and started pedaling as hard as he could. He had everyone cracking up." Sadly, several Blackhawks witnessed Farley's increasingly destructive drug and alcohol abuse and were with him at a downtown Chicago bar the night before he died. On the lighter side, Chelios spent a lot of time with Michael Jordan and Dennis Rodman. Jordan liked having Rodman around because his antics attracted so much attention that it took the spotlight off Jordan, at least for a while. After one NBA playoff game in Salt Lake, Chelios agreed to join Rodman for a post-game jaunt to Las Vegas. The Blackhawks defenseman hoped to escape notice and so he snuck out to the limousine before Rodman. As the vehicle pulled away from the arena and headed to the airport, an irate Bulls coach Phil Jackson yelled, "I see you in there, Chelios!"[270]

The Birth of Emily

Weino would not have been inclined to be running wild with Rodman like JR and Chelios under any circumstances, but with toddler Ben and wife Tracy at home he was even less likely to be living the celebrity lifestyle. Going into the summer break after the 1996 play-off showdown with Colorado, he had an additional reason to stay at home (or at least close to home). Tracy was about eight months pregnant with the couple's second child. On 26 June as Eric played golf with his pager turned off, their friendly neighbor Dennis drove Tracy to the hospital. Dennis rolled her into the Emergency Room yelling "I'm not the father, I'm not the father!" Meanwhile, Eric had called home and his mom Sandra exclaimed, "She's in labor!" Eric arrived at the hospital in time, just as Tracy started to push. Eric brought Sandra along, and she promptly told the doctor that she really wanted a granddaughter since she had three sons and one grandson already. Emily Martin Weinrich was born healthy, weighing 7lbs and 11 ounces. Grandma Sandra and Emily's godmother Susanne lit up cigars. Upon first meeting Emily, young Ben called her "Emmy" and the nickname stuck.[271]

After a busy summer chasing toddler Ben and helping Tracy with baby Emily, Weino returned to training camp ready to roll. Coach Hartsburg explained to the defensemen that he planned to turn them loose to join the action in the offensive end more often. The new philosophy was exciting, and it immediately paid off in a 5-2 win over Washington in the season opener on 5 October 1996 as Eric scored about half-way into the first period to give Chicago a 2-1 lead. He tickled the twine once again three weeks later in a 6-4 win over St. Louis, giving the Blackhawks a 4-3 lead four minutes into the second period. Hartsburg looked like a strategic wizard for unleashing Eric and the other blueliners on 29 October, during a tie in Tampa Bay. After the Lightning took a two-goal lead, Weino scored near the end of the second period and again seven minutes into the third period to even the game and earn Chicago a valuable point.

After the first fifteen games, Weino ranked second on the team with four goals, had three assists, and in the plus/minus statistic was at a strong positive six. According to *Tribune* sportswriter Rich Strom, up to that point in the season Eric had played "quietly spectacular." Coach Hartsburg echoed the sentiment and observed, "He's been outstanding." It was not a shock to the coach though, who added: "We've always noticed him as a good player. If you do a lot of little things right, teammates and coaches notice."[272] Weino explained that he had been very excited during camp when Coach Hartsburg announced his plan to encourage offensive participation by the defensive corps. "I've probably had better scoring opportunities in these 15 games than I've had in nine years," he commented. According to journalist Tim Sassone, Eric had "easily been the Hawks' second-best defenseman behind Chris Chelios." Regardless of his play, or more likely because of his play, Weino had been subject to trade rumors swirling in the Chicago winds. He understood that it was a reality of professional sports, but nevertheless did not like the trade talk. "I love it here," he said. "I hope nothing happens because we've bought a house and everything." It was impossible to ignore the rumors, especially when off the ice. "It does weigh on your mind when you're away from the rink, sitting at home with your kids," he added.[273] Wisely the Blackhawks would hold onto Eric for a couple of more years.

It continued to be a successful season for Eric as the holidays approached. On 22 November 1996, he had two assists in a 5-2 win at Calgary. After Tracy and Eric's first New Year's Day with two children, Weino chipped in with an important goal against his former team New Jersey and Chicago earned a point in a 3-3 tie on the road. Two weeks later, on Long Island, Eric notched a goal and an assist in a 3-2 loss to the Islanders. On 3 February 1997, he contributed three assists in a 4-2 victory in San Jose. On 20 February, he scored late in the first period to give Chicago a 2-0 advantage over Boston in a game the Blackhawks went on to win 5-3.[274]

When the regular season ended, Chicago had won 34 games against 35 losses and thirteen ties which put them in eighth place in the Western Conference and slated them for a rematch with the high-flying Colorado Avalanche. The steady Weino had played in 81 out of 82 games. His 32 points on seven goals and 25 assists put him sixthg on the team, and second among Blackhawk defenseman behind only Chelios. He ended up at positive nineteen in the plus/minus category, which was third on the squad. When the playoffs kicked off in Denver, the Avalanche won the first two matches but then the Blackhawks bounced back for a victory in game three in Chicago. Weino assisted on his team's second goal, scored by Amonte and giving the Blackhawks a 2-1 lead, in a battle they ended up winning 4-3 in overtime at home. Chicago again triumphed two nights later in game four at home to even the series. Back in Denver, the Avalanche smashed the Blackhawks in the fifth game by a humiliating 7-0 score. Valeri Kamensky from Russia, whom Eric had befriended at the Junior World Championships back at the end of 1984 in Finland, scored a hat-trick for the Avalanche. While recording a shutout, Patrick Roy registered his 89th NHL playoff win and thus set a record.[275] Joe Sakic and Kamensky each notched two goals in game six and the Avalanche moved on to face Detroit in the next round, while Chicago started summer vacation earlier than they hoped.

Between 1991 and 1997, Eric Weinrich established himself as a dependable NHL defenseman who skated and passed well, was not afraid to play physical hockey, and who occasionally displayed an offensive flair. After another campaign with the cosmopolitan Devils, he was traded to the Hartford Whalers where he started slowly but displayed his high-level skills nicely during the second half of the season. The next year, in the fall of 1993, the Chicago Blackhawks acquired Weino and he immediately felt at home in the Windy City. For five seasons he played a key role on a strong Blackhawks team that included many "home-grown" players born in the USA. While he occasionally displayed his offensive ability, in key times of games and especially in the playoffs, Eric mostly played a conservative, defensive-minded style of hockey. As a stay-at-home defender, as a homeowner, and more importantly as a husband to Tracy and father of Ben and Emily, Eric Weinrich increasingly embraced the concept of home during his five years in Chicago.

Weino's Wisdom

This period in my life and career was a turning point for many reasons. Going through my first trade was unsettling but also gave me a chance to play with some different players and make some new friendships as well as offering me some new opportunities on the ice. Tracy and I started to get settled in Hartford while she was working on her master's degree, and it appeared that we would be part of the Whalers organization for a while. I then suffered a knee injury at the start of the 93-94 season, after coming into the season in the best condition of my life. The setback was disappointing, but early in the season I had a chance to come back and play most of the season. To my surprise, not long after I started back in the line up, I was traded to Chicago. This move would change my career and bring many of the best moments in our lives.

Chicago was a team that intrigued me when we played there that season. While I still was recovering but made the trip, I sat watching the game wondering what it would be like to play alongside some of the USA's best, Chelios and Roenick, along with other top players like Steve Smith, Michel Goulet, Brent Sutter and Eddie Belfour. At the same period, the Chicago Bulls were the talk of the town and Michael Jordan was the most famous athlete in the world. Chicago was an exciting city compared to where we were previously and there was always something happening in the city and the area. It was a popular place for movies and concerts as well as the many sports teams in the city. There wasn't much more a person could ask for, especially an athlete playing for one of the teams. The fans in Chicago were very supportive and Chicago Stadium was one of my favorite venues to play in as a visiting player.

Tracy and I were blessed during our time in Chicago with the birth of our two children. Ironically, the year our son was born was during a work stoppage in the NHL which allowed us more time together after he was born. Later, when I heard the news Tracy had given birth to a girl, I couldn't have been happier.

We had some very successful seasons in Chicago, making the conference finals one year. Coming so close to the finals was heartbreaking. One of the most memorable things that happened during our years in Chicago was a friendship I made with one of hockey's all-time greats, Vladislav Tretiak. Vlad is known as one of the best goaltenders in the history of the game. Most people of my generation only remember him as the goalie who was pulled in the 1980 Olympic match against the USA, in the greatest upset in sports. One always wonders what the outcome would have been if he remained in the game that day. I'm not sure how it came to be that Vlad became the goaltending coach for the Blackhawks, but we never imagined how lucky we were to have him working with the goalies and his being around the players when he was in town. Vlad had a presence about him, not intimidating at all, but a warm and inviting persona. As famous a person as he was, he remained humble and friendly. Having played with some of his former teammates in NJ, we shared stories about them and started a friendship. I wanted to talk to Vlad as much as I could, and Vlad was always happy to talk hockey and about Russia. I never asked him about his experience in Lake Placid but had read his book and learned about his perspective during the tournament at the Olympic Games. Vlad was a very proud person and I never felt it was a subject he liked to reflect on. I would just spend time with him and listen to what he spoke about very intently. Every moment we spent together I relished as special and felt fortunate that he wanted to take time and speak with me. Over the years we were in Chicago I looked forward to his visits. One thing I loved about Vlad was he would watch our games and often gave advice or his *perspective. During the playoffs against Colorado, I had to face an old friend often during the games, Valeri Kamensky. We had come up through the ranks in the same age group, and he was one of the best talents of that era. Kamensky had a lot of speed and change of pace. I struggled figuring out how to handle his rushes against me. Vlad came up to me one night and told me a tactic that the coaches taught their players on the CSKA team in Moscow. Instead of skating backwards, Vlad told me to try taking the rush skating forward and match the speed of the oncoming forward — a simple but brilliant solution and a method you see young players use in today's game. Although Val often got the better of me, I used this maneuver the rest of my career if I was experiencing the same issues. During one of the World Championships that was held in St. Petersburg, formerly Leningrad, Vlad learned that I was playing for the USA, and he set up a dinner for the team at one of his friends' restaurants. Just think, not many years ago we often referred to the Soviets as our enemies and the thought of a Soviet player befriending a player from the US would have been unheard of. But I feel very fortunate as an athlete to have been exposed to many opportunities, having the ability to meet people from other countries. Of these memorable moments, my friendship with Vlad was one of the most special.*

CHAPTER 6

"Going for Global Goals
Again, 1997-2001"

Starting in the spring of 1997, the focus for Eric Weinrich shifted slightly from the emphasis on "home" which defined his first four seasons in Chicago to a rejuvenated pursuit of global goals. He ended each of the next five seasons by suiting up for the United States at the World Championship tournament and established himself as "Mr. Dependable" for USA hockey, for which he was honored with a Bob Johnson medallion. Perhaps his greatest contribution to the national team came in 2000 during the World Championships in Russia. Coach Lou Vairo counted on Weino to spearhead the blueline corps, and the former Maine Black Bear delivered for his old friend. The United States did not have a lot of high-profile superstars, but the lunch-pail crew played tough and disciplined hockey and humiliated the host Russians 3-0 before a sellout crowd in St. Petersburg. Beating the Russian Bear in his own cave, and the strong showing by the United States overall in the 2000 tourney, demonstrated as much as anything Eric Weinrich's contributions to USA hockey as he continued to pursue global goals.

Another Stint for the USA and then a
Disappointing Blackhawks Season

After the Colorado Avalanche eliminated the Chicago Blackhawks from the 1997 playoffs on 26 April by defeating them 6-3, most of the Blackhawks headed for the lakes and golf courses that provided the backdrop for their summers. Eric "Weino" Weinrich, as he so often did, instead accepted the call from USA hockey and laced up his skates for his country. The 61st Ice

Hockey World Championships took place in Finland, where Eric joined his teammates for game three against Italy on 30 April. The US won 4-2, and since they had won their first two games against Latvia and Norway, they were positioned to advance to the knockout round. They lost their last two group stage matches to Canada and Sweden, but then acquitted themselves well in the next round by beating the Czech Republic 4-3 and tying Russia 1-1 before dropping their final game to Finland, 2-0. Weino had played in six of the team's eight games and registered four assists.

After a busy summer with Tracy and their two young children, Eric returned for another training camp with the Blackhawks in great shape as usual. Chicago looked forward to the new season with high hopes, but unfortunately, they stumbled out of the gate and lost their first seven games and would never be able to dig themselves out of that hole. On the bright side for Weino he suffered no serious injuries and played in all 82 games. He had a few memorable moments, such as giving his team a 2-1 lead with a first period goal in a 5-2 win over Buffalo to end the season-opening slump and notching two assists in a 3-0 win over Vancouver including an assist on Tony Amonte's powerplay winner in the first period. In a 4-2 win over Phoenix in early February 1998, Weino assisted on the first two Chicago goals. On 25 March against the Mighty Ducks of Anaheim, Eric netted the opening goal two minutes into the first period, his second and final goal of the season. The Ducks came back to win 3-2, when Teemu Selanne blasted home his 50th goal of the campaign. The officials sent Weino to the box for two minutes early in the game and then charged him with a ten-minute misconduct near the end. For the entire season, Eric accumulated a career-high 106 penalty minutes, which probably reflected his frustration with the Blackhawks' poor play.

Chicago ended up with a disappointing record of 30 wins, 39 losses, and 13 ties for fifth place, and they failed to make the playoffs. Coach Craig Hartsburg was given his walking papers. In the press conference announcing Hartsburg's firing, general manager Bob Murray pointed the finger at captain Chris Chelios for not playing his best and seeming "distracted." Rumors swirled that Chelios and Hartsburg did not get along. Chelios challenged this interpretation in his autobiography and contended that no one wanted the Blackhawks to play well and qualify for the playoffs more than he did.[276] Based on his record, it is hard to argue with Chelios on this point. Nevertheless, Chicago's season ended without any post-season excitement.

Global Goals and Charity Efforts

Once again, Weino donned a USA sweater and took to the ice for his country at the World Championships, in Switzerland. Eric played in all six games for the United States, who beat Switzerland but lost the other two games in the group stage and then lost two and drew one in the consolation round. Sweden took the title, led by a couple of superstar forwards whom Eric knew all-too-well, Peter Forsberg and Matts Sundin, who each amassed eleven points in the tournament to top the scoring chart. The low point for Team USA was a 4-0 loss to Italy on 10 May 1998. Weino notched two assists in the six games he played but was also charged for sixteen penalty minutes to continue a theme of frustration from the regular season.

The poor performance by the United States in Switzerland had serious ramifications, as it meant that the USA would need to cobble together a team in November (when both the professional and college ranks were in the throes of their seasons) to compete in a preliminary round to qualify for the 1999 championships. As it turned out a youthful USA squad managed to win all three games in November (against Kazakhstan, Estonia, and Austria) and earn a spot in the 1999 tournament. The struggles by the USA in Switzerland clearly reflected a problem of not being able to get a lot of participation by NHL players. Weino, who never needed to be asked twice to skate for the USA and served as captain at the 1998 tournament, expressed his opinion. "All the other countries are getting their best players, and we're not getting ours," stated Eric. "We do everything we can, but we've got a lot of young guys, and we're playing against players in the NHL in other countries. Maybe I'm not in the right position to say this, but unless players from the United States start showing a little pride for their country, we're going to be in the same position every year."[277]

Eric was not the only Weinrich pursuing global goals in the spring of 1998, as his brother Alex was just completing a season as a defender with Sonthofen in the first division in Germany. Al played in 59 games, notching an impressive ten goals, and adding eight assists. Living in a town of less than 20,000 nestled in the Bavarian Alps on the southern end of Germany near the border with France was a wonderful opportunity for the Maine native, for sure. His greatest overseas experience had been the year before, however, when he played for Milan in the Italian A-League and got to compete in the Champions League. Milan traveled to some amazing places for games, including Helsinki and Prague. According to Al, "The Czech Republic was the best. They knew hockey. Finland was a close second." Al had nothing but good things to say about his time living in Milan and joked that if he had not been playing so much hockey, he would have gained thirty pounds. Al would go on to play for two teams in Denmark, where he met his wife Irene and retired from hockey to take a job for Thomson Reuters.[278]

Family, as usual, was front and center for Eric in the summer of 1998. After his stint as captain for Team USA at the World Championships in Switzerland, he and Tracy and the kids spent quite a bit of time on Round Pond near Damariscotta, Maine, relaxing and getting ready for another training camp with the Blackhawks. He and Tracy were also busy working on the final planning for the first annual Eric Weinrich Celebrity Golf Tournament, which they organized to raise money for the Alzheimer's Association. It was a personal issue for Eric, because one of his grandfathers had died from Alzheimer's disease in 1990. Several big-name players turned up, including goalie Mike Richter of the Rangers and high-scoring forward John Leclair of the Flyers. Fellow former Black Bears such as Keith Carney,

Garth Snowe, and Mike Dunham put a strong University of Maine stamp on the event. After opening the festivities with a steak and lobster dinner, the participants hit the links at the Woodlands Country Club in Falmouth and raised $72,000 for the fight against Alzheimer's. The event came as no surprise to Weino's former coach in Orono, Shawn Walsh. "He's just a guy who likes to give back," said Walsh. "And when you come in contact with people like that, you really appreciate them."[279]

Traded to Montreal

Eric and Emily in Montreal; Ben and Emily in Montreal

Weino showed up at the Blackhawks' training camp in his typical great shape and there were high hopes in Chicago for a Stanley Cup run, but the season instead started out very badly. On 17 November 1998, the Montreal Canadiens traded defenseman Dave Manson and goalie Jocelyn Thibault to Chicago in exchange for Eric and goalie Jeff Hackett. "A blockbuster trade Monday between a pair of struggling NHL clubs," wrote journalist Ben Sturtevant, "has brought veteran defenseman Eric Weinrich closer to his Maine hockey roots." Sturtevant interviewed Eric by phone as he was packing a bag in hopes of flying to North Carolina in time for that night's game against the Hurricanes. "It's a good opportunity for me," explained Weino. "All the tradition and history they have up there, it's a great hockey town... now I'm going to play where hockey is king."[280]

Eric expressed his hopes that the Canadiens, whose top scorer Saku Koivu was injured, would be able to turn things around and start winning. He and Tracy were excited about the move, which would put them a lot closer to both sets of grandparents and were not at all worried about selling their home in Hinsdale, Illinois. They were a little worried about their young children, Ben (4) and Emily (2), living in a French-speaking city such as Montreal. Eric was very excited to live in a European-style cosmopolitan place such as Montreal but admitted that although he had studied French in high school, he would need to work hard on brushing up. "I don't want to boast about my French because some of my French teachers will probably remember how bad it was," he commented. As for the high-pressure fans and long hockey tradition in Montreal, for Weino it was a motivator. "It's kind of like playing for the New York Yankees," he observed. "You're in the shadow of greatness." The Canadiens management, for their part, were happy to be bringing Eric on board. According to general manager Rejean Houle: "We feel he's a defenseman who will move the puck. That's something we need. He can also provide some leadership for the younger defenseman."[281]

Providing Leadership and Key Goals

During his first season for Montreal, Eric Weinrich did indeed provide leadership to younger defensemen and show them how to move the puck, beginning in his first game as a Canadien on 17 November in North Carolina when he assisted on a goal that gave Montreal a 2-1 lead. He also showed he would stand up for his teammates by joining in a fracas at the end of the game and being charged with a five-minute fighting penalty. Two nights later in his first home game in Montreal, Weino assisted on the goal that knotted the game against Calgary at 2-2 and the Canadiens ended up on top, 4-3. On 30 November in a 3-1 home win over Los Angeles, Eric chipped in with one assist.

Following the pattern which held throughout his NHL career, Weino did not frequently tickle the twine for the Canadiens but many of the goals he did score were clutch. His first Montreal marker tied Toronto 1-1 in the first period on 26 December 1998, and the Canadiens won 2-1. The year ended on a great note for Eric and the matchup was once again in the Saddle Dome in Calgary where he often played well. He assisted on Montreal's first goal and then scored the powerplay winner in the second period of a 2-1 victory. Weino notched the Canadiens second goal in a 4-4 home draw with Washington on 18 January 1999, opened the scoring with powerplay blast in a 3-2 win over Buffalo in Montreal on 6 February, and hammered home another powerplay goal in a 1-1 tie with San Jose on 22 March. His seventh and final goal of the season came in a 2-1 loss to the Flames on 25 March, once again in the Calgary Saddle Dome. Although Eric had played well for his new team, the Canadiens finished with a sub-par record of 32 wins, 39 losses, and eleven ties and failed to qualify for the playoffs.[282]

Competing again for the USA and Buying a Home

Instead of starting his summer break immediately, Weino once again suited up for Team USA. This time it was for the 1999 World Championships in Norway, which the United States was lucky to be a part of based on great play by a very young team at the November 1998 qualifying round. The USA opened the first round on 2 May with a thumping 7-1 win over Japan, followed by a sound 5-2 defeat of Austria on 4 May. Eric and his teammates lost 4-3 to the Czech Republic on 6 May but finished second in their group and qualified to the next round. Finland and Canada both beat the USA in the next group stage, and the final game for Eric in Norway was a win over Switzerland. When asked why he continued to extend his season and travel great distances to don the USA sweater, Weino explained that it was because he had had so many great international experiences before, and he wanted to continue doing so. He enjoyed the chance to see former teammates and spend more time with the guys. Eric appreciated the opportunity for overseas travel for himself and his family. "Honestly, Andy," he reminisced,

"I just loved playing and wanted to keep playing." Tracy supported his view and always encouraged him to participate in World Championships.[283]

During the summer of 1999, Eric and Tracy purchased a beautiful home on Cousins Island in Yarmouth, Maine. It is in an incredible location next to the Atlantic Ocean, and Eric would soon acquire a boat and start learning how to navigate on the sea. Their wonderful summer vacation, as all good things must do, came to an end and the Canadiens' training camp started in early September. Tracy, somewhat apprehensive about another dark and cold winter, returned to Montreal with the kids. Ben, for his part, prepared to begin kindergarten which would be 75% French. "He will translate the paper for daddy," predicted Tracy.[284]

Stalwart Warrior for the Canadiens

In mid-September, the Canadiens journeyed to Portland, Maine to battle the Boston Bruins in an exhibition game. Eric agreed to sit for a lengthy interview with Scott Martin, a journalist from the *Kennebec Journal* which had been the Weinrich family's local newspaper during his middle school and high school years in Gardiner. According to Martin, "Eric Weinrich has been around hockey long enough to have seen and done just about everything." He then asked Weino what his role would be with the Canadiens in the new season. Eric responded that Coach Alain Vigneault had spoken with him and told him that he expected him to be a "leader in the room." Martin then questioned Eric about the pressure of playing for a fabled franchise like Montreal, and Weino responded that it was a positive motivation for him to work harder. "When you put on the Montreal Canadiens jersey you get a tremendous sense of pride. I just read a thing in *Sports Illustrated* about the top 20 franchises and they've got Montreal as one of the greatest franchises of the century. When I look back on my career and know that I played for the Montreal Canadiens, I'll remember it as a special time."[285]

Throughout the 1999-2000 season, Eric played hard every night to live up to the expectations of the Montreal fans. The team started slowly, and would soon be cursed with injuries, but on 14 October Eric helped them earn a 5-4 win in Philadelphia by assisting on the goal by Brian Savage that tied the game at 4-4. Two nights later he assisted on Savage's winner in a 2-1 home victory over Buffalo. On 30 October, Eric assisted on the tying goal by Saku Koivo in a 2-2 draw against the Rangers in the Molson Center in Montreal. On 10 November, Eric registered his first goal of the season in a 5-4 loss to Pittsburgh. Three nights later he notched two assists in a 4-2 home victory over the Atlanta Thrashers. With several players, including a few defensemen, out with injuries Eric was being asked to play a lot. For example, in an October game against Toronto he skated for nearly 33 minutes, which was well over half of the game. According to the *Sporting News*, Weino had been "placed at a disadvantage because of the Canadiens' injury problems."[286]

On 20 November in Los Angeles, Eric assisted on the opening goal in a 5-4 win. Two nights later he assisted on the first goal in a 2-1 victory in Anaheim against the Ducks. On 23 November, as the road trip in California continued, Eric assisted on the winning goal in a 3-2 victory in San Jose. Back on the east coast on 13 December, he assisted on the only goal in a 1-0 triumph in Washington against the Capitals. After the holidays, the Canadiens traveled to Colorado and faced off against the Avalanche on 7 January (the author was in attendance). Weino scored a goal in the first period to even the score at 1-1. Unfortunately, the high-flying Avalanche scored 3 straight after that to win by a 4-1 margin. Four nights later in Montreal, Eric chipped in with two assists in a 3-0 victory over Detroit. On 6 March, he scored the tying goal in a 3-2 home win against Atlanta.

As the Canadiens' most dependable defenseman who was continuing to play a lot of minutes night-in and night-out, assistant captain Weino was a key reason for the team's seven-game winning streak in February which put them back in the playoff chase. It was quite an accomplishment just to climb into the race after they had started the season winning only twelve out of their first 37 games. In a 17 March interview with the *Kennebec Journal's* Scott Martin, Eric attributed Montreal's resurgence to holding other teams in check. "Our defense was limiting teams to hardly any chances," he commented. "That is a pretty good recipe for wins, when you can limit teams to few chances and get great goaltending." In the opinion of sportswriters such as Martin, "Weinrich and fellow defenseman Craig Rivet" were the "anchors for the Canadiens defense." Eric admitted, however, that he was really starting to feel the effects of being on the ice so much every game; but, letting up or slacking off were not options for the intense competitor. "But now at this point of the season," he explained, "I have to keep playing hard. I've played with guys like Chris Chelios who had to play these types of minutes all the time and always played hard."[287]

Season Ending Injury?

In a mid-March battle with the Broad Street Bullies in Philly that ended in a 1-1 draw, Weino evidently "picked up a hair-line fracture" in his foot. With so many teammates out with injuries and the pain not bothering him much, he decided to keep playing. "I figured I could… I should play through it because of the players we were missing." He toughed it out two nights later versus Carolina and again two nights after that against Buffalo; however, during a 22 March 2000 game in Atlanta, the injured bone in his foot gave out. "I don't know if I stopped a shot or I turned the wrong way… it just snapped," explained Eric. "The pain became pretty bad late in the second period," he added. "I knew I was done when we were taking the x-rays… the bone was sticking out." Doctors outfitted him with a "walking boot" the next day, and the Canadiens medical staff predicted he would not be able to return to action for the rest of the regular season.[288]

Eric joked with the media that he would stay with the team on the rest of their road trip and serve as a cheerleader, but of course his injury was no laughing matter to him or the Montreal Canadiens. The team had lost 500 man-games to injury during the campaign; nonetheless, they were still in the playoff race with eight games remaining. According to Patrice Brisebois, Eric was the one guy whom they could not afford to lose. Fellow defender Scott Lachance wondered, "How do you replace the 25 minutes Eric has been giving us all season?" He elaborated: "Now we've got to get the job done without a guy who's been giving us all those minutes, who's on the power play and the penalty kill." Goalie Jeff Hackett, another star for the Canadiens and a close friend of Weino, made a similar observation. "Eric has been our best defenseman all season, played the most minutes, has worked the hardest," Hackett stated. "Losing him now could be the worst thing that's happened to us all year."[289]

The team was devastated to lose Eric for the season, and that made him even more determined to defy the odds and return to action. Despite having a broken bone in his foot, he only missed 5 games over 12 days. Like Timex, he would take a lickin' and keep on tickin'! "Last time we saw him," wrote Montreal journalist Jack Todd, "it looked like he could barely walk." But Weino insisted on giving it his all for his teammates and for Canadiens' tradition. "Fast forward to Madison Square Garden last night," wrote Todd on 6 April. "Weinrich may still have trouble walking, but he can play hockey. He picked up right where he left off last night – killing penalties, working on the power play, steadying a defense that was more than a little scrambly at times, but never when Weinrich was out there." Eric played almost 24 minutes in the 3-0 win over the Rangers, which was more than any other Canadien. It was his first game back after sitting out 5 with the broken foot. His blast on a first period power play was tipped into the net by Brian Savage, giving him an assist on the winning goal. For his effort, the media named him the number two star of the game.[290]

His coach, Alain Vigneault, exclaimed that "he's been one of our great warriors all year." Vigneault predicted that Eric would be in terrible pain that night but would just take a couple of painkillers and be ready to play the next night at home against Tampa Bay. "He's a symbol of this team, for him to come back like that, you know what it means," concluded Vigneault. Eric had played without taking a shot in the foot for pain and had instead just taken regular painkillers and used ice for the swelling afterwards. "I feel after tonight that I can still contribute, so I want to be there," he offered. In the view of sportswriter Todd, "Weinrich is doing everything in his power to get his team to the post-season dance." Weino was going above and beyond the call of duty, for sure.[291]

Playoff Quest and Media Recognition

Back at the Molson Center in downtown Montreal, the Canadiens hosted the Tampa Bay Lightning on the evening of 6 April. A flurry of goals by the Canadiens put the game out of Tampa's reach early on, with Eric assisting on the fifth Montreal marker on a power play in the second period. With the match safely in hand, Eric sat out the third period of the 5-1 victory. The following night the Pittsburgh Penguins beat the Buffalo Sabres, which meant Montreal would go into its regular season finale still having a slim chance to make the playoffs. Eric and daughter Emily were pictured prominently on the front page of the *Montreal Gazette* the next morning, watching the Pittsburgh/Buffalo game under the bold headline "Weinrich family cheers Penguins." When queried about the team's mindset going into their last regular season game against the Senators, Eric observed that "It's out of our hands now and all we can do is play our best against Ottawa and hope to get some help." He explained that he still had considerable pain in his foot when walking, but not when skating. "When I'm out there on the ice, I don't even think about the injury," concluded the consummate team player.[292]

Weino's yeoman-like effort had attracted the attention of media personnel who covered the Canadiens, and they voted to award him the Jacques Beauchamp Trophy, which has been awarded annually since 1982 to the Montreal player who "played a dominant role" for the club. Eric's buddy Jeff Hackett, moreover, won the Molson Cup for having earned the most star-of-the-game selections. It was fitting that the two anchors of such a stingy defense would be honored. "There's no doubt that the best trade Canadiens general manager Rejean Houle ever made was the one that brought Eric Weinrich and Jeff Hackett to Montreal," contended journalist Pat Hickey. Both Weino and Hackett downplayed the awards when interviewed by Hickey. "I'll never score a lot of points or be very flashy, but I always try to be consistent," said Eric. "I try to give my best whenever I'm out there." During the 1999-2000 season, he had been on the ice a lot. His average ice time of 25.2 minutes per game was among the highest in the NHL. He had put his body on the line, blocking over 150 shots which was also among the league leaders.[293]

Sadly, the season ended on a disappointing note, with Ottawa winning the last game 3-1 and ending Montreal's postseason hopes. The result meant that the Canadiens missed the playoffs in back-to-back seasons for the first time in 78 years. On the bright side, according to local journalist Jack Todd, the Canadiens "have reclaimed the loyalty of their legion of fans with a display of courage, heart and teamwork worthy of any of their famous predecessors among the teams responsible for the 24 Stanley Cup championship banners that hang from the ceiling of the Molson Center." Eric had once again given his best effort and logged a team-high 23 minutes on the ice. He was impressed by the enthusiastic ovation from the hardcore fans who stayed until the bitter end. "The people who stuck around," he characterized as "pretty classy."[294]

Montreal finished the season with a record of 35 wins, 34 losses, and thirteen ties. It was a remarkable record when you consider their terrible start (only twelve wins in the first 37 games). Eric had played in 77 games, missing only five with a broken foot. He had played tough but clean hockey, being whistled for only 39 penalty minutes while blocking over 150 shots. He registered a positive four in plus/minus and notched four goals and 25 assists to finish sixth on the team in scoring with 29 points. The leading scorer for the Habs, Martin Rucinsky, only had 49 points so it was obviously defense and goaltending that allowed Montreal to compete for a playoff spot. The Canadiens finished with the fourth best goals-against average in the NHL and tied for the second-fewest goals allowed in the Eastern Conference. Arguably this was one of the most impressive seasons in Weino's long career, and the best was yet to come back on the global stage.

Global Goals Again

After a very short break, instead of heading for summer vacation on Cousins Island in Maine, Weino opted to go for global goals again. When USA hockey called, as usual he said yes. The 2000 Ice Hockey World Championships were going to be played in Russia. The United States was being coached by Lou Vairo, who had known Eric for nearly 20 years since the junior camps in Colorado Springs. When the boss of USA Hockey asked Lou to coach the team, he admitted that Lou was not the first choice. They laughed and agreed that Lou would make it fun and the US team would win a game or two. His first question was: who is on defense? When the boss answered Eric Weinrich, Lou felt relieved. He looked forward to seeing Eric again and working with him. Lou's strategy was that he would bring a team and stick with it. He would not replace people with latecomers from the NHL mid-tourney. He told the team to give 100% and they will all get to play.[295]

Team USA opened the tourney in Saint Petersburg at the Ice Palace, which held over 12,300 fans, in a 3-3 draw against Switzerland on 29 April. Two days later they squared off against the host Russians in front of a sold-out crowd. Weino assisted on the opening power play goal. The Russians had a lightning-fast lineup with Pavel Bure, Valeri Kamensky, and Alexei Yashin; however, the USA defense anchored by Weino, Hal Gill, and Phil Housley was rock solid and did not let them score a single goal. The United States triumphed 3-0, silencing the capacity crowd. Eric, who had been to Russia and the Soviet Union a few times in previous years, noticed a lot of changes. People spoke out a lot more, and not always in positive ways. The new hotels and arena were impressive, but when the crowd yelled at the USA players on the bus and gave them the finger it was not pleasant. After the 3-0 US victory while the American national anthem played, fans blasted airhorns and threw bottles at the US players. Eric kept his helmet on and concluded that perhaps this was an example of how things had gotten worse in Russia after the disintegration of the Soviet Union. His old friend Alexei Kasatonov often told him that things had been better under Soviet rule, and in this circumstance it seemed true.[296]

On 3 May 2000, the USA beat France 3-2 and thus advanced to the second group stage. In this round they beat Belarus 1-0, tied Latvia 1-1, and then overcame a powerful Swedish side 5-3. The defensive corps led by Weino and the two goalies, Damian Rhodes and Robert Esche, were going above and beyond, and the team was exceeding expectations. Lou Vairo and his boys certainly were having fun, and they had won a lot more than one or two games. Indeed, after the first two group stages they were undefeated with two ties and four wins, including the shocking defeat of host Russia. A lot of the credit for this great run went to Eric and the other defenders. According to Coach Vairo, it was a "thrill" to have Eric on the squad in Russia. He was such an "efficient" player that as a coach you did not need to teach him anything. Playing in this 2000 tourney, according to Vairo, was Weino's greatest ever contribution to USA hockey. He had an incredible long-term record of service and "never said no" to the national team. Vairo believes Eric has been very underrated for his accomplishments and has not gotten the recognition he deserved. He added that you could take Eric's amazing success on the ice and multiply it by ten to understand his impact as a person off the ice.[297] In the knockout stage the USA ran into a red-hot Slovakian buzz-saw spearheaded by Miroslav Satan (the tourney's leading scorer) and was eliminated from the tourney by a 4-1 score to finish in fifth place. It did not diminish the great run that they had in the two group stages.

Life in Montreal

After a wonderful summer in Maine, the Weinrich family migrated north
for the beginning of another season on the St Lawrence River in the Great
White North. Playing in Montreal was a real thrill for Eric, who said it
was the closest he ever came to celebrity status. "Being part of something
everyone got behind" was incredible. At the same time, it could be very tough
"living up to the franchise standards." Former Canadien superstars such as
Guy Lafleur and Maurice "Rocket" Richard regularly attended games, and
comparisons to the past championship teams were tough. His biggest regret
was failing to make the playoffs with Montreal. Tracy and the kids had a
very positive overall experience living in the Canadian metropolis, but there
were challenges. In terms of hockey, Tracy recalled how amazing it was to
be part of the Canadiens franchise. "It was like being a New York Yankee,"
she said. "We were treated like gold." On the personal side for Tracy, it could
sometimes be challenging living in a foreign country without citizenship.
Finances and health care were a little complicated. At the same time, it was
exciting to have Ben and Emily attend schools where they learned French.
Ben, for example, was able to read the newspaper stories for his parents.
Tracy's French was not quite as strong as Ben's, and during one interview she
mistakenly told the reporter that she had twelve children instead of two![298]
She enjoyed activities with the other players' wives such as playing tennis.
Eric praised life in Montreal overall: great restaurants, nice neighbors, and
wonderful schools for the kids. "We really like it here," he concluded.[299]

The Montreal fans and the Canadiens' administration appreciated
having Weino as part of their organization, and as the 2000-01 season got
underway it was clear that he would once again be on the ice as much or more
than anyone else on the team. As usual, he played steady and dependable
defensive hockey with an occasional flash of offense (often in clutch
situations). On 14 October 2000 in a 5-4 home victory over his former
Blackhawk teammates, Eric assisted on three goals including the winner in
overtime and logged over 26 minutes on the ice. In a 24 October 2-2 draw

with Minnesota in the Molson Center, Weino scored the tying goal on a third period powerplay. By the end of the night, he had been on the ice for just under 28 minutes. A week later, on 1 November in a home game against Detroit he played over 26 minutes and chipped in with two assists in a 4-2 loss. Unfortunately for Weino, his solid play and yeoman work ethic could not compensate for injuries and weak spots in the lineup, and after the first twenty games of the season Montreal's record stood at a dismal five wins, thirteen losses, and two ties.

Toe-to-Toe with Jagr and Super Mario

On 16 December in the Molson Center against the explosive Pittsburgh Penguins, Eric blasted one into the net to give the Habs a 2-0 lead in the second period. The mighty Jaromir Jagr turned on the jets and notched a quick hat trick, resulting in a 4-4 tie. After celebrating his 34th birthday on 19 December, Weino played 24 minutes in a 4-2 home victory over the Nashville Predators, contributing to the offense with a pair of assists. As another New Year's Day approached, the eyes of the hockey world focused on Pittsburgh, where Mario Lemieux returned to the ice after a three-year break to battle Hodgkin's lymphoma and focus on recuperation. His first game back was 27 December, and he quickly returned to his hall of fame form. By the end of the regular season in just 43 games, he would register an incredible 35 goals. He and Jagr would lead the Penguins on an impressive playoff run that would take them as far as the Eastern Conference finals.

When Pittsburgh hosted Montreal on 5 January 2001, the star of the 4-3 Canadiens' win was not Super Mario or big number 68; instead, it was none other than Weino. The former Maine Black Bear scored two goals and logged more ice time (over 27 minutes) than anyone else on either team. Not even Eric's biggest boosters would have expected him to out-shine Lemieux and Jagr on the Penguins' home ice! His scoring spree against the Pens ended abruptly on Montreal's next trip to Pittsburg on 24 January,

145

when Eric played 23 minutes in a 3-1 loss that saw Super Mario notch a hat-trick. The man who scored 690 goals in just 915 career regular season NHL games would not be overshadowed by Weino this time. Nonetheless, Eric had played a star role in a three-game drama between Montreal and Pittsburg over a six-week period. Jagr scored a hat trick in the first, Weino scored one goal in the first and had a brace in the second, and Lemieux notched a hat trick in the last encounter. It really was a memorable run, with each team winning one, losing one, and tying one and with Lemieux, Jagr, and Weinrich each scoring three goals!

Personally, for Eric, the timing of his offensive bonanza could not have been better because his contract only ran until 1 July 2001 and so he was boosting his stock for a possible free agent contract. As a hockey player at age 34, it was now or never for one last big contract. Financial matters were not his highest priority but with a wife and two children, working in a career that would be short even in the best of circumstances, these considerations must come into play. His stock was certainly rising, and in a 3-0 home win against the Atlanta Thrashers on 12 January, he scored Montreal's second goal. Back at the Molson Center on 10 February, Weino skated for a team-high 27 minutes, scored the first goal, and added an assist on Trevor Linden's game-winner in a 5-3 victory over the Islanders.

Requesting a Trade

By this point in the season, there was little doubt that Weino would be traded. It was a win-win situation in that the Canadiens organization wanted to get something for such a dependable player instead of just losing him to unrestricted free agency in the summer and Eric wanted to end the season with a contender (which Montreal was not) before testing the free-agency waters in July. The morning after his strong performance against the Islanders, the *Montreal Gazette* praised him to the skies. "There wasn't a better player for the Canadiens on the ice last night," commented journalist

Pat Hickey. He provided significant analysis of Weino's circumstances and the very high chance that he would be moving on. "Being a selfish sort," wrote Hickey, "I'm going to miss Eric Weinrich." According to Hickey, his opinion was widespread among the media who covered the Habs. "Weinrich is not only a solid hockey player, but he's a professional when it comes to dealing with the media. He makes himself available even in the most difficult circumstances and he answers questions in a straight-forward manner that is rare in the world of sport."[300]

During a tough 4-0 shellacking in Ottawa on 18 February, Eric logged nearly 26 minutes, which was more than any other Canadien. It turned out to be his last game in a Montreal uniform, because a few days later, on 21 February 2001 the Canadiens dealt Weino to the Boston Bruins in exchange for younger and less-accomplished defenseman Patrick Traverse. "The Eric Weinrich odyssey is finally over," commented journalist Herb Zurkowsky, "Now let the second-guessing begin." The one clear positive for Montreal in the trade was budgetary, as Traverse was making about $500,000 annually while Weino's salary was around $2 million per year. Andre Savard, general manager of the Canadiens, contended that he had been in talks with six or seven teams and that this was the best deal he could get. He had worked with Traverse in Ottawa and argued that he was a solid player who could contribute in Montreal, "but obviously he's not the same caliber as Weinrich." During the press conference, one media pundit quipped that Savard had traded a dollar for a quarter. "The difference isn't that much," replied Savard. "It's impossible to replace Eric Weinrich, but you've got to understand the situation. He was going to be a free agent, and 50 cents is better than nothing."[301]

Savard also had attempted to convince Eric to sign a new contract with Montreal and offered a raise that would give him a three-year deal for between $7 million and $7.5 million. There was no doubt that Montreal appreciated Weino's worth; however, he believed he could get at least that much from another team as a free agent. More important than money on Eric's list of priorities, moreover, was that he had the chance to sign with a Stanley Cup contender instead of remaining with the rebuilding Habs. "This was the hardest decision I've had to make, in hockey or life," explained Weino. "But it's my only chance at unrestricted free agency." He elaborated on the unique situation: "This isn't the first time I've been traded, but it's the first time such a big deal was made about it in the papers. And it was my decision, so it's a different feeling." He was excited to put on the Boston jersey, and it was special because he had watched a lot of Bruins' games growing up in Maine. Still, departing from Montreal left him with mixed emotions. "I played for arguably the greatest franchise in sports, certainly one that's recognized as the greatest in hockey," he said. "It was a great fit and I enjoyed it. I definitely benefitted from playing in Montreal."[302]

Briefly a Bruin

Eric flew to Texas and met his new teammates in Dallas for a 23 February contest against the Stars. While it did not seem possible, he got even more ice time than his usual heavy load in Montreal. He led both teams with over 32 minutes of action in a 5-4 overtime loss for the Bruins. On 1 March in Boston he scored his first point as a Bruin, contributing an assist in a 3-1 victory over the Tampa Bay Lightning. Two nights later in another home win, this time 3-2 over San Jose, Weino played a whopping 31 minutes and chipped in with another assist. Two weeks later, Eric scored his first (and only) goal as a Bruin in a 3-2 win at Montreal. His blast came on a powerplay which had been initiated when Patrick Traverse committed a penalty. Undoubtedly fans and media in Montreal were reminded of the quarter versus dollar debate!

As the race for the final playoff spot in the Eastern Conference headed down to the wire, Weino contributed an assist in a home victory over the Islanders on 31 March. He continued to log lots of ice time, leading the team with 24 minutes. In the last three regular season games, the Bruins won two of them. They won 3-2 in Buffalo, lost 5-2 in New Jersey, then returned home and triumphed 4-2 over the Islanders. They finished with a respectable record with 88 points which was the same number as Carolina, but on the tie breaker the Hurricanes took eighth place and the last post-season position. Since arriving from Montreal in late February, Eric had played a lot of ice time in all 22 of the Bruins' games. He contributed a goal and five assists. During that stretch, Boston had eleven wins, six regulation losses, two ties, and three overtime losses. The Bruins had made a solid effort boosted by Eric's steadying presence on defense, but sadly they had fallen short of their goal by a whisker.

Team USA's Mr. Dependable

After logging lots of minutes in 82 NHL regular season contests, which tied his career high for games played, and especially considering the enormous ice time he had gotten during the last 22 games as Boston battled intensely for the post-season but barely missed out, it would have been completely understandable if Weino had made a beeline for Cousins Island and spent the summer sailing the Atlantic. Not surprisingly, however, he accepted another call from United States Hockey and once again donned a jersey for Team USA at the World Championships in Germany. It was the ninth time he represented his country in a senior international competition – the 1988 Olympics, the 1991 Canada Cup, and seven World Championships.

In their opening game at the 2001 World Championships on 28 April, the USA beat Ukraine 6-3. After a loss to Latvia, Eric and his teammates tied powerful Sweden and that was enough to get them into the second group stage. On 5 May, the USA thrashed Finland 4-1. After a disappointing 3-0 loss to Austria the USA rebounded to beat Slovakia soundly and advance to the final knockout round, which determined medals. On 10 May in the quarterfinals, Weino and his comrades impressively edged Canada, 4-3, and moved into the semi-finals against Finland. The Fins got revenge with a 3-1 win, and then fell to the Czech Republic in the finals to finish second. Team USA lost 3-2 to Sweden in the bronze medal contest and finished in fourth place. The Americans had acquitted themselves well in the tourney with four wins, four losses, and a tie. Eric played in all nine games and contributed two assists. A very busy season had finally come to an end and now Weino could return to the coast of Maine and relax. The big question for the unrestricted free agent over the summer was who would make him the best offer for a new contract?

Before signing a lucrative new deal, Eric journeyed to Colorado with his dad in June to attend the President's Awards banquet at the USA Hockey facility in Colorado Springs. The USA Hockey organization presented Weino with a Bob Johnson medallion for outstanding effort in international competitions. Bob Johnson was the famous coach of the Wisconsin Badgers, Pittsburgh Penguins, and Team USA. Eric had played for Johnson briefly in 1991 before Johnson died from brain cancer. "Just to be connected with Bob Johnson is something special," explained Eric. The administration at USA Hockey considered Eric's efforts over the years to be special, too. They were very aware of his dedication and the amazing number of international tournaments in which he had played. "When duty calls," wrote a journalist in his story about Eric winning the award, "Weinrich is there to answer the call." When asked about his incredible record of participation, Weino responded: "Any time I was asked to play for the U.S., I wasn't going to pass it up. They call me every year."[303] Fittingly, Eric's dad Jack attended the award ceremony in Colorado Springs. The next day they met up with Andy DeRoche and his roommate Rob Rehder at a Colorado Rockies baseball game in Denver. Eric and Andy had played baseball together as kids, so watching the Rockies game brought back some great memories. Afterwards Jack and Eric headed for the airport and their flight back to Maine.

Conclusion

Starting in the spring of 1997, the focus for Eric Weinrich shifted slightly from an emphasis on "home" which defined his first four seasons in Chicago to a rejuvenated pursuit of global goals. He ended each of the next five seasons by suiting up for the United States at the World Championship tournament every year and established himself as "Mr. Dependable" for USA hockey, for which he was honored with a Bob Johnson medallion. Perhaps his greatest contribution to the national team came in 2000 during the World Championships in Russia. Coach Lou Vairo counted on Weino to spearhead the blueline corps, and the former Maine Black Bear did not disappoint his old friend. The United States did not have a lot of high-profile superstars, but the lunch-pail crew played tough and disciplined hockey and humiliated the host Russians 3-0 before a sellout crowd in St. Petersburg. This game, and the strong showing by the United States overall in the 2000 tourney, demonstrated as much as anything Eric's contributions to USA hockey as he pursued global goals.

In addition to skating on the global stage for the US, Weino's pro career also took an international turn during these five years when he was traded to the Montreal Canadiens in the fall of 1998. There would never be a dull moment for Eric, Tracy, and their kids living in the cosmopolitan city that is Montreal. During his three seasons there, Weino logged a staggering amount of ice team and proved that he could still compete with the best in the NHL, most notably going toe-to-toe with Jaromir Jagr and Mario Lemieux during a string of three games in the middle of the 2000-01 campaign. Each team won a game, and they tied the other. The leading scorers with three goals apiece were Super Mario, Jagr, and Weino. With his stock on the rise and his contract set to expire, Eric was in the driver's seat in the last few months of that season and requested a trade from the hapless Habs to a playoff contender. He briefly became a Bruin and, incredibly, logged even more ice time in Boston than his 25-minutes per game in Montreal. The Bruins barely fell short of a postseason berth, but Weino certainly had given it his best shot. He again summoned the energy to play for Team USA at the 2001 Worlds in Germany, then headed home to Cousins Island as a sought-after free agent to await the inevitable offers.

Weino's Wisdom

This was a very special time in my career for many reasons. Getting an opportunity to play in Montreal during what I would consider the prime of my career was one of the highlights in our hockey journey. Although the successes of the team were few we discovered that the Montreal fan base was well educated in their hockey knowledge. Even in losses the crowd and city were very supportive and appreciated the effort of a weakened line-up riddled with injuries, and often we would be in the game until the end. It was appreciated by the players more than anyone could imagine.

Our family had set our roots in Chicago, with both our children born there and starting to make friends, so it was unsettling when the trade was announced. As usual, I went early, and Tracy and the kids had to move on their own. Luckily, we found a nice rental for our time in Montreal and made some nice friends there. We grew to love the international feel of Montreal and its bilingual and diverse customs and traditions, one of which was following the Canadiens. Our children quickly were immersed into the community of both the Quebecois and English language. In no time our son was understanding his Francophone friends. Tracy started her French lessons as well and I picked up what I could around the locker room and amongst the press and staff.

The city had a European feel to it with the restaurants, the fashion, the culture, and the architecture. The unique thing about Montreal which was new for us was the Canadiens were the only game in town. The press and TV broadcasts covered the team inside and out and everyday was a story about something surrounding the team. As a newcomer, it took me some time to get used to all the coverage and in time I observed the pressure on some teammates of being a French-Canadian player in Montreal. Of course, it was a dream scenario for most French Canadians but had its challenges. After my previous seasons I just tried to make myself available to the press and answered as honestly as I could. If I could throw in some French words I would do my best. The one aspect that Tracy and I will never forget was the way the city embraced the team. We have always enjoyed traveling in Europe and enjoyed the various parts such as the old city and the different sections with the various ethnic groups. As you walked through the downtown streets you would always hear many languages spoken, although primarily French and English.

Because of the number of injuries we incurred as a team, I was often playing much more than I ever had previously and felt more responsibility. In any event, it was a significant moment in my career as a player. It provided an opportunity to explore what I was capable of night to night. We also had a very international group of players, including French Canadians, Canadians from other provinces, players from the Czech Republic, Finland, Russia, Latvia, Sweden, and the United States. It was quite possibly the most international team I had played for. I made many good friends in my time with Montreal. My biggest regret was that we never qualified for the playoffs, in great part due to the injuries to our captain, Saku Koivu. I often wonder what we could have achieved with a healthy Koivu in those years. He was such a fierce competitor and leader, I'm sure he would have made all the difference.

Another special moment in this period of my career was my trip to St. Petersburg, Russia. The last time I was in the Soviet Union was when it was still Leningrad, back in 1987. My recollection from the last trip was vague, only really recalling the hotel and small area around there where I took a few strolls. In honesty I was a little intimidated about going too far. My best description of the city was that it reminded me of a black and white movie, with our team dressed in our red, white, and blue track suits every day. I remember passing a tram in the city jammed with people looking very gray and somber. Also, we saw the bread lines every day we bussed to the arena. In 2000, as we were traveling to Russia for the tournament, I wondered how different the city would look this trip? Would we be able to walk around and feel more at ease?

The US delegation was fortunate to have a member very familiar with the city that year. Misha Manchik, who grew up in Leningrad, was hired to be our massage therapist and a liaison throughout the tournament helping with the interpretation and coordination. Misha and I became fast friends, and our friendship remains strong to this day. He and I work for the New Jersey Devils, he in the scouting department and me, as part of the development staff. The team especially relies on his ability to travel within Russia during the difficult period during the war and during the Covid outbreak. He has been invaluable helping communicate with our draft picks who play within Russia in the recent years. Once we arrived in St. Petersburg, Misha took control and helped set up a dinner with a friend of Tretiak's who had invited us to his spot along the canal in the city. On the first night I had already ventured out more than during the previous trip. Our hotel was located outside the area of the city that was accessed over a bridge to the central part of the city. At night, the bridges went up and remained up until the morning. If you didn't leave before a certain time at night, you would remain stuck in the center until morning. Where we and some other teams were staying in a large hotel, we were outside of this area. When we went into the center, it was during the day. I went one day with Misha and a couple of other teammates. We went to his mother's apartment, on about the 7th floor with no elevator. When we arrived, we found a small apartment, no more than a couple of rooms where Misha and his family had lived. His mother was elderly but still walked up and down the stairs daily to collect groceries and leave the apartment. It was special to see a different side of the city other than what we were there for.

On another day, we went to the main shopping street, Nevsky Prospect, which had all the high-end shopping found in most major cities. It was a sharp contrast to the trip in 1987. Walking up and down the street felt like any other city in Europe, with older but rehabbed buildings and a newly paved road. Interestingly, we walked off the main drag for a little, not knowing exactly where we were going and behind the street on the next block we found a totally different looking area, with older, rundown shops and vacant storefronts. We were all a little nervous and quickly made our way back to the main street. Around this time, people started gathering along the street. We learned earlier there would be a parade, resembling our Veteran's Day parades. Many locals came out along with other military types lining the street to pay tribute. As we watched the parade procession roll by, the one thing that was evident was there were hardly any older veterans. We learned that during the war, many of the veterans, men, had been killed or died, leaving widows and children. A great many Soviets died during the war with Germany. Later in the day as we walked the street, we were encountered by a man in his twenties, dressed in military fatigues. He stopped us and noticed we were Americans. He then asked us for our passports which we didn't carry with us. We tried to explain but he pressed us. Finally, my buddy grabbed my arm, and we started running. Soon we had lost the man or maybe he didn't follow us. It was a little unnerving and my teammate probably did the right thing by getting us out of that encounter. As much as it had changed in the city, which I still consider one of the most beautiful cities in Europe, I sensed the feeling it was turning the corner but still had an element of the "wild West".

In all my years playing internationally, I can recall beating Russia and the Soviets maybe only 3 times. It was always a game we looked forward to because of the 1980 Olympic Miracle game. Even 20 years later, the Soviet/Russian 'big red machine' remained as one of hockey's superpowers and as a feared opponent. This year, mostly because they were hosting, they had assembled an all-star cast. Playing in the new arena built for the tournament and the home city team, SKA, they were there to win the gold medal. On the drive to the game, we passed a young man on the road who saw our bus and gave us the finger. We knew the rivalry was on.

Lou Vairo, the 1984 Olympic Team coach who was sort of a folk hero in Russia, having spent time with the legendary coach in Russia, Tarasov, was selected to coach our team that year. I think for him it was a special feeling coming back to Russia and leading our team in the tournament. He had many great tales and stories about his trips to the Soviet Union and we spent hours during that trip speaking with him and listening intently. I first met Lou Vairo in Colorado, during an under-18 camp. He made a point to come talk to me. He

155

had some unorthodox methods but made the practices fun and challenging. As a coach with us pro players, he kept the coaching light and mostly let us play. There were a few times he implemented a tactic, and they worked perfectly. To this day he remains one of the people in the game who has left a lasting impression as a teacher and friend.

One of our goalies, Robert Esche from the Utica, NY, area, who was getting his feet wet in pro hockey was a surprise selection to start the game for us. No one was more surprised than him, starting in his first game against the mighty powerhouse in their home arena. We all had faith in Robert, and maybe Coach Vairo reached into his coaching bag of knowledge on this choice. We went into the game apprehensive as always but as the game went on and we took the lead, we started believing. Robert played the game of his life and when the final horn sounded, we had defeated the home team in their backyard, 3-0. Amidst our excitement following, there was disappointment and despair on the Russian side. A good friend and former teammate in NJ, the great Alexei Kasatonov, was leading the Russian team that year. When Coach Vairo asked me to come to the press conference, I entered with mixed feelings. I could see the disappointment on the face of my good friend, Alexei, and it broke my heart. Getting to know Alex as a teammate and friend, I know how much this meant to him and having to face the press after what I would call a huge upset loss, I can't imagine how difficult that was for him. He was used to perfection and dominance for most of his career. I did my best to convey how big this win was for us against a seemingly unbeatable opponent. I wanted Alex to know the respect I had for him and what he meant to the game and his country. At this point it probably didn't matter much. That was one of the toughest things I've ever had to do in the game. My friendships with both Alex and Slava Fetisov made such an impact on my life moving forward as a player and person. I'll always have the greatest respect for them and their careers. Of all the games against the Russians and Soviets, that was probably one of the best, mostly for Robert Esche and Lou Vairo.

CHAPTER 7

"Flying High with the Flyers and Moving Back to Maine, 2001-2008"

family photos during the years in Philly

During the last seven years of his playing career, Eric Weinrich accomplished several more "global goals," most notably skating in his 1,000th regular season NHL game and helping Team USA win a bronze medal at the 2004 World Championships in Prague by defeating the host Czech Republic team. Signing as a free agent in July 2001 with Philadelphia, Eric would fly high with the Flyers for two and a half seasons. Some memorable moments in Philly included a 3-point effort in his first game and two spectacular goals in a 2003 playoff series against Toronto. Weino also notched three assists in that series and helped the Flyers advance to the next round. Traded to St. Louis in February 2004, Eric logged lots of ice time and played solid, dependable defense to aid the Blues' successful fight for a playoff spot. On the international stage, in addition to his key role in USA Hockey finishing third at the 2004 World Championships, Weino also played in the 2002 tourney in Sweden and the 2004 World Cup of Hockey. When a labor dispute wiped out the 2004-05 NHL season, Eric took advantage of a wonderful opportunity to play for a few months in Austria in spring 2005.

After a difficult and disappointing final season in the NHL mostly with St. Louis and then briefly with Vancouver, Weino announced his retirement in front of family and friends in Portland, Maine in August 2006. He joined the Portland Pirates in the AHL as an assistant coach, and then returned to the ice as a player early in 2007 and skated for a season and a half before a severe and scary set of injuries sustained during a fight in the spring of 2008 ended his playing career. Having his career ended by fisticuffs was a tragic twist of fate for a classy player like Weino, who had never instigated fights, resorted to unnecessary violence, or delivered cheap shots at any point in his career. Sportswriters and knowledgeable observers, who had showered Eric with well-deserved praise at the time of his 2006 retirement from the NHL, once again sang his praises when he was inducted into the Maine Sports Hall of Fame in 2015. As a cornerstone recruit who helped put University of Maine hockey on the national map, a reliable performer for Team USA who played in more World Championships than anyone else, a dependable and durable NHL defensemen, and a cultural ambassador during the final years of the Cold War, Eric "Weino" Weinrich accomplished a long list of global goals both on and off the ice.

Flying High with the Flyers

Having demonstrated his stamina and grit during his years in Montreal and months in Boston, Weino became a free agent when the 2001 season ended. Home on Cousins Island in late June, Eric soon began weighing the offers from teams seeking his signature. There were multiple options for Weino, described as "one of the most sought after free-agent defenseman." On 5 July 2001, Eric signed a three-year contract with the Philadelphia Flyers for approximately $8.5 million. His main reason for picking a Flyers jersey was their talented roster, which made them a championship contender. "My top priority right now is to win the cup," explained Eric.[304] Eric was not the only free agent signed by the Broad Street Bullies; moreover, the acquisition who generated the most headlines was his former Blackhawk teammate Jeremy "JR" Roenick.

Just a few days before Weino inked his deal, JR agreed to terms with Philadelphia on a five-year contract worth $37.5 million. He could have gotten more money from other teams such as Boston, but like Eric he picked the Flyers because he thought they could make a run at the Stanley Cup. JR believed that Philadelphia wanted him to deliver both goals and hard hits; moreover, he felt they needed an energy boost and a sense of humor that could lighten things up. He kicked things off in style at his first Flyers' press conference, when his signing was announced, by hugging owner Ed Snider. JR then exclaimed to the assembled media, "You'd hug him too if he gave you that kind of money." His routine included a disco ball that he lit up in the locker room before every game, while dancing to 1970s disco songs such as "Party Train." You could never question his toughness and will to win on the ice, however, and those were characteristics that he and Weino shared. Indeed, they were roommates for some of their time together in Philly.[305]

Both free agent signings were fired up to get the new season underway, and they started off with a bang against the Florida Panthers in the First Union Center in Philadelphia on 4 October 2001. Weino scored the team's first goal of the season to tie the game at 1-1 in the first period, beating

Florida goalie Trevor Kidd. The play started when JR won a face-off in the corner and then Justin Williams passed the puck across the high slot to Eric, who "rifled a shot high over Kidd's left shoulder." Both Weino and JR assisted on the go-ahead goal scored by Williams early in the third period, JR scored Philly's fourth goal, and then Eric assisted on the last goal which was also scored by Williams. It would be hard to script a better beginning with the Broad Street Bullies than this for Weino, who according to a journalist was "superb at both ends."[306] Two nights later, on 6 October, the Flyers hosted the Columbus Blue Jackets and battled to a 3-3 tie in which Eric registered two more assists.

On 20 October 2001, Weino hammered home a goal in the second period giving the Flyers a 4-2 lead and they ended up winning 6-3. On 30 October, Eric played seventeen minutes and was a plus one in a 3-0 win over the Washington Capitals; however, he sustained an injury. He sat out the next two games with a bruised shoulder. Through the first eleven encounters the Flyers had won five, lost three, and tied three. Weino had started the season nicely with two goals and five assists, clocking a plus six in plus/minus. Journalists covering the Flyers witnessed a happy and smiling Eric Weinrich. "This is fun for me," he commented. The Flyers signed him in hopes of adding an experienced defender who could skate with the puck, and they were certainly not disappointed after the first month of the season.[307]

After sitting out two contests due to injury, Weino returned to action on 6 November in his old stomping grounds, the United Center in Chicago. The Flyers lost to the Blackhawks 2-1, and Eric logged just under 25 minutes of ice time. He would not miss another game the rest of the season. Starting in mid-December, Philadelphia went on a hot streak winning eighteen, losing six, and tying five, which catapulted them into first place in their division. Eric played steady defensive hockey and contributed some key offense. On 8 January 2002, Philly beat Atlanta 7-4, and Weino notched two assists. In the next game on 10 January, he again chipped in two assists, in a 3-2 win over the Devils. After not scoring in another victory on the 12th, Eric provided two more assists in a 5-3 Flyers win in the Molson Center in Montreal on 14 January. At that point in the campaign, red-hot Philadelphia had won 26 games, tied five, and lost six.

Comfortable On and Off the Ice

As the Flyers passed the mid-season point, there was absolutely no doubt that Eric's move to Philadelphia was working out well. According to one feature article on his contributions, Weino "brought solid, steady play along with veteran leadership skills." His style of play, unlike fellow free agent signing JR, did not make the news on a nightly basis, but it did "not go unnoticed by his teammates and coaches." According to right wing Mark Recchi, who had been teammates with a lot of incredible players, "Eric's such a steady guy back there." Goaltender Brian Boucher marveled at how Weino managed to keep his game simple but occasionally mixed it up and this kept the opposition on edge. Boucher had a great view of Eric's play from the goaltender's crease and considered him a pleasure to watch. "He's helped this team out tremendously," concluded the goalie.[308]

In addition to fitting in well with his teammates, Eric was popular with fans and made a positive impact in the community. In February he visited the Holy Name School in North Camden, New Jersey. The event had been set up by neighbor Nancy Jerome, a lifelong Flyers fan and season-ticket holder who volunteered regularly at Holy Name. Eric spoke to about 200 elementary school children in the cafeteria/gym and admitted that he was more nervous than when playing in front of 20,000 screaming fans. He told them about himself and answered questions. School principal Pat Munyan explained that all the pupils had been learning about hockey for two weeks, and that Eric's visit meant a lot. "Hockey is not a big inner-city sport, but they love it," Munyan said. North Camden was a low-income part of Camden, with a population that was almost 70% Latino and 25% African American. The visit by a Flyer was a special event, for sure. Many of the kids were most impressed by the fact that Weino had suffered a broken jaw, while others praised him for his handwriting. According to Charlene Perez, age nine, it was "very neat."[309]

Back on the ice, Weino played a key role in a 3-1 victory in Los Angeles against the Kings on 4 February 2002, assisting on the first Flyers' goal and scoring the winner in the second period. At the end of the night he had skated for 22 minutes and was a plus two. About a month later, on 8 March, Eric tickled the twine in Tampa to tie the score at two in a game that finished with a 4-2 Philadelphia win. The last month of the season was a bit rough for the Flyers, but they still finished in first place in the Atlantic Division with 97 points from a 42-win, 27-loss, 10-tie, and 3-overtime-loss record. Eric played in eighty games and registered twenty assists and four goals. He recorded a remarkable plus 27 in the plus/minus category, putting him third on the team and seventh in the entire league. It was a career best for him.

Playoffs and World Championships in Sweden

Eric surely would have traded all his positive statistics for a Stanley Cup, but he would not get very close to a championship in 2002. The Flyers were knocked out of the playoffs in the first round by the Ottawa Senators in just five games. Eric played in all the playoff games but did not register a point. He was not alone, as the Flyers offense sputtered badly. "We only scored two goals in those five games," recalled JR. "The Flyers started the 2001-02 NHL season with great promise, but it didn't go the way any of us expected."[310] Their brief postseason foray concluded with a 2-1 overtime loss to Ottawa on 26 April. Coach Billy Barber was subsequently fired, and his replacement Ken Hitchcock was hired in May. Meanwhile, Weino again accepted an invitation from USA Hockey to compete in the World Championships (for the eighth time). He joined his comrades in Sweden during the second group stage and helped them advance to the knockout round. Finland beat the United States in the quarterfinals on 7 May, 3-1, eliminating the Americans from the tourney and ending Eric's season.

The Weinrich family spent another wonderful summer on Cousins Island in Maine. Eric enjoyed navigating up and down the coast, checking out historic sights and watching wildlife such as seals. The children, Ben and Emily, were at the fun ages of six and eight that summer. Tracy was energetic and enthusiastic, as always. The captain and crew often took oceanic excursions and stopped on little islands for picnic lunches. "There's a lot of history on those islands," Eric explained to an interviewer. "We'll take a book out with us and read about World War I and tell the kids about it. It's a history lesson every day." He also expounded on the allure of the sea: "Every time we're out there, I just say to my wife 'I can't imagine doing anything else.' For some reason for me, it is a real peaceful feeling."[311] In such a wonderful location, they got lots of visitors that summer (including the author after his first trip to southern Africa). Having all four grandparents within a reasonable drive, and Eric's brother Jason nearby, made things even better. In addition to relaxing and spending lots of quality time with family, Weino worked as hard as ever to stay in tip-top physical condition. In September 2002, he headed to his second training camp with the Flyers ready to rock and roll on the ice (although not necessarily ready to boogie with JR under the disco ball in the locker room).

Dependable Part of a Tough Defense

The 2002-03 edition of the Broad Street Bullies was a very good team overall, and their defense played especially well all season. The Flyers started out on a hot streak, losing only one of their first eight games. They tied two and won five of those, ending with a 6-2 victory over the New York Islanders on 26 October 2002 in which Weino notched three assists. The team kept up the good work, and their record stood at fourteen wins, seven regulation losses, six ties, and one overtime loss after a 2-2 tie with Toronto on 12 December. Eric provided helpers on both Flyer goals in that draw. Philadelphia's performance improved over the holiday season, and they won ten out of eleven before losing to the Islanders on 24 January 2003. At that juncture of the campaign, Eric had one goal and eleven assists. Most impressive, though, was his plus/minus rating which stood at plus-21. That figure led the Flyers and was tied for fourth in the entire NHL. "While he doesn't always garner headlines," assessed a journalist, "those in the know appreciate his contribution." That included his teammates and his coaches. "It doesn't matter who we play Weino with on defense, it's a good pair," Flyers coach Ken Hitchcock said. "He's having an exceptional year and playing with a lot of confidence."[312]

In early March, Philadelphia acquired another of Eric's former Blackhawk teammates, Tony Amonte, from Phoenix in a trade. A week later, on 17 March, the Flyers went to New Jersey and beat the Devils on their home ice, 4-2. Eric and JR both assisted on the third Philly goal, which was scored by their buddy Amonte. Half-way through the second period, Weino registered the Flyers' fourth goal, short-handed, which was a rare accomplishment for him (or any defenseman). Notching two points in an away win against his original team made for a nice night for Eric. At that point in the campaign, the Flyers had won 38, tied eleven, and lost 22 (four in overtime).

1,000th Game

On 31 March 2003 at the Mellon Arena in Pittsburgh, a location where Weino had enjoyed some of his best moments, he accomplished the admirable feat of skating in his 1,000 regular season NHL game. He assisted on the tying goal in the first period and the Flyers ended up cruising to a 6-1 victory. At that time fewer than 200 players had suited up for over 1,000 NHL games, and by any account Eric had reached one of his most significant global goals. "In the past few years, it has been a goal of mine to reach 1,000 games," Weinrich explained to a journalist. To log such longevity, teams clearly needed to continue to want you around. When questioned about Eric's value to the team, Flyers' Coach Ken Hitchcock observed that while in past years as an opponent he had been impressed by Weino's offense skills, as his coach he realized how much more valuable Eric was as a steady presence in the defensive end. "He is part of the glue that makes up what you really look for in a team," concluded Hitchcock.[313] The NHL Players' Association, furthermore, praised Weino for passing the 1,000-game milestone in a nice congratulatory letter and hoped Eric had "enjoyed the special day along with Tracy, Benjamin, and Emily."[314] Undoubtedly, he did.

The campaign concluded a week later as the Flyers hammered Florida, 6-2. Eric took the night off, which was the only game he missed all year. He had played in 81 contests during the regular season, registering two goals and eighteen assists, and ended up with a very strong plus/minus score of positive sixteen. His biggest contribution, as Coach Hitchcock had pointed out, was in the defensive end of the ice. He helped solidify a blueline unit that only surrendered 166 goals, which ranked first in the NHL. Combine that with a solid offense led by John Leclair and Jeremy Roenick, and the result was a very good record of 45 wins, 13 ties, and 24 losses. It was good enough for fourth place in the Eastern Conference, which meant Philadelphia would face 5th-place Toronto in the opening round of the playoffs.

Knocking Out Toronto

The Eastern Conference quarterfinal series began on 9 April 2003 at the First Union Center in Philadelphia. The Maple Leafs got on the board first about eight minutes into the match when Alexander Mogilny scored a short-handed goal. Mogilny was one of the most talented of the players who came to the USA from the Soviet Union at the end of the Cold War and amassed over 1,000 points in his NHL career. Not to be outdone by the Russian superstar, Weino tied the game with a beautiful goal which he blasted past his former teammate Eddie Belfour. "Weinrich a chance," observed Gary Thorne on ESPN, "scores!" Thorne, a lawyer who was born in Bangor and got his hockey broadcasting start describing University of

Maine games on the radio, had seen a lot of Eric's play over the year including a couple of seasons announcing Devils' games. His partner on ESPN for the Philly/Toronto series was former Blackhawk Darren Pang. "Eric Weinrich surprised everybody. It was a perfect, perfect laser to the top corner over Belfour's shoulder to tie it," stated Pang.[315] Toronto regained the lead on another Mogilny goal a couple of minutes later, and the Russian scored the final goal for a hat-trick in the 5-3 Maple Leafs' victory.

Two nights later, on 11 April, the teams squared off once more in the City of Brotherly Love, and first period goals by Simon Gagne and JR put the Flyers up 2-0. Early in the second stanza, Mogilny struck again to pull the Leafs within one. Two minutes later, veteran winger Mark Recchi scored to put Philly up 3-1, and then on a powerplay halfway through the period John LeClair netted an insurance goal for the Flyers with an assist by Weino, and the score ended 4-1 for the home team to even the series.

April 14 found the two rival squads tangling in Toronto. About four minutes into the game Weino dumped the puck towards the goal and was promptly dumped himself, by the always aggressive Tie Domi. As the Flyers started another push out of their zone, Domi leveled Simon Gagne with a nasty hit. Philadelphia played on as the referees prepared to call Domi for a penalty. JR found Amonte, who looked up from the wing and saw Eric all alone in the middle. He hit him with a quick pass and Weino burst in unmarked on Belfour, whom he beat on the goalie's right side with a wrist shot. "Weinrich in, shot, score," exclaimed Gary Thorne on ESPN, "Eric Weinrich on the delayed penalty call, and a 1-0 Philadelphia lead." Darren Pang added, "Two Flyers all alone on Eddie Belfour, and Eric Weinrich had a practice shot at him."[316] After Philly increased their lead to 2-0, Toronto battled back with 3 straight scores including another from Mogilny. The Flyers tied it in the third but then Toronto won in the second overtime. Eric would have gladly traded his goal for a win.

On 16 April in Toronto, the Flyers beat the Maple Leafs 3-2 in triple overtime when Mark Recchi scored his second goal of the contest. Three nights later in Philly, the Flyers took a 3-2 lead in the series with a lopsided 4-1 victory. Weino assisted on the final goal. Back at home on the 21st, Toronto forced a seventh game showdown with a 2-1 win. The teams returned to Philly for the rubber match on 22 April, and the Flyers smoked the Leafs 6-1 to progress to the second round of the postseason. Weino assisted on Philly's fifth goal, and for the seven-game series against Toronto he finished with an impressive five points (tied for second on the team) on two goals and three assists.

Battling Ottawa

Philadelphia's next opponent was top-ranked Ottawa, where the Flyers and Senators faced off in game one on 25 April. The Broad Street Bullies got on the board first thanks to Amonte, and then took a 2-0 lead before the first period ended. The explosive Senators' offense struck back ferociously, however, and registered four unanswered goals to win by a 4-2 margin. Two nights later, still in Ottawa, the Flyers again started strong with goals from Gagne and Recchi. This time their defense stayed stout and contained the mighty Senators frontline, winning 2-0. Weino logged just under 25 minutes and was positive two in plus/minus. Game three in Philly on 29 April was a see-saw affair in which the Flyers scored first, Ottawa tied it, the Flyers took a 2-1 lead, then the Senators tied it again in the 3rd. Sadly for Weino and his comrades, it was the Senators who scored in OT for a 2-1 advantage in the series. Philadelphia would not quit, however, and they once again shut down the fierce Senators offense in game four, winning 1-0 on a first period goal by Michal Handzus. Weino played just over twenty minutes, partly because he spent four minutes in the penalty box for two minor infractions. Through the first four games Philadelphia had put up an admirable fight; nevertheless, Ottawa flexed their offensive muscles and scored five goals in each of the next two games, winning 5-2 and 5-1 to eliminate the Flyers from the playoffs.

A longer run into the series, during which Weino played in 13 playoff games, meant that he would not be able to play in the 2003 World Championships. Refreshed by a couple of months on Cousins Island, he headed to his third training camp with Philadelphia in the fall. The Flyers started out the season on a hot streak, and after twenty games had only lost three, with five ties and twelve wins. Eric was getting plenty of ice time and playing dependable defensive hockey; however, he was less involved in the offense than usual and only had a single assist up to that point. During the next week he joined the attack a bit more and notched a couple of key assists, and then on 3 December 2003 he scored his first goal of the season in a 5-2 win over the Penguins.

Weino's World

During the 2003-04 season, Eric wrote weekly autobiographical essays for the *Kennebec Journal*, entitled "Weino's World," and these resembled the journal entries he had submitted for publication during his 1987-88 stint with Team USA leading up to the Calgary Olympics. Eric's career and personal life had gone through an incredible number of changes over the years, and so had the everyday life of people due to the high-tech revolution. The internet, cell phones and laptops had not existed in 1987, but they were increasingly prevalent and dominant in daily life by 2004. "Another thing the new year has brought for this old school player is a computer for the road," explained Eric. "Yes, I have converted to the electronic age finally. And I even can get on the Internet in hotels by myself!" It truly was incredible how much the world had changed since his days with the U.S. Olympic Team. It made his part-time journalist job much simpler. "This makes writing this much easier and sending in these stories very quick," he pointed out. "Before, on the road, I was handwriting each article and then faxing to the newsroom." Eric also appreciated the benefits for him and his family. "The thing I will really enjoy is hooking up the camera device to my laptop and talking to home while we see each other on the screen," he elaborated. "It seems so space age and to think when I first started playing there weren't even cell phones!"[317]

A week later in his next installment, partly prompted by a family trip to see the film *Cheaper by the Dozen*, Eric (admittedly a bit of a "sap" regarding movies) pondered his future both personally and professionally. "Now don't get me wrong," stated Weino. "I am not writing off my life as a hockey player just yet, but when you turn 37 and you are at the end of your current contract you must prepare for all circumstances." His preference was to secure another contract with the Flyers and stay in Philadelphia, primarily because he believed they had a shot to win the Stanley Cup in the next few years. By continuing to work hard and play solid defensive hockey he could improve his chances of staying in Philly; however, at the end of the day it would be up to general manager Bobby Clarke. "There are other teams that could be interested," continued Weino, "but that would mean a new city, new home, new schools, new friends, and a new support system for Tracy and the kids."[318] How much of a shot at the championship a potential next team had would be a factor, and of course the option of retiring to Maine was not a bad backup plan.

On 28 January 2004 in Florida, Eric scored his second goal of the season to tie the score at 2-2 in a game that ended up in a 3-3 draw. (As things turned out this was his last goal as a Flyer.) Philadelphia thus earned a good point on the road and were battling for a high seed in the Eastern Conference. "The race for first in the East continues, with Toronto, Ottawa, New Jersey and us all with a chance of claiming the top spot," explained Eric in his 2 February column. "We know how important it is because the seedings change every round of the playoffs."[319] That evening Eric sustained a bruised foot in a 2-1 home loss to Tampa Bay. An x-ray indicated a potentially serious injury, so Weino did not travel with the team on their next trip and instead had an MRI done on his foot. By this point Eric was sure that management was keeping him out of action so he would be healthy enough to trade, and on 9

February the deal was done. Weino went to the St. Louis Blues in exchange for a draft pick, and he was informed just before that day's practice. "The news was a relief, and I immediately called Tracy to give her the news. She, too, was relieved," concluded Eric in his first column as one of the Blues.[320]

Meet Me in St. Louis

Two weeks after joining St. Louis, Weino provided an overview of why this transition to a new team and city had gone very smoothly. Players in the Blues locker room had welcomed him and quickly started joking around. This had usually been his experience when joining a new squad, but in this case, it was a particularly friendly onboarding. In addition, soon after he arrived on the banks of the Mississippi, Ben and Emily started their February vacations from school, so Tracy was able to take them out for a week to visit Eric and see him play for his new team. Helping the team win a few games also eased the adjustment. In his first outing with the Blues, they were beaten soundly by a tough Colorado outfit, but then they won the next three games. In the 3-2 victory over Pittsburgh on 14 February he assisted on an overtime goal by Eric Boquniecki, on the 16th he skated 24 minutes in a 4-2 win over Phoenix, and then in another overtime victory on the 19th against Tampa Bay he again assisted on the winner, this one scored by Doug Weight. "It feels great to factor in some of the offense again," he admitted, "and play a significant role on the team… Twenty-plus minutes a night sure is fun to play again."[321]

One special aspect of playing for the Blues was getting to watch their number one defenseman, Chris Pronger, night after night. Pronger was one of the best players in the world, and he had a league MVP trophy in his collection to show for it. At six foot six inches tall and with an incredible wingspan, it was nearly impossible for opponents to get around him. "He also possesses that unflappable ability to hold onto the puck in the tightest situations and make a great play," added Eric. "The great ones can do this every shift."[322] As St. Louis started down the home stretch locked in an intense fight for a playoff spot, they required every amazing play Pronger could give them. First, they would need to survive a grueling road trip around the west playing their conference rivals, starting on 20 February in Detroit.

The challenging journey had a rocky beginning that night, as the Blues got thumped by the Red Wings, 5-1, with Weino skating about 23 minutes. Two nights later in the Windy City, Eric's old stomping grounds, he scored his first goal for St. Louis and gave the Blues a 2-1 lead in the second period. Unfortunately, the Blackhawks battled back to tie the game and then eventually won it in overtime. The Blues' next stop was the Mile-High city to face the dangerous Avalanche, whose lightning quick offense featured such speedsters as Milan Hedjuk, Joe Sakic, Teemu Selanne, and fellow former University of Maine Black Bear Paul Kariya. Colorado bolted out to a 2-goal lead thanks to two markers by Hedjuk; however, the Blues did not give up and managed to earn a point from a 2-2 tie. Weino played 28 intense minutes at high elevation, doing his part to contain the Avs' potent attack.

From Denver on Thursday night, the Blues flew to Vancouver for a Saturday game and then south to San Jose for a Sunday matchup. They lost both of those contests, 2-0 and 1-0, perhaps partly due to the draining itinerary. "It has definitely been a wild ride in St. Louis, but I have gotten spoiled by the travel in Philly," explained Eric. "Now, this weekend I got a taste of the travel in the Western Conference again." He emphasized the difficulty of going from Denver to Vancouver to San Jose: "If you think this is a couple of short flights, take a look at an atlas." At that juncture of the campaign the Blues ranked ninth, two points out of the last western playoff slot. "It's going to be a real track meet for the next month, and hopefully the offseason training will pay off now. Too bad we don't get frequent flyer miles anymore."[323]

The impact of the brutal weekend road-trip, which saw the Blues return to St. Louis at 3am on Monday 1 March and then host Calgary the next day, may well have also contributed to their 2-4 loss to the Flames on the 2nd. After finally getting a chance to rest a bit, the Blues earned a hard-fought 1-1 tie against Edmonton at home on 4 March. Weino skated 23 minutes and assisted on the loan Blues goal, a strong contribution to the team earning an important point in a playoff hunt. There would be no rest for the weary and the Blues hit the road again, playing on Long Island on 6 March. Eric assisted on the first marker of the match and played 23 minutes again as St. Louis beat the Islanders 4-2. The very next night the Blues beat the Sabres in Buffalo, 5-1, and Weino ranked plus-two in 23 minutes of action. He had helped his new team pick up six crucial points in two days on the road.

Happy Birthday Lumpy

Two days later back on the banks of the Mississippi, the Blues beat the Islanders 3-2 and Eric notched a helper on a powerplay goal in the second period that tied the game at two apiece. St. Louis prevailed in overtime to pick up three more crucial points in the standings. On 11 March, the Blues hosted the Nashville Predators, who were also gunning for one of the final postseason positions in the Western Conference. The Preds took a 1-0 lead in the first on a powerplay goal; however, the Blues stormed back and tied it on a blueline blast by Weino in the second period. The game ended in a 1-1 tie and the Blues had another important point. This author attended the game with his college roommate, John "Lumpy" Lemkemeier, a lifelong resident of St. Louis and Blues fan. We were also celebrating Lumpy's birthday that evening, so it was nice of Eric to score a goal in Lumpy's honor![324]

Earning a Playoff Spot

After the 11 March draw with Nashville, the Blues had a dozen games remaining in the regular season and needed to win at least half of them to have a shot at the playoffs. They started well two nights later by beating

Columbus, 5-3, and ended up winning seven, tying one, and losing only four of the final twelve. Weino logged a lot of ice time and contributed assists in three of the wins, including his helper against the Predators in Nashville on 3 April. The Blues triumphed 4-1 and clinched a playoff spot with one game remaining. Eric had accurately predicted that the home stretch would be a track meet, and the Blues had run a solid race. His hard training in the offseason had paid off once again. St. Louis finished in seventh place with 39 wins, 32 losses, and eleven ties. Their 91 points were just two ahead of ninth place Edmonton, so every point since Eric joined the Blues had been important.

Seventh-place St. Louis encountered 2nd-place San Jose in the opening round of the 2004 NHL playoffs, and the Sharks hosted game one on 8 April. The Blues played tough defense but could not manage a goal, so regulation ended with the score knotted at zero. San Jose netted one about ten minutes into overtime to win the intense battle. Eric played 26 minutes, second on the Blues only to Pronger, who played a whopping 36. Game two took place on April 10 and the Sharks scored the first three markers. Doug Weight's goal for the Blues with two minutes left in the third stanza was too little, too late, and the Sharks took a two-game lead in the series as the squads journeyed to St. Louis where they laced up the skates again on 12 April. Weino assisted on the Blues 2nd goal and was plus-2 in the 4-1 victory, which resuscitated the Blues' chances.

The following evening in game four, San Jose took an early lead but then St. Louis tied it up about halfway through the first period. Unfortunately for Weino and his comrades, the Sharks scored two unanswered markers in the second period and held off a Blues comeback in the third. San Jose won, 4-3, and seized a commanding 3-1 lead in the series. Back in San Jose for game five on 15 April, the Sharks again struck first. The Blues Brian Savage, who had scored many goals while Weino's teammate in Montreal, found the net to tie it later in the opening stanza. The Sharks hammered home two more in the second period, ending the season for St. Louis. If the Blues had gotten just one lucky bounce and prevailed in game 1, which they had lost 1-0 in overtime, perhaps the series would have turned out differently. It was not to be, however, and this turned out to be Eric's last chance to do battle in the NHL playoffs.

Checking the Czechs in Prague

After exiting the postseason earlier than he had hoped, initially it appeared that Weino was heading back to Cousins Island for a long summer vacation. Team USA was playing in the World Championships in the Czech Republic and managed to squeak through the opening round with one win, one draw, and one loss. They opened round two by beating Russia. In their next game they lost to Sweden, and during the contest a key defenseman, Aaron Miller, took a hard hit and suffered a mild concussion. At that point, USA Hockey once again called on Eric to don his nation's jersey, and without hesitation he was on his way to Prague. This stint would be his record-setting ninth time playing for the USA in a World Championship tourney, surpassing Mark Johnson's previous high of eight appearances.[325] Weino arrived in time to play against Denmark on 4 May, and he helped the United States to a lopsided 8-3 victory which guaranteed them a place in the knockout round.

To reach the semi-finals and get closer to a medal, Team USA would first need to get past the host Czech Republic, who had won all five games so far by a combined score of 19-5 and was led by the future Hall-of-Famer Jaromir Jagr. The squads faced off in the late game on the evening of May 5 in front of a capacity crowd of 17,360 fans in the Sazka Arena in Prague. A preview article by John Sanful predicted a fierce showdown between Jagr and the Czech offense on one hand, and Weino and the USA defense on the other. "This is the most meaningful hockey Jaromir Jagr has played this season," Sanful commented. Jagr's NHL season with first Washington and then the Rangers had been a major disappointment, but now he had a "chance to salvage the season by leading the Czech team into the semi-finals."[326]

Sanful's insightful analysis of Eric's role in the showdown noted that he had a long and admirable record of dependable service to USA Hockey, and in the medal round of this year's tourney he was needed more than ever. "With the absence of Aaron Miller due to a concussion, Eric Weinrich will have to be the main defensive cog in the American engine," he surmised. With all the deadly Czech firepower, "Team USA needs someone who brings great experience and intangibles to a game like this." According to Sanful, the worth of Weino was "measured in his ability to play positional hockey, especially around his own net. Guys like Weinrich have a calming effect on their goaltenders." Sanful concluded his feature on Eric with a prescient prediction: "Expect Weinrich to play safe, fundamental hockey as the Americans look to pull off an upset today against the highly-favored Czechs."[327]

The opening period featured solid defense on both sides, physical play resulting in several penalties, and no goals. Early in the second stanza the Czech Republic took the lead on a blast by Colorado Avalanche defender Martin Skoula, and then increased their lead to a seemingly insurmountable 2-0 on a powerplay marker from the great Jaromir Jagr. The capacity crowd erupted, anticipating a victory and a shot at gold. Team USA did not surrender, however, and Richard Park found the net to pull them within one a few minutes after Jagr's goal. Weino asserted himself and was whistled for a roughing penalty a few minutes later, but no harm came on the powerplay. About halfway through the third period, the United States tied the match on a goal by Erik Westrum, and Weino and his blueline comrades held the Czech attack at bay through the third period and then also through a sudden death overtime period. The game would be decided on a penalty shootout, and the USA won on a successful penalty by defender Andy Roach. Weino had played the solid defensive hockey that journalist Sanful had predicted and earned a plus-two ranking by being on the ice for both USA goals.

Contributing to this victory, which knocked the mighty Czech hosts out of the World Championships without a medal, was one of the great successes of Eric's long career. By playing dependable defense and giving the USA a chance at a medal, he accomplished an admirable global goal. Reminiscing about the event over ten years later, he remembered it like it was yesterday. When his teammate scored the penalty to win, the sellout crowd was "dead silent." Later, when the US players went out for dinner and a beer, "the people looked so devastated that he felt bad about winning."[328] Two nights later, on 8 May, Sweden beat the USA in a tough 3-2 battle to advance to the final. On 9 May in the third-place showdown, Eric and his comrades beat Slovakia on another penalty shootout to take home the bronze medal. Surprisingly, the winner again came from defender Andy Roach, who would play a total of five NHL games during his long career which was mostly in the minor leagues and Europe. In many ways, winning a medal in this tourney represented a small victory for unsung heroes everywhere.

World Cup, Lockout, and Austria

After collecting his bronze medal, Weino headed back to Cousins Island for another wonderful summer enjoying life on the Maine coast. The months passed quickly as days were filled with piloting boat rides, entertaining company, and working out. In late August, Eric joined Team USA for the second Hockey World Cup. Essentially a collection of all-stars, Weino's teammates donning the red, white, and blue included Chris Chelios, Brian Leetch, Mike Modano, Brett Hull, Scott Gomez, Chris Drury, and Keith Tkachuk. As the seventh or eighth defensemen on the squad, Eric did not play a lot, but he did see action in the opening game on 31 August against Team Canada in Montreal. The Canadian squad featured superstars such as Mario Lemieux, Vincent Lecavalier, Joe Sakic, Jarome Iginla, and Martin Brodeur. Sakic scored the winning goal in a 2-1 Canadian victory. Eric got into one other game, and the USA finished fourth after beating Russia in the quarterfinals but losing to Finland, 2-1, in the semifinals on 10 September. This tournament remarkably represented Weino's fourteenth and last dance with Team USA after previously competing in two junior Worlds, the Olympics, nine senior Worlds, and the 1991 Canada Cup.

After the Hockey World Cup, Eric would have attended his first training camp with St. Louis; however, a labor dispute between players and owners prevented the NHL season from starting. Since it was the owners who refused to concede, the situation was classified as a lockout. As fall turned into early winter, Weino was still at home in Maine with Tracy and the kids. He stayed in shape and hoped for a settlement so the season could get underway. But in February 2005, the season was cancelled entirely and there would be no Stanley Cup awarded for the first time since 1919. Eric was getting cabin fever and going a bit stir crazy, which of course was not easy for his family. Tracy strongly encouraged him to "go somewhere!" Many NHL players signed short-term deals with teams in Europe, and Weino did the same. His agent had contacts in Austria, so Eric inked a contract with Villacher SV in the small city of Villach, located in the south-central part of the country near the borders with Italy and Slovenia, surrounded by lakes and mountains. Looking back, Eric described the short-term move to Villach as a "great opportunity."[329]

During his three-month stint with Villacher, Weino registered eleven points (on three goals and eight assists) in ten games. Most of the matches were in Austrian cities, but the team did venture into Slovenia a few times. All travel was done on a bus, which would stop at diners for meals and pull over on the roadside so the guys could pee. One member of the team regularly slept with the luggage under the bus. Villacher had no trainer or equipment guy, and one of the player's fathers sharpened the skates. Compared to life in the NHL, in Eric's opinion playing in Austria was a "breath of fresh air." The way the team operated, in many respects, resembled the youth leagues he had played in while growing up in Rumford and Gardiner. Life in Austria away from hockey was also special, as the players lived in lake houses with incredible mountain views. Eric's wife and kids came for a nice visit, and Tracy was particularly pleased by the proximity to Italy.[330]

Final NHL Season

When his partial campaign with Villacher SV concluded, Weino returned to Cousins Island for another summer with his family. Hosting friends, sailing around Casco Bay, and working hard to stay in tip-top condition kept Eric busy. Soon it was late August, which meant it was time to head to his first training camp with St. Louis. He had a one-year contract and would be turning 39 in December, so it was a real possibility that the 2005-6 season would be his last in the NHL. It would not be a particularly enjoyable experience for Eric and his teammates on the banks of the Mississippi, as the Blues got off to a terrible start and never recovered. On 28 October in a 6-4 loss in Anaheim, Weino scored on a powerplay in the third period that pulled the Blues within one, but then the Ducks scored again to seal the win. As things turned out, that was his last NHL goal. About a week later, he notched two assists in a 6-5 home loss to the Blackhawks, and at that point the Blues had won only two out of their first twelve contests. Three more times between late November and 10 December, Eric registered a pair of assists in a game; however, the Blues lost every time.

Moving through the holidays and into the new year, things did not get any better for St. Louis. On 9 January 2006 in Denver, the Avalanche thrashed the Blues 6-1. Having just returned to Colorado after spending a year teaching and researching in Zambia, I attended the game with my wife Heather. Born and raised in Zambia, Heather not surprisingly had never attended a hockey game before this one. It was my last time in person witnessing Eric in the NHL, after seeing him in many memorable games in New Jersey, Hartford, Chicago, Denver, Montreal, Philadelphia, Los Angeles (with my uncle Mike!) and St. Louis over the years since 1990. It was interesting to ponder the different stages of life as Eric neared the end of his days in the NHL, and I was in the second year of marriage to Heather and a massive research project on USA/Zambia relations that would last for over a decade. For Eric and the other Blues, of course, the pressing reality after their game in Denver was that their record stood at a dismal ten wins, five ties, and 25 losses. Weino, with a contract running out at the end of the year, was again (as he had been in Montreal in 2001) in the position of wanting to be traded to a contender. On 1 March he contributed an assist in a 4-2 win at Edmonton, which would be his last point as a member of the Blues. As things turned out, it was his last point in the NHL.

The Blues traded Weino to the Vancouver Canucks on 9 March 2006 for defenseman Tomas Mojzis and a draft pick. On 11 March, Eric suited up for the first time as a Canuck in a 2-1 home loss to the Dallas Stars. The Canucks were in contention for a playoff spot but did not play quite well enough down the stretch to make it into the postseason. In the eighteen games after Weino joined Vancouver, the Canucks won just seven and lost eleven. Eric played in sixteen of those games, averaging about nineteen minutes per match, but contributed no goals or assists. The Canucks ended up ninth in the Western Conference, three points out of the playoffs. Their final game was a 4-3 overtime victory over Colorado, and Weino logged fifteen minutes in what would be his final NHL contest. He packed up and headed back to Cousins Island to consult with Tracy, ponder the future, and weigh the options.

Retiring from the NHL

Home on the Maine coast, Eric as usual worked hard to stay in shape and prepare for another NHL season. The Calgary Flames, perhaps remembering the many great games Weino had played in their Saddledome, offered him a one-year contract. The Boston Bruins also expressed some interest, and that of course would have been a much better geographical and logistical situation for the family. In mid-July, the Bruins decided to move "in another direction." Eric talked with his agent, Steve Bartlett, who was also the agent for Kevin Dineen, head coach of the Portland Pirates of the AHL. Bartlett had recently been informed by Dineen that Portland would be looking for an assistant coach, and he encouraged Eric to pursue that chance. "This is a great opportunity," explained Eric in his 7 August press conference and retirement celebration at the Cumberland County Civic Center in Portland. "I can live right at the house."[331]

Andy, Eric, Christy and Pat Feeney
Portland, Maine on 12/31/2007

The decision had not been an easy one for Weino, but ultimately it came down to putting his family first. The previous season, as he played in St. Louis and Tracy and the kids lived in their home in New Jersey, had been very difficult for everyone. It got even worse after the trade to Vancouver, which was a considerably longer and more difficult trip than St. Louis when Tracy wanted to bring the children to visit their dad. "This year was not fun," admitted Tracy, adding that "It wasn't easy to juggle life and hockey." During the retirement celebration with 12-year-old Ben leaning on his shoulder, Eric remarked: "It's going to be awesome to be in Maine for the whole year. I have not spent an entire year in Maine since my sophomore year at the University of Maine."[332] He summed up his thought process as follows: "The timing was right. I had received a good offer from Calgary, but I didn't want to move my family again for just one year."[333]

During a brief and emotional retirement speech in front of friends and family, he quoted from a 1910 address by Teddy Roosevelt who had stated: "It is not the critic who counts... the credit goes to the man who is actually in the arena, whose face is marred by dust and sweat and blood, who strives valiantly, who errs and come short again and again... who at the best knows in the end the triumph of high achievement and who at the worst, if he fails, at least he fails while daring greatly." It was a very fitting quotation for a farewell speech by the man who had toiled in the trenches as a workhorse NHL defenseman in over 1,000 games and who had represented the USA in more World Championships than any other player. Perhaps his contributions off the ice, as a "good citizen," had been even more important over the years. His youngest brother Jason attended the ceremony and explained to the press afterwards: "He brought me into a lot of locker rooms with him, and I can tell you, his teammates loved him. To a man." In response to a comment about Weino not getting publicity or credit, his father Jack responded: "No, people in hockey know Eric. They know him well."[334]

Sportswriters across the state of Maine paid their tributes and tipped their caps, starting with Larry Mahoney, who worked for the Bangor newspaper and announced radio broadcasts of University of Maine hockey for over forty years. In his article entitled "Weinrich was epitome of NHL pro," Mahoney praised Weino as "the consummate professional, quietly efficient, dependable, resourceful, and durable." According to Mahony, Eric "typified the stay-at-home defenseman." He pointed out that Weino played in at least 75 games in thirteen of his final fifteen seasons, and rightly attributed that to "off-season conditioning." Not surprisingly given Mahoney's close connection with University of Maine hockey, he paid attention especially to Eric's role in turning the Black Bears into a national powerhouse. In conclusion the five-time Maine sportswriter of the year characterized Weino as "a classy, intelligent individual who puts his family first."[335]

Raising the bar even higher in its encomium and panegyric for Weino was the insightful, thoughtful, and well-written essay by long-time *Lewiston*

Sun Journal sportswriter Kalle Oakes. Another award-winning and respected journalist (like Mahoney) and one who knew Maine sports figures as well as anyone, Oakes would spend 27 years toiling for the Lewiston newspaper before eventually taking his typewriter to Kentucky to ply his trade in the south. The day after Eric's retirement celebration in 2006, Oakes penned a wonderful ode to Weino entitled "Forgotten Mainer perhaps best ever." He asked his readers to ponder the question: who was the most accomplished athlete from Maine in the past 25 years? He identified some of their likely answers, naming legendary athletes from the Pine Tree State such as distance runner Joan Benoit Samuelson, baseball pitcher Billy Swift, women's basketballer Cindy Blodgett, and boxer Joey Gamache. "And that's a wrap, right?" Oakes asked his readers. "Wrong!" he answered. "You could make a case that now-retired National Hockey League defenseman Eric Weinrich of Gardiner belongs at the top of the mountain."[336]

Oakes speculated, however, that if you stopped random sports fans on any Maine street, two-thirds of them would not mention Weino in their list of the best athletes from Vacationland. He placed most of the blame for Eric's lack of notoriety in his home state on the NHL for completely failing to promote itself in the USA. It was also partly due to Weino's approach to his craft, though. "He has merely played one of the most thankless positions in professional sports without fanfare or complaint for eight different franchises," explained Oakes. "He has done it without whining about the size of his paycheck" and "maintained said value without flaunting otherworldly offensive talent and without devolving into a belligerent thug," added the sportswriter. "Basically, he was everything we collectively cried that professional sports should be, and then it slipped our mind that he existed," contended Oakes convincingly.[337]

Offering analysis of the Cumberland County Civic Center ceremony and Eric's long career, Oakes argued: "There was no hint of 'me' or 'I' in Monday's retirement speech or in the nearly two decades of professional hockey that preceded it." Speculating on why the farewell event took place at all, Oakes offered: "It's safe to say that his new employer, the Portland Pirates, made him do it." The praise from the Lewiston scribe was clearly heartfelt, and frankly as one who watched Eric's career closely over the decades, I could not agree more with Oakes' final analysis about Weino. "He was a gentleman enforcer. He didn't score many goals, but he scored many meaningful ones," concluded Oakes. "Eric Weinrich never had a glamorous job on the ice. To an entire generation of hockey enthusiasts, however, he was one of the best in the business at what he did." For those reasons, Oakes closed by proposing Eric's photo for the cover of a mythical Encyclopedia of Maine Sports History.[338]

Portland Pirates

Eric Weinrich served as an assistant coach for the Portland Pirates through the fall and early winter of 2006, working closely with the team's young defenders. Head coach Kevin Dineen appreciated his efforts. "Eric has brought a vast array of experience and knowledge to our organization," commented Dineen. On 26 January 2007, however, Portland announced that Weino would be donning a Pirates' jersey and returning to the ice as an active player. When asked by the press if Eric would suit up that evening, he dryly quipped, "He would be a good option."[339] During the remainder of the season, Weino saw action in 36 games, chipping in with two goals and twelve assists. The Pirates finished with a record of 37 wins and 43 losses and missed out on a playoff spot. While spending another sunny summer on Cousins Island with friends and family, Eric was not certain what the next season would bring, but as usual he stayed in top condition. As training camp approached, the Pirates' parent organization, the Mighty Ducks of Anaheim, offered him a contract to play another season in Portland and he gladly accepted.[340]

The Pirates did well during the first half of the season, and Weino not only contributed solid defensive play on the ice but also served as a leader and a role model to the younger players. "In the locker room, whether it's practice or whatever, he brings that leadership," commented rookie defenseman Brett Festerling. "He works hard every day. He is a guy who sets the tone. People do not understand how hard he really works when he gets off the ice and in the gym. That kind of thing shows all the guys all the little things it takes to be a pro," concluded Festerling.[341]

On New Year's Eve 2007, this author and his wife Heather attended a Pirates game in Portland to watch Eric play. We were accompanied by my cousin Patrick Feeney and his girlfriend at the time Christy (whom he married in 2010). We had a wonderful time riding down from Bethel to Portland and going out for dinner and drinks before the game. We cheered for Eric and the Pirates, who beat Lowell 3-0 and improved their record to nineteen wins and sixteen losses. After the game, we got a chance to visit with Eric and snap some photos. Christy, who grew up in New York as a diehard Rangers fan, remembered Weino very well from the old days and was particularly thrilled to meet him. As always, Eric was humble and gracious, even to a Rangers fan! The New Year's Eve matchup turned out to be last time I would see Weino skate in a competitive hockey game.

The Pirates played great hockey in the second half of the season to finish with a record of 45 wins and 35 losses, and advanced to the third round of the AHL playoffs. Sadly, Eric did not play a part in the exciting postseason run because he was seriously injured in a fight on 29 February 2008. During an intense surgery, three plates were placed into the area around his left eye. He had also sustained a broken jaw, for the second time in his career. This was particularly tragic, given the fact that Eric had never been an instigator of fights or played unnecessarily violent hockey. In mid-March, doctors gave him permission to start light workouts.[342] He hoped to return to action during the AHL playoffs, but it was not to be. During his final season he played in 52 games for the Pirates, registering one goal and seven assists. After sitting out the last couple of months of the season to recover and recuperate, Eric decided to step off the ice for good and work as a scout and developmental coach.

Maine Hall of Famer

On Sunday 3 May 2015 during a noon banquet at the Augusta Civic Center, Eric Weinrich was among a class of nine inducted into the Maine Sports Hall of Fame. Press coverage highlighted his role in helping to turn the University of Maine hockey team into a national powerhouse. "Eric was a great player at Maine and obviously fashioned a tremendous NHL career," stated Black Bears' coach Red Gendron. "More important than anything else, it's his quality as a human being. That goes all the way back to his family and being raised in Maine, and Maine values," added Gendron. Weino praised his fellow inductees and expressed his gratitude for being chosen. "It's probably one of the nicest honors any Maine person could accept," he concluded.[343] Eric had accomplished another impressive global goal, and this one was extra special because it was in his home state.

Induction into the Maine Sports Hall of Fame was very fitting for Weino, who learned to skate on a frozen pond in Poland, joined his first hockey team in Rumford, and later led North Yarmouth Academy to a state championship. During his high school years in Yarmouth, he first donned a Team USA jersey at the World Junior Championships in Finland and displayed not only his ability to compete against the best Under-20 players in the world but also an acumen for serving as a cultural ambassador. After earning All-American accolades and leading the Maine Black Bears to the NCAA Tournament, he earned a spot on the USA Olympic Team and played at the 1988 Games in Calgary. His professional career started in fall 1988 with the Utica Devils in the AHL, and his two years earned him a shot in the NHL in New Jersey, where he became teammates and friends with former Soviet Red Army superstars Fetisov and Kasatonov.

Weino's stellar tenure in the NHL saw him skate in over 1,000 regular season games, with his longest stint being in Chicago as part of a successful and exciting team that featured Chris Chelios and Jeremy Roenick. Other high points in the NHL included serving as assistant captain for the fabled Canadiens during a couple of seasons in the cosmopolitan city of Montreal and playing a key role in the Philadelphia Flyers ousting of Toronto in the 2003 playoffs. Even more than his admirable exploits in the NHL, however, Eric's incredible record of service to his nation in international competitions (two World Juniors, 1988 Olympics, nine World Championships, a Canada Cup, and a Hockey World Cup) demonstrated the distance he had traveled from the frozen lakes of his youth. During his amazingly successful international hockey life during the last days of the Cold War and beyond, most notably as a dependable member of Team USA, Eric Weinrich accomplished a long list of impressive global goals and served as a respected cultural ambassador for his country.

Weino's Wisdom

This part of our life was the first chance we could "choose" where we would play to some extent, and for the remainder of my career the family resided in New Jersey, Haddonfield, just outside of Philadelphia. In all the family lived there for five years and made many lifelong friends as a result. I played on a very international team in Philadelphia, and we had some good success in the regular season all three years. I had teammates from all over the globe including Roman Czechmanek, Jiri Dopita and Jan Hlavac, three of the top players of the Czech Republic at the time and whom I had faced before they came to the NHL in World Championships. Michael Handzus was from Slovakia, Sami Kapanen from Finland, Kim Johnsson from Sweden and one of my favorite teammates, Dmitri Yuskevich, from Russia. Dmitri was a throwback to the Soviet-era style players, with good skills and toughness. During one playoff run, he sustained a separated shoulder, but told the doctors he was playing. His shoulder was a massive bruise of black and blue, so he taped it up and played with what I imagine was some unbearable pain. He even scored a big goal for us in the game and he went on to play all of the series. That was the kind of character I remember from my early years against the Soviet players. "Yusky" appreciated where he had come from and gave his all every game and we all admired that.

The year I was traded to the St. Louis Blues, it came as a bit of a shock. I was visiting family and got the call from the GM. St. Louis seemed like a good spot if it had to happen and I knew some of the players there from my past. We made a strong run towards the end of the season and made the playoffs to face a tough San Jose team. After getting knocked out in five games, our GM Larry Pleau, advised me to skip the World Championships and go home to the family. After arriving safely, I settled in for a couple of days in some nice warm weather and enjoyed time with the family. Not long after, I received a call from an old friend and teammate from the "88 Olympic Team," the US coach, Peter Laviollette. The team was competing at the World Championships in Prague, Czech Republic, and during one of the recent games Aaron Miller, a key part of the defense, had sustained a concussion. Peter explained what had happened and asked if I would be interested. In the end I said yes and joined the team for a game against Denmark. We moved into the crossover phase and faced the Czech team with Jagr. A win against the home country would put us in the medal round. After a 2-2 draw the game went to a shootout and Andy Roach was our hero scoring the winning goal on a fantastic move. After a tough loss to the Swedes, we went up against Slovakia where the game went to another shoot out. Again, Roach scored the winner with his patented move. In what would be my last World Championship, a long-awaited medal, Bronze, was a great way to go out. It was also a big moment for USA hockey, which has not had much success in the Worlds. I was happy for our team leader and former Olympic teammate, the late Jim Johansen, or affectionately known as "JJ." We had been part of many teams together in the past and for all his tireless work during the tournament and throughout the year, he deserved it as much as anyone. Also, there was another longtime staff member, Art Berglund, who I've known since 1985. We enjoyed a nice celebration dinner post-game and reminisced about the past and this medal.

When I received a call from my agent while visiting Rockland, Maine in late July, he asked if I wanted to join the USA World Cup of Hockey Team, replacing an injured Derian Hatcher. I had reservations about going since I hadn't really started much on-ice training which I usually did in August. But it was a hard opportunity to say no to and so I packed up what I had with us in Maine and joined the team in Columbus. I didn't feel prepared for the games and the tournament was a disappointment for us, finishing fourth. As we played the games in August the looming possibility of a work stoppage was eminent. And when it happened, most players stayed at home although some chose to find a team in Europe. Early on there were a small number of the top young players without families who signed with teams in Switzerland and Sweden. Some European players joined their previous clubs back in their hometowns, as did some Russian players in their country. I chose to stay with my family in NJ for the time being, hoping a resolution could be worked out. We couldn't use our facility where we normally practiced but we did skate with a small group a few times a week. I used a local gym to train. As the lockout stretched to January, I really wanted to play. My agent informed me there was a team in Villach. Austria, which needed a player. We discussed it as a family, and we decided it would be a fun experience. The family would make a trip and stay with me for part of the time I was playing there. Playing in Europe had always been something we talked about doing post-career and maybe this would be the chance to try it. Little did I know, the team also included Ethan Moreau, a teammate from Chicago, former UNH star and Hobey Baker winner, Jason Krog, another outstanding college player, Rob Doyle, and a St. Louis teammate, goalie Rheinhard Divis. It was also the town from where the Raffl boys, one of who played 500+ NHL games, started their careers. Villach had a great history of hockey, and the city and alumni were big supporters. It was a fun experience playing for Villach, the derby games against Klagenfurt, playing against the Red Bulls of Salzburg and visiting the surrounding areas of Austria, Slovenia and Italy. It is truly one of the most beautiful places on earth. We met my brother and family in Venice one weekend and went to a spa in Slovenia as well as skiing in Zell Am See. After getting spoiled in the NHL for so many years, it was refreshing to see players who often had jobs during the day come to practice and games and play so hard with pride in their city's team. I'll never forget how the players and city embraced us foreigners into their community.

My last NHL season playing for St. Louis was a year of mixed emotions. I missed my family who remained in NJ for the last year of my contract. They came for brief visits, but it was hard on me, and even harder for Tracy. As much as I loved the game, I would never put her through this again. If I was to play the next season somewhere we would go as a family. At the end of that season, walking into our place in Haddonfield was a welcome sight. With the future up in the air, we focused on a house renovation in Maine which would be our next home.

I was fortunate to get an offer to coach with the local team in Portland, Maine, after a few NHL opportunities didn't pan out. I joined Kevin Dineen and his staff as an assistant coach of the American League franchise of the Anaheim Ducks. Little did I know I would be back playing halfway through the season and into a couple more before an injury ended my playing days forever. Those couple of years back in the AHL were an interesting time for me. As the oldest and most experienced player, I was given an opportunity to play with rookies every game and work with them side by side rather than behind them as a coach. After that couple of seasons playing, I resumed coaching with Dineen and we took over the Buffalo AHL franchise which had moved into Portland when Anaheim moved their team closer to the NHL team. Kevin was a great mentor and I appreciated how he handled the young players and how he approached their development. When Kevin was offered an NHL head coach position in Florida, I decided I was staying in Maine and took a scouting role with Buffalo. After several seasons of scouting and one year off from work, I was offered a development staff position with my first pro team, the New Jersey Devils, which is my current role now. Working primarily with drafted prospects who haven't turned pro in North America, including European players, it has been a nice transition and a chance to stay involved in the game. Over the past eight years I have made trips throughout Europe including several back to Russia, Finland, Sweden, Czechia and Switzerland. Traveling to Russia, especially Moscow and St. Petersburg, connecting with some former teammates and friends was very interesting. Seeing how much the country has changed since I was first there in 1987 and not feeling as threatened or intimidated allowed me a chance to explore the cities and take in some extraordinary sights and history. Now, with the war with Ukraine and Russia, travel for a USA citizen to those areas is impossible. We have relied on our Russian scouts and my good friend, Misha Manchik, to keep us informed about our players there. Everyone hopes for a quick resolution as the world watches intently.

Along with the Bronze medal in Prague and my experience in Austria, I received a nice honor from USA Hockey, the Bob Johnson Award, given annually to recognize excellence in international hockey competition. My father and I made the trip to Colorado Springs for the ceremony. I was honored to receive the award, more so because the presenter was Lou Vairo. It was an emotional moment for me. Lou was a special friend, and I had the honor of playing for Bob Johnson briefly during the 1991 Canada Cup before Coach Johnson suffered a stroke during the tournament. During the pre-tournament games and practices Coach Johnson was such a calming and positive voice. No matter what the situation he always managed to make us feel like we had everything in control. His famous quote, "It's a great day for hockey" exemplified his spirit towards the game. After all the games and travel overseas, I was humbled and touched with the recognition. International hockey has given me an opportunity to experience the world and make many great friends. One thing that always stands out is although the competition is fierce and emotional, when it's over we can be friends and laugh together. I will never take that for granted and hope one day I can give back to the game what it has given me.

ENDNOTES

1   Author's interview (assisted by his wife Heather and daughter Ellen) with Jack and Sandra Weinrich, Cousin's Island, ME., 30 December 2018.

2   Bill Brill, "Hey, who is dis Eric Weinrich from Roanoke, anyway?" *Roanoke Times & World News*, 25 May 1985. Clipping from Weinrich Family Collection (hereafter WFC), Cousins Island, Maine. Photocopies of all the Weinrich Family Collection documents cited here are in the author's possession. Thanks to Eric, Tracy, Jack, and Sandra for granting me access to these materials. Thanks also to my parents, Wayne and Mary Corkum, for allowing me to use their office facilities in Bethel, Maine to photocopy the documents.

3   Author's interview with Jack and Sandra Weinrich, Cousin's Island, ME., 30 December 2018.

4   Ian McCaw, "Eric Weinrich: Local Boy Makes Good in Maine," *Let's Play Hockey*, (Jan. 23-29, 1987), 30, WFC.

5   John Banks, "Family Skates to Greatness," <u>Unknown Publication</u>, undated (but probably 1997), WFC.

6   For his insightful account of his own life see Bobby Orr, *Orr: My Story* (New York: G.P Putnam's Sons, 2013).

7   Steve Dandy, "Skating in the Shadow of old No. 4," *Portland Evening Express*, 25 February 1984, 18, WFC.

8   Eric Weinrich, "Let Nature Take Its Course," *American Hockey* (January 2003), 6, WFC.

9   "The Right Road Taken," official website of the National Hockey League Players' Association, www.nhlpa.com accessed 29 January 2003, printout of article in WFC.

10 "Outstanding Players Get Trophies at Hockey Dinner," *Rumford Falls Times*, 23 March 1976, WFC.

11 This is based on the author's personal recollection. My attempt to make the Rumford Point Little League team in spring 1976 was unsuccessful, but after another year in the "minor league," I would become Eric's teammate in the summer of 1977.

12 "Hockey Programs Gear Up," *Rumford Falls Times*, 4 November 1976, WFC.

13   For more discussion of the elementary school experiences of Eric, and this author, see Andy DeRoche, "Embracing Ubuntu: How a White Gen Xer from Maine Learned about Race and Married a Zambian," in Elwood Watson, editor, *Generation X Professors Speak: Voices from Academia* (Lanham: Scarecrow Press, 2013), 95-116, especially 98-99.

14   "Squirts now 10-1 in league play," *Rumford Falls Times*, 27 January 1977, WFC.

15   Joe Clark, "Weinrich Trio: At Home on the Ice," *Kennebec Journal*, undated but probably November 1982, WFC.

16   "PeeWees win another, 6-3," *Rumford Falls Times*, undated, but probably from winter of 1977-78, WFC. People in Gardiner would soon give a sigh of relief when the Weinrich family left Rumford and moved to their community.

17   Dandy, "Skating in the Shadow," 18, WFC.

18   Andy DeRoche phone interview with Alex Weinrich (was living in Denmark), 5 October 2019.

19   Andrew DeRoche, "A Role Model," *Western Maine Spectator*, August 1991, WFC. My late uncle John Willard was the founder, publisher, and editor of the *Spectator*.

20   Ernie Stallworth, "Weinrich reaches for new level," *Unknown Publication*, undated but probably Sept. or Oct. 1987, WFC.

21   Eric Lucey, "Veteran Weinrich Trades Time for Success," USA Hockey Website, www.usahockey.com (August 2001), printout of page in WFC.

22   Banks, "Family Skates to Greatness," WFC.

23   "Weinrich hurls perfect game," *Kennebec Journal*, 26 June 1979, WFC.

24   Joe Clark, "Weinrich Trio: At Home on the Ice," *Kennebec Journal*, undated but probably November 1982, WFC.

25   John Banks, "Family Skates to Greatness," Unknown Publication, undated (but probably 1997), WFC.

26   Dandy, "Skating in the Shadow," 18, WFC.

27   Nicholas Sarantakes, *Dropping the Torch: Jimmy Carter, The Olympic Boycott, and the Cold War* (Cambridge: Cambridge University Press, 2011), 1-14.

28   For the story of USSR hockey in the 1980s and many former Soviet players' migration to the NHL at the end of the Cold War, see the superb film directed by Gabriel Polsky, *Red Army* (Sony Pictures Classics, 2014). Thanks to Eric for suggesting this film, and loaning me his copy. Also consult Tal Pinchevsky, *Breakaway: From Behind the Iron Curtain to the NHL – The Untold Story of Hockey's Great Escapes* (Mississauga: John Wiley & Sons Canada, Ltd., 2012).

29   Andy and Heather DeRoche interview with Eric and Tracy Weinrich, 25 July 2017, Cousins Island, Maine.

30   Joe Clark, "Weinrich Trio: At Home on the Ice," *Kennebec Journal*, undated but probably November 1982, WFC.

31   "Cool: Eric Weinrich," *Les Canadiens* magazine (January 2000), 19, WFC. Globensky's book *A Little Knock Won't Hurt Ya!* was recommended by Al Weinrich during our interview and is high on my list of future reads.

32   Eric Weinrich, "Let Nature Take Its Course," *American Hockey* (January 2003), 6, WFC.

33   John Banks, "Family Skates to Greatness," <u>Unknown Publication</u>, undated (but probably 1997), WFC.

34   Jerry Crasnick, "Weinrich hockey's worst-kept secret," *Maine Sunday Telegram*, 8 July 1984, WFC.

35   Tom Perkins, "Eric Weinrich: Gardiner's gift to Maine hockey has a bright future," <u>Unknown Publication</u>, undated but probably late 1986 or early 1987, WFC.

36   Joe Clark, "Weinrich Trio: At Home on the Ice," *Kennebec Journal*, undated but probably November 1982, WFC.

37   Joe Clark, "Weinrich Trio: At Home on the Ice," *Kennebec Journal*, undated but probably November 1982, WFC.

38   Ernie Stallworth, "Weinrich reaches for new level," *Unknown Publication*, undated but probably Sept. or Oct. 1987, WFC.

39   "Area Skaters Represent Maine team," Unknown Publication, undated but probably early 1983, WFC.

40   Joe Clark, "Weinrich Skates On: Defenseman an Olympic Hopeful," *Kennebec Journal*, 14 July 1983, WFC.

41   Joe Clark, "Weinrich Skates On: Defenseman an Olympic Hopeful," *Kennebec Journal*, 14 July 1983, WFC.

42   Author's interview with Jack and Sandra Weinrich, Cousin's Island, ME., 30 December 2018.

43   Author's phone interview with Lou Vairo, 19 July 2018.

44   Vairo's significance is briefly discussed in Stephen Hardy and Andrew C. Holman, *Hockey: A Global History* (Urbana: University of Illinois Press, 2018), 387.

45   Jeff Z. Klein, "Coach Helped Hockey Flourish beyond Asphalt," *The New York Times*, 3 December 2014, accessed at www.nytimes.com on 19 July 2018.

46   Author's interview with Lou Vairo, USA Hockey Facility, Colorado Springs, CO., 27 July 2018.

47   For example see the 4-minute video "U.S. Hockey Hall of Fame – Lou Vairo" on YouTube. It was Eric Weinrich who suggested the author research Lou Vairo and contact him about an interview. Thanks Eric!

48   Joe Clark, "Weinrich Skates On: Defenseman an Olympic Hopeful," *Kennebec Journal*, 14 July 1983, WFC.

49   Ernie Stallworth, "Weinrich reaches for new level," *Unknown Publication*, undated but probably Sept. or Oct. 1987, WFC.

50   Steve Dandy, "Skating in the Shadow of old No. 4," *Portland Evening Express*, 25 February 1984, 18, WFC.

51   For his story of battling health problems resulting from numerous concussions, as well as inspirational stories of many other people facing adversity bravely, see Pat LaFontaine, *Companions in Courage: Triumphant Tales of Heroic Athletes* (New York: Warner Books, 2001).

52   Chris Chelios with Kevin Allen, *Made in America* (Chicago: Triumph Books, 2014), 88.

53   For convincing analysis of Kasatonov's emergence in the early 1980s see Pinchevsky, *Breakaway*, 147. Regarding the career of Fetisov, particularly his experiences after moving to the USA, peruse Keith Gave, *The Russian Five: A Story of Espionage, Defection, Bribery and Courage* (Ann Arbor: Gold Star Publishing, 2018), especially chapter 10 entitled "Viacheslav Fetisov: 'A King of Man,'" 147-157.

54   Jerry Crasnick, "Weinrich hockey's worst-kept secret," *Maine Sunday Telegram*, 8 July 1984, WFC.

55   Svobada's defection detailed in Pinchevsky, *Breakaway*, 75-77.

56   For details on this truly remarkable draft see the Wikipedia entry "1984 NHL Entry Draft," at https://en.wikipedia.org/wiki/1984_NHL_Entry_Draft (accessed on 27 August 2017). When Glavine and his Braves defeated the Chicago Cubs 19-5 on 15 April 1994, Eric and several other Blackhawks (and this author) attended the game and briefly met the great pitcher afterwards. Glavine and Eric recalled their shared experience as New England schoolboy skaters.

57   For details and analysis regarding the growth of the Hockey Night in Boston tournament, see Hardy and Holman, *Hockey: A Global History*, 383.

58   Jerry Crasnick, "Weinrich hockey's worst-kept secret," *Maine Sunday Telegram*, 8 July 1984, WFC.

59   Joe Clark, "NYA cruises past St. Doms," *Lewiston Sun Journal*, 25 September 1984, WFC.

60   Gary Hawkins, "Weinrich has bright hockey future," Unknown Publication, undated (but probably early fall 1984), WFC.

61   Joe Clark, "Weinrich named to U.S. Junior hockey team," *Lewiston Sun*, undated but either late November or early December 1984, WFC.

62   Jerry Crasnick, "Weinrich to compete in Finland," unknown publication, undated but either late November or early December 1984, WFC.

63   Clark, "Weinrich named to U.S. Junior hockey team."

64   Postcard from Eric (in Suomi, Finland) to Mom, Dad, Al and Jay (in Gardiner, Maine, USA), 18 December 1984, WFC.

65   Andy DeRoche phone interview with Al Weinrich, 5 October 2019. Al ended up to be quite a cultural ambassador himself, playing in several European leagues and marrying Irene, from Denmark, where they now live.

66   Postcard from Eric, WFC.

67   Bill Brill, "Hey, who is dis Eric Weinrich from Roanoke, anyway?" *Roanoke Times & World News*, 25 May 1985, WFC.

68   Andy and Heather DeRoche interview with Eric and Tracy Weinrich, 25 July 2017, Cousins Island, Maine.

69   Andy and Heather DeRoche interview with Eric and Tracy Weinrich, 25 July 2017, Cousins Island, Maine. During my research in the Weinrich Family Collection, I discovered the set of Soviet hockey cards and told Eric, who was quite happy to hear that the cards were still around.

70   NCAA hockey's decision to brand their semifinals as the "Frozen Four" was an attempt to cash in on the widespread and lucrative popularity of the NCAA basketball tournament's Final Four, and it certainly did not hurt. By the end of the 1990s, the men's hockey tournament was the 2nd highest revenue generator for all NCAA sports. See Stephen Hardy and Andrew C Holman, *Hockey: A Global History* (Urbana: University of Illinois Press, 2018), 459-461.

71   Steve McKibben, "Eric Weinrich Skates to Stardom," Interview for *Maine-ly Sports*, 21 January 1985, Clipping from Weinrich Family Collection (hereafter WFC), Cousins Island, Maine.

72   Larry Woodward, "Weinrich Will Lace Skates at Maine," *Portland Press Herald*, 15 January 1985, WFC.

73   Larry Mahoney, "Weinrich Commits to U-Maine," *Bangor Daily News*, 15 January 1985, WFC.

74   Larry Mahoney, "Experience 'Fascinating' for Weinrichs," *Bangor Daily News*, 15 January 1985, WFC.

75 McKibben, "Eric Weinrich Skates to Stardom."

76 *Lewiston Daily Sun*, 1 March 1985 and 6 March 1985, www.sunjournal.com/archive accessed 20 November 2017.

77 Eric Weinrich text message to author, 19 November 2017.

78 Ken O'Quinn, "Devils Draft Weinrich," undated clipping from unidentified newspaper mid-June 1985, WFC.

79 For an insightful discussion of Larionov's career see Keith Gave, *The Russian Five: A Story of Espionage, Defection, Bribery and Courage* (Ann Arbor: Gold Star Publishing, 2018), especially chapter 11 entitled "Igor Larionov: A Tale of Two Anthems," 159-168.

80 Larionov would struggle initially with the Vancouver Canucks, but eventually become an NHL star there and even more so later with Detroit. He would help the Red Wings win 3 Stanley Cups. For a fascinating documentary on the experience of the Soviet players coming to the NHL, see the Gabe Polsky film *Red Army* (2014).

81 Letter from New Jersey Devils' management to Eric Weinrich, 20 June 1985, WFC.

82 Gary Hawkins, "Eric Weinrich: NHL draft pick plans busy hockey summer," *Kennebec Journal*, undated clipping but probably mid-June 1985, WFC.

83 Game Program, *The Battle of the Bears*, 12/20/85, 30, WFC.

84 Author's interview with Eric Weinrich, 27 January 2017, Boulder, CO.

85 Mike Schroeder, "Thanks, We Needed That," *American Hockey Magazine*, February 1986, 8, WFC.

86 Larry Woodward, "Devils keep close tabs on their 1985 draft pick," *Portland Express*, 11 March 1986, WFC.

87 Bill Porter, "Making the Grade: UMO's Weinrich earns high marks," undated clipping from unidentified newspaper, probably spring 1986, WFC.

88 Tom Perkins, "Eric Weinrich: Gardiner's gift to Maine hockey has a bright future," undated clipping from unidentified newspaper, probably January 1987, WFC.

89 Ernie Stallworth, "Weinrich reaches for new level: Olympics next step on path to excellence," undated clipping from unidentified newspaper, probably late July or early August 1987, WFC.

90 *Lewiston Daily Sun*, 25 October 1986 and 1 November 1986, www.sunjournal.com/archive accessed 23 November 2017.

91 Dave Brenner, "Weinrich's 55-foot shot sinks UNH," undated clipping from unidentified newspaper, probably 16 November 1986, WFC.

92 *Lewiston Daily Sun*, 12 March 1987, www.sunjournal.com/archive accessed 24 November 2017.

93   Larry Mahoney, "Weinrich scoring an added plus," *Bangor Daily News*, undated but probably late November 1986, WFC.

94   Ian McCaw, "Eric Weinrich: Local Boy Makes Good in Maine," *Let's Play Hockey* (Jan.23-29, 1987), 30, WFC.

95   David Conte letter to Shawn Walsh, 9 April 1987, WFC.

96   Bob Johnson letter to Eric Weinrich, 8 July 1987, WFC.

97   Ernie Stallworth, "Weinrich reaches for new level."

98   Maxwell McNab letter to Jack Weinrich, 20 August 1987, WFC.

99   Eric Weinrich, "Olympic Diary: U.S. Olympic coaches just right contrast," *Maine Sunday Telegram*, undated but probably mid-September 1987, WFC.

100   Eric Weinrich, "Olympic Diary: NHL exhibition games test Olympians' mettle," *Maine Sunday Telegram*, undated but probably late September 1987, WFC. The author and his friend Bob Cameron attended the game in Philadelphia.

101   Eric Weinrich email to the author, 2 October 2017.

102   Eric Weinrich, "Olympic Diary: NHL exhibition games test Olympians' mettle," *Maine Sunday Telegram*, undated but probably late September 1987, WFC.

103   Eric Weinrich, "Olympic Diary: Returning to Orono will be emotional," *Maine Sunday Telegram*, 11 October 1987, WFC.

104   Ibid.

105   Ibid.

106   Larry Mahoney, "Weinrich returns 'home' Friday as member of U.S. Olympic Team," *Bangor Daily News*, undated but probably mid-October 1987, WFC.

107   Eric Weinrich, "Olympic Diary: Maine, Michigan State tough teams on tour," *Maine Sunday Telegram*, undated but probably late November 1987, WFC.

108   "Weinrich adjusts to Olympic pace," *Portland Press Herald*, 11 November 1987, WFC.

109   Eric Weinrich, "Olympic Diary: Hockey Players learn to live with fights," *Maine Sunday Telegram*, undated but probably late October 1987, WFC.

110   Ibid.

111   Eric Weinrich, "Olympic Diary: After a loss in Calgary, Thanksgiving break in the sun," *Maine Sunday Telegram*, 29 November 1987, WFC.

112   Ibid.

113   Eric Weinrich, "Olympic Diary: Illness one more hurdle to Calgary," *Maine Sunday Telegram*, 13 December 1987, WFC.

114   Paul Abramowitz, "Weinrich sidelined for time being," undated clipping from unidentified newspaper, but probably around 13 December 1987, WFC.

115 Eric Weinrich, "Recovery made easier with a touch of home cooking," *Maine Sunday Telegram*, 20 December 1987, WFC.

116 Eric Weinrich, "Opportunity for Olympic team berth resumes Dec. 29," *Maine Sunday Telegram*, 27 December 1987, WFC.

117 Ibid.

118 Paul Abramowitz, "Weinrich content with bit part in Prime Time," *Maine Sunday Telegram*, 14 February 1988, WFC.

119 Eric Weinrich, "Olympic Diary: Soviets tough as they come," *Portland Press Herald*, 17 February 1988, WFC.

120 Eric Weinrich, "Olympic Diary: Olympics sure wasn't a vacation," undated clipping from unidentified newspaper, but probably 26 February 1988, WFC.

121 Weinrich, "Olympic Diary: Soviets tough as they come."

122 Eric Weinrich text message to the author, 19 December 2017.

123 "Soviets overcome third-period rally," *Kennebec Journal*, 18 February 1988, WFC.

124 Tal Pinchevsky, *Breakaway: From Behind the Iron Curtain to the NHL – The Untold Story of Hockey's Great Escapes* (Mississauga: John Wiley & Sons Canada, 2012), 147.

125 Weinrich, "Olympic Diary: Soviets tough as the come."

126 Weinrich, "Olympic Diary: Olympics sure wasn't a vacation."

127 Ibid.

128 *Lewiston Sun Journal*, 22 February 1988, www.sunjournal.com/archive accessed 21 December 2017.

129 Weinrich, "Olympic Diary: Olympics sure wasn't a vacation."

130 Tom Perkins, "Weinrich, Bears bury Friars, 10-2," *Lewiston Daily Sun*, 29 February 1988, www.sunjounral.com/archive accessed 15 December 2017.

131 Eric Weinrich text message to the author, 15 December 2017.

132 *Post-Star* (Glens Falls, NY), 7 October 1988, 15. This preview article noted that Eric was a key addition to the Utica club. This article, and most of the others in this chapter, were accessed via www.newspapers.com.

133 Rich Chere, "'Visionary' NJ Devils general manager Lou Lamoriello set for Hall of Fame induction," www.NJ.com, 8 November 2009, accessed on 15 November 2017.

134 Ibid.

135 "Devils GM says Soviets near release of Fetisov," *South Florida Sun Sentinel* (Fort Lauderdale, FL), 14 July 1988, 34. Coincidentally, a paragraph at the end of this article primarily about Fetisov noted that Eric Weinrich had signed a contract with NJ.

[136] Robinson quoted in Nate Dow, "A Worldly Opinion," *Lewiston Daily Sun* (Lewiston, ME), 23 February 1988, 15.

[137] For insightful analysis of the historical Canada/Soviet rivalry see John Soares, "'Our Way of Life against Theirs:' Ice Hockey and the Cold War," in Heather Dichter and Andrew Johns, editors, *Diplomatic Games: Sport, Statecraft, and International Relations since 1945* (Lexington: University Press of Kentucky, 2014), 251-296. For personal recollections of the rivalry from two of Canada's all-time best see Wayne Gretzky with Rick Reilly, *Gretzky: An Autobiography* (New York: HarperCollins, 1990), 151-61 and Bobby Orr, *Orr: My Story* (New York: G.P. Putnam's Sons, 2013), 136-38 and 179-81.

[138] Dow, "A Worldly Opinion."

[139] "Story #65: Igor Larionov Openly Revolts Against Coach, System," International Ice Hockey Federation, *100 Year Anniversary, 100 Top Stories*, published 2008 on www.iihf.com, accessed on 14 July 2018.

[140] Ibid.

[141] *Democrat and Chronicle* (Rochester, NY), 1 October 1988, 2d.

[142] *Press and Sun-Bulletin* (Binghampton, NY), 3 and 5 November 1988.

[143] *The Post-Star* (Glens Falls, NY), 15 December 1988, 1C.

[144] Author's phone interview with Tracy and Eric Weinrich, 7 July 2018.

[145] Ibid.

[146] *The Sentinel* (Carlisle, PA), 19 January 1989; "Weinrich's hat trick sinks Bears," undated article from unidentified paper (but probably in Portland, ME), clipping from Weinrich Family Collection (hereafter WFC), Cousins Island, Maine.

[147] *Democrat and Chronicle* (Rochester, NY), 21 January 1989, 4d.

[148] Eric's slip described in *Daily Record* (Morristown, NJ), 24 January 1989, 1c; another good article mentioning that it was Eric's first NHL game is in *Asbury Park Press* (Asbury Park, NJ), 24 January 1989.

[149] *Baltimore Sun*, 1 March 1989.

[150] *Democrat and Chronicle* (Rochester, NY), 3 April 1989.

[151] Chere, "'Visionary' NJ Devils general manager Lou Lamoriello."

[152] "Story #65: Igor Larionov Openly Revolts."

[153] "Story #63: Alexander Mogilny Becomes the First Soviet-NHL Defector," International Ice Hockey Federation, *100 Year Anniversary, 100 Top Stories*, published 2008 on www.iihf.com, accessed on 14 July 2018.

[154] "One on One with Viacheslav Fetisov," 27 February 2006, The Official Site of the Hockey Hall of Fame, https://www.hhof.com/htmlSpotlight/spot

oneononep200101.shtml, accessed 20 July 2018. The interview was conducted when Fetisov was inducted into the Hall, which is in Toronto.

155   The showdown with Yazov and the departure for the USA soon after are depicted dramatically in Gabe Polsky's film *Red Army* (2014), which is essentially a biography of Fetisov.

156   *Press and Sun-Bulletin* (Binghampton, NY), 6 October 1989, 5c.

157   *Daily Record* (Morristown, NJ), 30 October 1989, 5b.

158   George Herring, *From Colony to Superpower: U.S. Foreign Relations since 1776* (Oxford: Oxford University Press, 2008), 905-906.

159   *New York Daily News*, 15 December 1989; "Weinrich named Player of the Week," undated clipping (probably around 12/15/89), unidentified newspaper, WFC.

160   Heather and author Andy DeRoche's interview with Eric and Tracy Weinrich, 25 July 2017, Cousins Island, ME.

161   For a careful examination of the Fetisov/Kasatonov relationship and how other Devils felt about it see Larry Brooks, "From USSR best buds to NHL enemies: How politics divided 2 ex-Devils," http://nypost.com, 24 January 2015, accessed 14 August 2017.

162   Colin Stephenson, "Devils have a surplus of defensemen," *Asbury Park Press* (Asbury Park, NJ), 7 January 1990, 136. This article demonstrates that at least some U.S. journalists were aware of the Fetisov/Kasatonov feud, which in the film *Red Army*, Fetisov claimed was completely ignored in the USA.

163   *Press & Sun-Bulletin* (Binghampton, NY), 21 January 1990.

164   Alex Yannis, "Weinrich may be in the NHL to stay," clipping from unidentified newspaper, undated (but probably 18 or 19 February 1990), WFC.

165   *New York Daily News*, 18 February 1990.

166   Yannis, "Weinrich may be in the NHL to stay."

167   *Asbury Park Press* (Asbury Park, NJ), 26 February 1990.

168   Heather and Andy DeRoche interview with Eric and Tracy Weinrich, 25 July 2017, Cousins Island, ME.

169   Gretzky with Reilly, *Gretzky*, 156-7.

170   Ken Dryden, *The Game: 20th Anniversary Edition* (New York: Wiley, 2003), 282-3.

171   *Philadelphia Inquirer*, 26 March 1990, 2d.

172   *Asbury Park Press* (Asbury Park, NJ), 28 March 1990.

173   Ike Kuhns, "Devils tune up with rout of Wings, 5-1," undated (but late March 1990), clipping from unidentified newspaper, WFC.

174   For the amazing Stastny defection tale see "Story #46: Hockey Escape of the Century – Stastnys Land in Quebec," International Ice Hockey Federation, *100*

Year Anniversary, 100 Top Stories, published 2008 on www.iihf.com, accessed on 14 July 2018.

[175] Heather and Andy DeRoche interview with Tracy and Eric Weinrich, 25 July 2017, Cousins Island, ME.

[176] James Roark, etal., *The American Promise A Concise History Volume 2: From 1865* 5th Edition (Boston: Bedford/St. Martins, 2014), 867.

[177] "Devils shove past Capitals, even series," *Chicago Tribune*, 8 April 1990, 56.

[178] Stats from 1990 playoffs from www.hockey-reference.com, which is a super resource.

[179] Heather and Andy DeRoche interview with Tracy and Eric Weinrich, 25 July 2017, Cousins Island, ME.

[180] *Post-Star* (Glens Falls, NY), 13 June 1990, 3c.

[181] Dave Greely, "Weinrich takes new attitude to camp," undated clipping (but probably late August 1990) from unidentified newspaper, Weinrich Family Collection (hereafter WFC), Cousins Island, ME.

[182] Ibid.

[183] Ibid.

[184] *The Record* (Hackensack, NJ), 9/17/1990, p44, accessed at www.newspapers.com on 4 February 2019.

[185] *The Record* (Hackensack, NJ), 9/28/1990, p38, accessed at www.newspapers.com on 4 February 2019.

[186] *Courier-News* (Bridgewater, NJ), 9/30/1990, pp27-28, accessed at www.newspapers.com on 4 February 2019. For an insightful discussion of Kasatonov and Fetisov when they joined the Devils see Tal Pinchevsky, *Breakaway: From Behind the Iron Curtain to the NHL – the Untold Story of Hockey's Great Escapes* (Mississauga: John Wiley & Sons Canada, Ltd, 2012).

[187] *The Record* (Hackensack, NJ), 10/4/1990, p116, accessed at www.newspapers.com on 4 February 2019.

[188] *The Record* (Hackensack, NJ), 10/5/1990, accessed at www.newspapers.com on 4 February 2019. For a thorough discussion of Federov's journey from the USSR to the NHL see Keith Gave, *The Russian Five: A Story of Espionage, Defection, Bribery and Courage* (Ann Arbor: Gold Star Publishing, 2018), 57-79.

[189] Jeffrey Engel, *When the World Seemed New: George H.W. Bush and the End of the Cold War* (Boston: Houghton Mifflin, 2017), 372.

[190] James A. Baker, III, with Thomas DeFrank, *The Politics of Diplomacy: Revolution, War & Peace, 1989-1992* (New York: G.P. Putnam's Sons, 1995), 258-9.

191 Robert McMahon, *The Cold War: A Very Short Introduction* (New York: Oxford University Press, 2003), 168.

192 *The Record* (Hackensack, NJ), 10/12/1990, p7, accessed at www.newspapers.com on 4 February 2019.

193 John Dellapina, "Weinrich one baffled Devil," *The Record* (Hackensack, NJ), 10/14/1990, p11, accessed at www.newspapers.com on 4 February 2019.

194 Ibid.

195 *The Record* (Hackensack, NJ), 10/21/1990, 10/24/1990, and 10/28/1990 accessed at www.newspapers.com on 4 February 2019.

196 *The Record* (Hackensack, NJ), 11/14/1990, p18, accessed at www.newspapers.com on 4 February 2019.

197 *Daily Record* (Morristown, NJ), 11/16/1990, and *Central New Jersey Home News* (New Brunswick, NJ), 11/18/1990, accessed at www.newspapers.com on 4 February 2019.

198 *Daily Record* (Morristown, NJ), 11/22/1990 and 11/29/1990, accessed at www.newspapers.com on 4 February 2019.

199 *The Courier-News* (Bridgewater, NJ), 12/2/1990 and *Daily Record* (Morristown, NJ), 12/4/1990, accessed at www.newspapers.com on 4 February 2019.

200 *The Record* (Hackensack, NJ), 12/7/1990, accessed at www.newspapers.com on 4 February 2019.

201 *Daily Record* (Morristown, NJ), p71, 12/23/1990, accessed at www.newspapers.com on 4 February 2019.

202 *The Record* (Hackensack, NJ), p19, 12/31/90, accessed at www.newspapers.com on 4 February 2019. This author recalls very well being bamboozled by Eric's ricochet passes off the boards during floor hockey games in physical education class at the Rumford Center School in the late 1970s.

203 McMahon, *The Cold War*, 168.

204 *Central New Jersey Home News* (New Brunswick, NJ), 1/7/1991, p19 and *Asbury Park Press* (Asbury Park, NJ), 1/9/91, p48 accessed at www.newspapers.com on 4 February 2019.

205 Dave Greely, "A definite plus: Weinrich shines for Devils," undated clipping (but probably 8 or 9 January 1991) from unidentified newspaper, WFC.

206 Ibid.

207 Colin Stephenson, "Plus/minus stat a plus to Cunniff," *Asbury Park Press* (Asbury Park, NJ), 1/6/91, p107 accessed at www.newspapers.com on 6 February 2019.

208 Ibid.

209 Ibid. At season's end it would be Chicago goalie Ed Belfour who won the Calder Trophy.

210 Ibid.

211 *Asbury Park Press* (Asbury Park, NJ), 1/23/91, p47 accessed at www.newspapers.com on 6 February 2019.

212 *Asbury Park Press* (Asbury Park, NJ), 1/27/91, p111, and *Daily Record* (Morristown, NJ), 1/29/91, p48, accessed at www.newspapers.com on 6 February 2019. The story of Fetisov joining the Red Wings and collaborating with the other former Soviet players for a Stanley Cup is dramatically told in Gabe Polsky's 2014 film *Red Army*. For a detailed examination in print see Gave, *The Russian Five*.

213 *The Record* (Hackensack, NJ), p39, 2/11/91, accessed at www.newspapers.com on 6 February 2019.

214 Ibid., 2/15/91.

215 *The Record* (Hackensack, NJ), p12, 2/19/91, accessed at www.newspapers.com on 6 February 2019.

216 John Dellapina, "Devils running out of time: Trying to raise their level of play as season winds down," *The Record* (Hackensack, NJ), p22, 3/13/91, accessed at www.newspapers.com on 8 February 2019

217 John Dellapina, "Devils step forward," *The Record* (Hackensack, NJ), pp40-42, 3/14/91, accessed at www.newspapers.com on 8 February 2019.

218 *The Record* (Hackensack, NJ), 3/24/91, accessed at www.newspapers.com on 8 February 2019.

219 Patrick Roy was at the top of his game in 1990-91, but had missed more starts than usual due to injury. Coincidentally, Roy had strong connections to the state of Maine. On summer trips from Quebec to the Atlantic coast, the Roy family often passed through Madison, Maine, a small paper-mill town on the Kennebec River where Patrick Roy's maternal grandfather Edward Miller was born in 1910. This author's dad Daniel DeRoche also grew up in Madison. See Michel Roy, *Patrick Roy: Winning. Nothing Else.* (Mississauga, Ontario: John Wiley and Sons, 2008), 28-30 and 279.

220 *Central New Jersey Home News* (New Brunswick, NJ), p21, 27 March 1991, accessed at www.newspapers.com on 8 February 2019.

221 Statistics from www.hockey-reference.com accessed 9 May 2019.

222 John Dellapina, "Puck just doesn't bounce their way," *The Record* (Hackensack, NJ), pp31 and 36, 4/8/91, accessed at www.newspapers.com on 8 February 2019.

223 Bill Pennington, "One of those crazy things," *The Record* (Hackensack, NJ), p31, 4/8/91, accessed at www.newspapers.com on 8 February 2019.

224 "Devils: Can't deep-six Pens," *The Record* (Hackensack, NJ), p140, 4/14/91, accessed at www.newspapers.com on 8 February 2019.

225 By the time his long career ended, Eric Weinrich competed in a 9 World Championships, more than any other USA player.

226 *Daily Record* (Morristown, NJ), p17, 4/18/91, accessed at www.newspapers.com on 8 February 2019.

227 "1991 Men's World Ice Hockey Championships" accessed at http://en.wikipedia.org on 15 May 2019.

228 "NHL's All-Rookie Team," *Central New Jersey Home News* (New Brunswick, NJ), p17, 22 June 1991, accessed at www.newspapers.com on 9 February 2019.

229 John Kreiser, "Hockey Digest's 1990-91 All-Rookie Team," *Hockey Digest* (June/July 1991), 38-41, WFC.

230 "A Soviet Sophomore Slump," *Hockey Digest* (June/July 1991), 40-41, WFC. Fetisov and Larionov both recovered from slow starts in the NHL and won multiple Stanley Cups together with Detroit in the late 1990s. The second wave of Soviet players such as Fedorov and Pavel Bure, moreover, were immediate NHL superstars.

231 This author also attended Eric and Tracy's wedding, and seeing Kasatonov there was incredible!

232 "Welcome to the Marriage of Terese Renee Martin and Eric John Weinrich," July Sixth Nineteen Hundred and Ninety-one, Hamilton College Chapel, Clinton, New York. Wedding program in possession of this author, who was lucky enough to attend!

233 Andrew DeRoche, "Role Model," *Western Maine Spectator* (July 1991), WFC. My late uncle, John Willard, was the editor of this short-lived newspaper and he gave me a chance to publish several articles which were very enjoyable to write. This one, about Eric and Tracy's wedding, was one of my favorites. The fact that Kasatonov was a guest was mentioned prominently.

234 Andy and Heather DeRoche interview with Eric and Tracy Weinrich, 25 July 2017, Cousins Island, ME. Slava Fetisov and his wife had a similar shopping experience when they first arrived in NJ, spending nearly $600 during their first visit to a grocery store. See Pinchevsky, *Breakaway*, 188.

235 Engel, *When the World Seemed New*, 440-473. The Soviet Union officially ceased to exist at midnight on 31 December 1991.

236 For the significance of the Canada Cup see Stephen Hardy and Andrew Holman, *Hockey: A Global History* (Urbana: University of Illinois Press, 2018), 410.

237 Larry Mahoney, "Canada Cup was 'dream come true' for Eric Weinrich," *Bangor Daily News*, p17, 19 September 1991, WFC.

238 Chris Chelios, with Kevin Allen, *Made in America* (Chicago: Triumph Books, 2014), 117.

239 Mahoney, "Canada Cup," WFC.

240 "Labatt Canada Cup 1991," www.hockeycanada.ca/en-ca/team-canada/men/world-cup/1991/home accessed on 17 August 2017.

241 Jeremy Roenick, with Kevin Allen, *J.R.: My Life as the Most Outspoken, Fearless, and Hard-Hitting Man in Hockey* (Chicago: Triumph Books, 2012), 164. I deleted the expletive that appeared in Roenick's original version.

242 Mahoney, "Canada Cup," WFC.

243 Ibid.

244 Rich Chere, "Weinrich thinks trade was whale of a break," *The Sunday Star-Ledger* (Newark, NJ), 13 September 1992, clipping in the Weinrich Family Collection (hereafter WFC), Cousins Island, Maine.

245 Joe Grant, "Weinrich improving game as Hartford still struggles," clipping from unidentified newspaper, undated but approximately 16 December 1992, WFC.

246 "Weinrich goal keys Whalers," *Kennebec Journal* (Augusta, Maine), 22 December 1992, clipping in WFC.

247 Viv Bernstein, "Weinrich's Offense Point of Concern," *Hartford Courant*, 9 January 1993, D1 and D3, clipping in WFC.

248 "Hockey," clipping from *New York Post*, 21 April 1993, in WFC.

249 Eric and Tracy Weinrich interviewed by Andy and Heather DeRoche, 25 July 2017, Cousins Island, Maine.

250 Bob Briggs, *University of Maine Ice Hockey: Images of Sports* (Charleston: Arcadia Publishing, 2008), 95.

251 Jason Weinrich interviewed by Andy DeRoche, Portland, Maine, 28 December 2019.

252 Clipping from *Yankee* (January 1994), p.52, WFC.

253 My grandmother Doris DeRoche and I watched the finals on TV, and we each celebrated with a drink at the end. Aunt Mary Margaret DeRoche, her daughter, was a Black Bears season ticket holder and at the game in Wisconsin in person. I attended many games in Orono during that season, and often ran into Jack Weinrich in the stands.

254 Jason Weinrich interview by Andy DeRoche, Portland, Maine, 28 December 2019. Jason had been drafted in the 6th round by the New York Rangers in 1990.

He was playing great hockey during his senior season at Maine in 1993-94, but unfortunately sustained two serious knee injuries and the Rangers released him. He persevered for a couple of seasons in the minor leagues and in Europe, but the injuries were too painful, and he retired in 2000.

255 Eric Weinrich to Andy DeRoche, 9 October 1993, letter in author's possession. The idea of opening a brew pub is one of very few goals of Eric's that he has not accomplished. Hey Eric, there is still time to do it!

256 "Weinrich sent to Black Hawks," undated (probably 3 November 1993) clipping from unidentified paper, WFC.

257 Joe Grant, "Weinrich takes one on the chin," clipping from unidentified paper, 2/25/94, WFC.

258 Robert Markus, "Hawks, Belfour Stop Skid, Flames," *Chicago Tribune*, 4 April 1994, www.chicagogtribune.com accessed 8 April 2020.

259 The author attended the last regular season game between Chicago and Toronto and the Cubs baseball game against the Braves, as well as lunch and shooting pool at Cheli's Chili Bar with several Blackhawks. What fun!

260 Text message from Tracy Weinrich to Andy DeRoche, 10 April 2020, and from Eric Weinrich to the Andy DeRoche, 11 April 2020.

261 Chris Chelios with Kevin Allen, *Made in America: Chris Chelios* (Chicago: Triumph Books, 2014), 144.

262 Ibid., 145.

263 Jeremy Roenick with Kevin Allen, *J.R.: My Life as the Most Outspoken, Fearless, and Hard-Hitting Man in Hockey* (Chicago: Triumph Books, 2012), 73.

264 Robert Markus, "Weinrich returns to top form," *Chicago Tribune*, 31 January 1996, clipping in WFC.

265 Chelios with Allen, *Made in America*, 145-46.

266 Ibid., 145-46.

267 Michel Roy, *Patrick Roy: Winning. Nothing Else.* (Mississauga: John Wiley and Sons, 2007), 385-86.

268 Jeremy Roenick with Kevin Allen, *J.R.*, 248-49.

269 Ibid., 74-77. Jordan personified the role of U.S. sports and entertainment in the new globalization as the Cold War ended in the 1990s as much as any athlete. For analysis of his significance see Walter LaFeber, *Michael Jordan and the New Global Capitalism* (New York: Norton, 1999).

270 Chris Chelios with Kevin Allen, *Made in America*, 139-141.

271 Tracy Weinrich text message to Andy DeRoche, 23 April 2020.

272 Rich Strom, "Out of Chelios' shadow: Trade spotlight plays on Weinrich's scoring," *Chicago Tribune*, 7 November 1996, clipping in WFC.

273 Tim Sassone, "Job Done in midst of trade rumors," *Daily Herald*, 7 November 1996, clipping from WFC.

274 These statistics and many others in this book were drawn from the Hockey Reference website at www.hockey-reference.com which is an excellent resource.

275 Michel Roy, *Patrick Roy*, 429.

276 Chris Chelios with Kevin Allen, *Made in America* (Chicago: Triumph Books, 2014), 146-7.

277 Erica Bulman, "Top NHL Players leave Team USA Scrambling," *USA Today*, 8 May 1998, clipping in WFC.

278 Author's phone interview with Alex Weinrich, 5 October 2019.

279 Mike Lowe, "Weinrich: Gardiner Native Returns to Home State to Host Charity Golf Tourney," *Maine Sunday Telegram*, undated clipping from summer 1998, WFC; "Eric Weinrich '89 giving back to his home state," *University of Maine Alumni Magazine* (Fall 1998), clipping in WFC.

280 Ben Sturtevant, "Weinrich sent to Canadiens," *Kennebec Journal*, 17 November 1998, WFC.

281 Ibid.

282 Statistics gathered from the Hockey Reference website at https://www.hockey-reference.com/teams/MTL/1999 games.html accessed on 9 May 2020.

283 Eric and Tracy Weinrich interviewed by Andy and Heather DeRoche, Cousins Island, Maine, 25 July 2017.

284 Tracy Weinrich email to Andy DeRoche, 7 September 1999, printout in possession of the author.

285 Scott Martin, "Q & A Eric Weinrich," *Kennebec Journal*, 19 September 1999, clipping in WFC.

286 Pat Hickey, "Road Trip: Canadiens Team Report," *The Sporting News*, www.sportingnews.com, printout of article in WFC.

287 Scott Martin, "The Workhorse: Weinrich anchors Canadiens defense down the stretch," *Kennebec Journal*, 17 March 2000, clipping in WFC.

288 Red Fisher, "Somebody Make it Stop: Pressure is on the defense now that Weinrich is gone for the season," *The Montreal Gazette*, 24 March 2000, clipping in WFC.

289 Ibid.

290 Jack Todd, "Habs keep on tickin'," *The Montreal Gazette*, 6 April 2000, clipping in WFC.

291 Ibid.

292 Pat Hickey, "Penguins do Habs a favour," *The Montreal Gazette*, 8 April 2000, clipping in WFC.

293 Pat Hickey, "The honour is yours: Weinrich wins Beauchamp Trophy, Hackett Molson Cup," *The Montreal Gazette*, 8 April 2000, clipping in WFC.

294 Jack Todd, "Habs lose with lustre," *Montreal Gazette*, 9 April 2000, clipping in WFC.

295 Andy DeRoche interview with Lou Vairo, Colorado Springs, Colorado, 27 July 2018.

296 Andy and Heather DeRoche interview with Tracy and Eric Weinrich, Cousins Island, Maine, 25 July 2017.

297 Andy DeRoche phone interview with Lou Vairo, 19 July 2018.

298 Eric and Tracy Weinrich interview with Andy and Heather DeRoche, 25 July 2017, Cousins Island, Maine.

299 "Eric Weinrich: Cool," *Les Canadiens*, 1999-2000 Magazine 4 (January 2000), 24. The feature story on Eric included questions and answers in both French and English and 13 wonderful glossy color photos of him and his family. The cover photo showed him dressed in black with sunglasses and his head shaved. Cool indeed!

300 Pat Hickey, "Weinrich will be missed," www.montrealgazette.com 11 February 2001, printout of article in WFC.

301 Herb Zurkowski, "Weinrich Traded," *Montreal Gazette*, 22 February 2001, clipping in WFC.

302 Ibid.

303 Eric Lucey, "Veteran Weinrich Trades Time For Success," www.usahockey.com (August 2001), printout of article in WFC.

304 Eric Lucey, "Veteran Weinrich Trades Time For Success," www.usahockey.com (August 2001), printout of article in WFC.

305 Jeremy Roenick with Kevin Allen, *J.R.: My Life as the Most Outspoken, Fearless, and Hard-Hitting Man in Hockey* (Chicago: Triumph Books, 2012), 145-150. After one game in Denver, Weino went out for a beer with Andy DeRoche and Rob Rehder. On the way back to the hotel, Eric asked if we could stop at a diner and pick up a cheeseburger for his roommate JR. We were happy to handle that important request!

306 Tim Panaccio, "Roenick has a blast in debut," *Philadelphia Inquirer*, 5 October 2001, clipping in WFC.

307   Tim Panaccio, "Frustration melting away for Flyers' happy Weinrich," *Philadelphia Inquirer*, 6 November 2001, clipping in WFC.

308   Jerry Burke, "Weinrich a perfect fit in Philly," www.nhl.com/cupcrazy2002/series/weinrich042602 posted on 26 April 2002, printout in WFC.

309   Kristen Graham, "A visiting Flyer, enthralled students," *Philadelphia Inquirer*, 12 February 2002, clipping in WFC.

310   Roenick, J.R., 152-3.

311   Dennis Austin, "Fine Weinrich," *Philadelphia Flyer Magazine* (Volume 19, Issue 29), 28 February 2003.

312   Marc Narducci, "His plus/minus totals make Weinrich a welcome addition," *Philadelphia Inquirer*, 25 January 2003, clipping in WFC.

313   Scott Martin, "'Weino' Reaches 1,000," *Kennebec Journal*, 31 March 2003, clipping in WFC.

314   Ian Culver, Associate Counsel of the National Hockey League Players' Association, to Eric Weinrich, 7 April 2003, letter in WFC.

315   Gary Thorne and Darren Pang, ESPN broadcast of Flyers vs. Maple Leafs, 9 April 2003, VHS tape recording from 2003 in author's possession. Yes, you read this correctly. VHS tape!

316   Gary Thorne and Darren Pang, ESPN broadcast of Flyers vs. Maple Leafs, 14 April 2003, VHS tape in author's possession.

317   Eric Weinrich, "Weino's World: Finally, Back Home," *Kennebec Journal*, 5 January 2004, clipping in WFC.

318   Eric Weinrich, "Weino's World: Pondering the Future," *Kennebec Journal*, 12 January 2004, clipping in WFC.

319   Eric Weinrich, "Weino's World: Hockey gets left out in the cold again," *Kennebec Journal*, 2 February 2004, clipping in WFC.

320   Eric Weinrich, "Weino's World: A journeyman's blues," *Kennebec Journal*, 16 February 2004, clipping in WFC.

321   Eric Weinrich, "Weino's World: Transition made easy by family and friends," *Kennebec Journal*, 24 February 2004, clipping in WFC.

322   Ibid.

323   Eric Weinrich, "Weino's World: Conference not easy," *Kennebec Journal*, 1 March 2004, clipping in WFC. This author was lucky enough to attend the 2-2 tie on 26 February in Denver. It was always a thrill to see Eric holding his own with the likes of Joe Sakic at the Pepsi Center!

324 Lumpy's wife Mary, another lifelong resident of St. Louis and Blues fan, also attended. She was gracious enough to host Eric and Tracy for dinner at the Lemkemeier home the next night. This author regaled them all with stories of my significant other in Zambia, Heather, who would soon be my wife. A good time was had by all!

325 Joeri Loonen, "Weinrich adds experience to US lineup," www.eurohockey.net/ news, 4 May 2004, printout of story in WFC; "Weinrich to set record by suiting up," USA Hockey Press Release, clipping in WFC.

326 John Sanful, "Can Weinrich and Co. shut down Jagr?" www.ihwc.net, 5 May 2004, printout of the story in WFC.

327 Ibid.

328 Eric and Tracy Weinrich interview with Andy and Heather DeRoche, 25 July 2017, Cousins Island, Maine.

329 Ibid.

330 Ibid.

331 Scott Martin, "Weino enters into a new world," *Kennebec Journal*, 8 August 2006, clipping in WFC; Kalle Oakes, "Weinrich retires, joins Pirates," *Lewiston Sun Journal*, 8 August 2006, clipping in WFC.

332 Scott Martin, "Weinrich finally has a home," *Kennebec Journal*, 8 August 2006, clipping in WFC.

333 Paul Betit, "Homecoming," *Portland Press Herald*, 8 August 2006, entire sports section mailed to this author by his beloved Aunt Betty Willard, known as "Betty Spaghetti."

334 Steve Solloway, "Here's to 18 seasons of daring greatly," *Portland Press Herald*, 8 August 2006, ibid.

335 Larry Mahoney, "Weinrich was epitome of NHL pro," *Bangor Daily News*, undated but probably 8 August 2006, clipping in WFC.

336 Kalle Oakes, "The Hot Corner: Forgotten Mainer perhaps best ever," *Lewiston Sun Journal*, 8 August 2006, clipping in WFC.

337 Ibid.

338 Ibid.

339 Paul Betit, "Weinrich ditches suit for a player's sweater," *Portland Press Herald*, 26 January 2007, clipping sent to the author by Larry Bennett, his wonderful uncle who passed away in 2020.

340 Rachel Lenzi, "There's really no doubt, he's still a player," *Portland Press Herald*, undated but probably late August or very early September 2007, ibid.

[341] Paul Betit, "Still playing, with passion," *Maine Sunday Telegram*, 16 December 2007, clipping sent to author by his aunt Betty "Spaghetti" Willard.

[342] Paul Betit, "Recovery a wait for Weinrich," *Portland Press Herald*, 14 March 2008, ibid.

[343] Evan Crawley, "Weinrich gets his due," *Kennebec Journal*, 4 May 2015.

Printed in the United States
by Baker & Taylor Publisher Services